11/3/00

The John Harvard Library

Fanny Kemble

Fanny Kemble's Journals

EDITED AND WITH AN INTRODUCTION BY

CATHERINE CLINTON

Harvard University Press

Cambridge, Massachusetts

London, England

2000

Library of Congress Cataloging-in-Publication Data

Kemble, Fanny, 1809–1893.
[Journals. Selections]
Fanny Kemble's journals / edited and with an introduction by Catherine Clinton.
p. cm. — (The John Harvard Library)
Includes bibliographical references and index.
ISBN 0-674-00305-5 (alk. paper)—ISBN 0-674-00440-X (pbk. : alk. paper)
1. Kemble, Fanny, 1809–1893—Diaries. 2. Kemble, Fanny, 1809–1893—Correspondence.
3. Actors—Great Britain—Diaries. 4. Actors—Great Britain—Correspondence. 5. Plantation
owners' spouses—Georgia—Diaries. 6. Plantation owners' spouses—Georgia—
Correspondence. I. Clinton, Catherine, 1952– II. Title. III. Series.
PN2598.K4 A25 2000
792′.028′092—dc21
[B]
00-035039

For

Susanna Delfino

Noi non potemo aver perfetta vita senza amici

Contents

Chronology

1809	*27 November:* Frances Anne Kemble (FAK) born in London to Charles and Maria Therese (de Camp) Kemble
1814	Sent to school in Bath
1815	Returns home to London
1817	Sent to Madame Faudier's school in Boulogne
1819	Returns home to Craven Hill, Bayswater, London
1821	Sent to Mrs. Rowden's School in Paris
1825	Returns to family home in Weybridge; formal schooling ends
1827	At Heath Farm; meets Harriet St. Leger
1828	Meets Anna Jameson in London; spends year in Edinburgh with Mrs. Henry Siddons
1829	*5 October:* Debut at Covent Garden in *Romeo and Juliet*
1830	Tours Bath, Edinburgh, Glasgow, Dublin, Liverpool, Manchester, Birmingham
1831	Sells *Frances the First* (drama)
	Summer: Tours Bristol, Exeter, Plymouth, Weymouth, Portsmouth, and Southampton
1832	*1 August:* Sails with Charles Kemble and Dall de Camp for America
	3 September: Lands in New York City and begins theatrical tour
	8 October: To Philadelphia
	13 October: Meets Pierce Butler (PB)
1833	*14 January:* To Washington
	30 January: To Philadelphia

16 February: To New York City; meets Catharine Sedgwick

April: To Boston

June: Holidays by boat to upstate New York; meets Edward Trelawney

July: Coach accident en route to Niagara Falls

1834   *April:* Dall dies in Boston

7 June: FAK marries PB in Philadelphia

9 June: Returns to New York to complete theatrical engagement

17 June: Retires from stage; Charles Kemble sails home alone while FAK and Butler honeymoon in Newport, R.I.

July: FAK and PB move in with PB's brother in Philadelphia while Butler Place is renovated

October: FAK learns she is pregnant

December: FAK and PB move in to Butler Place, Branchtown (suburban Philadelphia)

1835   *28 May:* Sarah ("Sally") Butler born

June: Journal of Frances Anne Kemble published (known as *Journal of America*)

Star of Seville (drama) published

1836   *April:* PB inherits plantations from Major Butler

October: FAK sails to England with Sally

1837   *September:* PB arrives in England; FAK, PB, and Sally return to America

October: FAK and PB in Harrisburg for Pennsylvania constitutional convention

December: Family returns to Butler Place

1838   *28 May:* Frances Anne ("Fan") Butler born

August: Family stays at Rockaway Beach, N.Y.

September: FAK travels with daughters to Lenox, Mass.; receives news of her mother's death

December: Family travels to Butler Island, near Darien, Georgia; FAK keeps journal for Elizabeth Sedgwick

1839	*February:* Family settles into Butler house at Cannon Point, St. Simons Island
	April: Family returns to Butler Place
1840	*February:* PB and his brother travel to Georgia, leaving FAK behind
	Summer: FAK to Lenox; PB to Hot Springs, Va.
	December: Charles Kemble ill; FAK, PB, and daughters sail for England
1841	*September:* FAK and PB accompany FAK's sister Adelaide on tour of Continent with Franz Lizst
	October: PB rents home on Harley Street, London
1842	*May:* FAK presented to Queen Victoria
1843	*January:* Adelaide Kemble marries Edward Sartoris and retires from stage
	May: With PB and daughters, FAK returns to Philadelphia, moves into boarding house
	Summer: Family holiday in Yellow Springs, Pa.
	October: Discovers letters confirming PB's infidelities
	November: Seeks legal separation from PB
1844	*March:* Schott scandal: PB accused by friend of illicit affair with his wife
	April: PB and Schott duel
	Summer: FAK in Lenox while PB and daughters in Newport; publishes *Poems*
	Fall: PB demands that FAK sign written contract if she wants to remain as his wife and have access to their daughters
1845	*March:* Fan breaks her arm; FAK signs contract and moves back into PB's household
	April: Quarrels with PB; departs
	September: Sails for England
	December: Travels to Italy
1846	*Winter–Spring:* In Rome
	Summer: In Frascati

Autumn: In Rome

December: Returns to London

1847   *January:* Sells *Year of Consolation*

16 February: Returns to the stage in Manchester

21 April: PB decides to sue for divorce; informs legal counsel

Summer–Autumn: FAK tours English provinces

1848   *February:* Appears with Macready in London

March: Begins career as Shakespearean reader

29 March: PB files for divorce in Philadelphia on grounds of desertion

24 April: FAK receives legal notice of divorce

Summer: Returns to Philadelphia

Autumn: Visits Lenox

1849   *Spring:* Buys house in Lenox, the Perch

April: Divorce proceedings postponed until September

Summer: Spends two months with Sally and Fan in Lenox

September: Divorce finalized, out-of-court settlement: FAK granted annuity and two months a year with daughters

Fall: Tours Boston and New York with readings; publishes *Poems*

1850   *Spring:* PB interferes with correspondence between FAK and daughters

FAK returns to London

1851   Continues career as Shakespearean reader

1852   *January:* Takes over care of Harry, her brother Henry's illegitimate son

1853   In Rome with Adelaide and Edward Sartoris

1854   Tours and lectures in England; brother Henry committed to Moorcroft Asylum

November: Charles Kemble dies

1856   *May:* FAK returns to U.S. when Sarah turns twenty-one

Summer: Tours the West with Shakespearean readings

1857	John Kemble (FAK's older brother) dies; Henry Kemble dies in asylum
1859	*February:* Debt forces PB to sell slaves in Georgia
	May: Fan turns twenty-one
	Sarah marries Owen Wister, Philadelphia doctor
	Summer: FAK travels to Europe with Fan
1860	*Spring:* Returns with Fan to Philadelphia
	14 July: Owen Wister, Jr. (FAK's first grandchild) born in Philadelphia
	December: South Carolina secedes
1861	*April:* PB and Fan go South
	August: PB arrested on charges of treason
	September: PB released
1862	FAK travels with Fan in England and Switzerland
1863	*May:* Publishes *Journal of a Residence on a Georgian Plantation* (American edition in June)
	Publishes *Plays,* which contains her third drama, *An English Tragedy*
1865	*April:* In London with Fan when Confederacy surrenders; Fan plans return to U.S.
1866	*March:* PB and Fan head to Georgia
1867	*July:* Fan returns to Philadelphia
	August: PB dies of fever in Georgia
	October: Fan and Owen Wister travel to Georgia
1868	*Spring:* FAK tours Great Lakes, gives Shakespearean readings
	August: Makes plans to live at Butler Place with daughters
1869	*November:* Fan meets James Leigh
1871	*June:* Fan marries James Leigh in London
	Autumn: FAK in Rome with Leigh, Wister, and Sartoris families
1872	In Rome
1873	*January:* Meets Henry James in Rome

1874	Returns to U.S. with daughters
	Harriet St. Leger returns correspondence; FAK begins to edit letters
	May: Moves to York Farm, Pa.
	July: Alice Dudley Leigh (granddaughter) born at York Farm
1875	*August: Atlantic Monthly* begins to serialize autobiographical articles
	October: FAK acquires typewriter
	Is contacted by British publisher Richard Bentley about expanding articles into a book
1876	*January:* Fan gives birth to a son, Pierce Butler Leigh, who dies shortly after
	June: Leighs decide to return to England
	Summer: FAK in Lenox
	Fall: Visits Boston; makes plans to return to England
1877	*January:* Sails for England with James, Fan, and Alice Leigh
	February: In Ireland; visits Harriet St. Leger
	Spring: Rents house in Connaught Square, London
	June: To Switzerland (and summers there most years until 1889)
	September: Returns to England
	October: Holidays in Wales with Harriet St. Leger
	December: Spends Christmas holidays in Stratford with the Leighs; Henry James visits
1878	*Fall: Records of a Girlhood* published in England (American edition, 1879)
	Harriet St. Leger dies
1879	*February:* Leases apartment in Queen Anne's Mansions, London
	June: Visits sister Adelaide before annual trip to Switzerland
	4 August: Adelaide dies while FAK is abroad
	2 November: Pierce Butler Leigh (grandson) born in England

1880	Pierce Butler Leigh dies

1880   Pierce Butler Leigh dies

December: FAK spends Christmas with Fan and Alice Leigh

1881   *May:* Is begged by Fan not to publish another installment of her autobiography, which would cover her married life; refuses

Publishes *Records of Later Life* (American edition, 1882), and *Notes of Some of Shakespeare's Plays*

Fall: Wister family visits London; travels with FAK and Henry James to Paris

1883   FAK publishes a more complete edition of *Poems;* Fan publishes *Ten Years on a Georgian Plantation*

1887   *Summer:* With Henry James, holidays at Lago Maggiore, Italy

1888   Moves in with the Leighs in their London home

1889   Publishes *The Adventures of Mr. John Timothy Homespun in Switzerland* and first novel, *Far Away and Long Ago*

1890   Publishes final installment of memoirs, *Further Records* (American edition, 1891)

1893   *15 January:* Dies at Fan's home in London and is buried at Kensal Green Cemetery

Fanny Kemble's Journals

Introduction

Talent gave English actress Fanny Kemble (1809–1893) access to the rich and famous while she was barely out of her teens. During her long and productive career over the course of half a century, she published six works of memoir totaling eleven volumes, which covered her life from her teenage years into her seventies. *Fanny Kemble's Journals* offers excerpts from this remarkable body of work.[1]

All those who knew her noted how witty and engaging Kemble was in person. Her captivating conversational style carried over into her writing. Kemble's distinctive prose allows us a window into her privileged world of White House audiences and London literary salons and takes us behind the scenes on a southern plantation and among Italian peasants. Reading her letters and journals is like being perched on Kemble's shoulder, being offered a ringside view of the nineteenth century.

Frances Anne Kemble was born in the first decade of the nineteenth century and died in the last. She was a member of the first family of the British theater, the niece of John Philip Kemble and Sarah Siddons, both so notable that the annals of the London stage have designated the turn of the nineteenth century as "the Kemble era." Fanny

---

1. For a full account of Kemble's life and work, see Catherine Clinton, *Fanny Kemble's Civil Wars* (New York: Simon & Schuster, 2000).

herself became an acclaimed actress in 1829, following her first stage appearance as Shakespeare's Juliet at London's Covent Garden. Her debut made her an overnight sensation. When she and her father, celebrated actor Charles Kemble, toured America three seasons later, she gained an international reputation as the rising star of her generation.

Kemble's ability to dazzle her audiences was legendary. But men and women alike commented that her offstage appearance was surprisingly plain. She was short and sturdy, not tall and lithe as she appeared on the boards. She possessed the prominent nose of the Kembles and her mother's dark, deep-set eyes. A female admirer joked that Kemble was both "the ugliest and handsomest woman in London!"[2] When the young Robert E. Lee, then a cadet at West Point, saw Kemble perform, he was smitten—until he later spied her in person at a ball, and confessed in shock that "she is next door to homely."[3] Author Washington Irving had a different response. As a young man, Irving, who was attached to the American Embassy in London when Kemble made her debut and later became acquainted with her, summed up her bewitching powers: "The nearer one gets to her face and to her mind, the more beautiful they both are."[4]

In 1834, at the age of twenty-four, Kemble retired from the stage following her marriage to Pierce Butler (1810–1867) of Philadelphia. Butler was due to inherit vast plantations in Georgia from his grandfather's estate. Fanny Kemble proclaimed that "as an Englishwoman" she had an aversion to slavery—presumably because the British had abolished slavery in 1831. Despite this potential incompatibility, and despite the reservations family and friends had expressed to the couple when they announced their engagement, Butler and Kemble succumbed to their strong mutual attraction. Passion blinded them to fundamental differences in temperament and interests. For better or worse, they tied the knot and proceeded to make a life together.

2. Frances Anne Kemble, *Records of a Girlhood* (New York: Henry Holt, 1879), p. 82.

3. J. C. Furnas, *Fanny Kemble: Leading Lady of the Nineteenth Century Stage* (New York: Dial Press, 1982), p. 91.

4. Dorothie Bobbé, *Fanny Kemble* (New York: Minton, Balch, and Co., 1931), p. 42.

The couple celebrated the birth of their first child, Sarah, in 1835. When he finally came into his inheritance in 1836, Butler's immense holdings made him the second largest slaveholder in Georgia. Kemble claimed she had no idea about the source of her husband's family money, which is highly unlikely. Although she was able to hold her tongue in public, Kemble's passionate opposition to slavery propelled her and her husband on a collision course.

Longing for a visit to her homeland, Kemble returned to England in 1836 with baby Sarah while her husband remained behind, tending to business. By the time Butler joined his wife abroad in 1837, absence had made her heart grow fonder, and the couple enjoyed a happy reunion. They sailed home together to America, and within nine months celebrated the birth of a second daughter, Frances, in May 1838.

Because Butler was apprehensive about his wife's animosity toward slaveholding, he did not want her to accompany him South on trips to his estates. But Kemble was determined to see for herself what plantation life was really like, and she begged to go with him on his next visit to Georgia. When news of her mother's death reached her in the autumn of 1838, Kemble was devastated. Butler felt he could not leave his grieving wife alone in Philadelphia for the winter; yet he knew he must take care of pressing plantation business. So in December 1838 he brought his entire family south with him to the Georgia Sea Islands. Butler hoped that an encounter with "the peculiar institution" would soften Kemble's radical views.

The plan backfired. Kemble's experiences in Georgia only strengthened her antislavery attitudes, as she documented in her *Journal of a Residence on a Georgian Plantation*. She detested slavery and hectored her husband about the wrongs she witnessed and about the improved conditions she sought for his wretched slaves. Butler grew deaf to her complaints, which only heightened the animosity between the two. By the time they returned to Philadelphia in the spring of 1839, the couple was disillusioned and estranged. Kemble felt that slavery was shameful and that her husband was diminished by his association with it; Butler had come to realize the implacability of his wife's antislavery sentiments and feared that she would be even more impossible on the subject after her southern sojourn.

The two frequently resorted to separate bedrooms (at Kemble's request) and fought constantly over the rearing of their children. Plagued by squabbles, spats, and trial separations, the Butler marriage slowly unraveled. During these years, unaware of the extent of Butler's infidelities, friends and family urged Kemble to appease her husband. Though the couple patched up their differences and promised to make a fresh start several times, hope of remaining together faded over time. The final straw for Kemble came in 1844, when her husband fought a duel with one of his friends over his alleged dalliance with the friend's wife. The scandal was the topic of gossip in Philadelphia for some months, but Butler seemed indifferent to both the public's and his wife's reaction.

In 1845 Kemble abandoned her husband's household for the last time. With this action, she also gave up legal rights to her children. She left her two daughters with their father in Philadelphia, while she sailed for England.

When Butler failed to pay the promised allowance pledged in their separation agreement, Kemble was forced to return to the stage to support herself. The comeback of this once-renowned actress generated box-office revenue. But a return to life on the boards proved too draining, and Kemble retired once again.

She did, however, continue performing—as a Shakespearean reader, moving from town to town, reading the bard's plays in rotation as a one-woman show. This successful second career was interrupted when her husband filed for divorce in 1848, charging her with desertion. Kemble sailed back to America in an attempt to redeem her reputation and win back her children.

Following a protracted and acrimonious legal wrangle, with documents leaked to the press and dirty linen aired on both sides of the Atlantic, the couple finally divorced in 1849. Pierce Butler was to retain sole legal custody of his daughters until each turned twenty-one. At the same time, he promised his former wife visiting rights for two months every summer, as well as a financial settlement. Kemble dropped the name Butler and began a new life, alone.

Kemble resumed her Shakespearean readings, which brought her more than financial reward. Her performances won her a new generation of fans—young Henry James, for one, heard her read— and renewed her popularity with audiences in both England and America. Yet professional success could not soothe the troubles of her personal life. Despite his promise at the time of the divorce, Butler interfered with Kemble's access to her children. To avoid renewed battles, Kemble abandoned the house she had bought in Lenox, Massachusetts, and settled back in England until her oldest daughter turned twenty-one in 1856.

During the late 1850s Kemble spent more and more time in America, dividing her time between friends in Boston, her house in Lenox and her daughters in Philadelphia. Her daughter Sarah married in 1859 and gave birth to Owen Wister, Jr., Kemble's first grandchild, in 1860. Sarah Butler had married into a Yankee family with antislavery sentiments, but her younger sister was devoted to her father's slaveholding interests. When war broke out, the family was divided.

Pierce Butler's suspected disloyalty to the Union led to his arrest by the federal government in August 1861. Although he was paroled from prison after only a few weeks, his daughters were rattled by this experience. Passionately devoted to the Rebel cause, Fan was warned by her sister Sarah to muzzle her Confederate sympathies. Sarah, a staunch Unionist, was active in the Sanitary Commission, and her husband, a surgeon, tirelessly ministered to Union soldiers. Kemble herself actively supported the Union cause, advocating the defeat of the Confederacy and an end to slavery.

The publication of Kemble's Georgia journal in 1863 was meant to strike a blow against the Rebels, to sway British public opinion against slavery and against southern independence. Kemble wanted to insure there would be no European diplomatic acknowledgment of the Confederacy. In fact, England did not offer the Confederacy the recognition they had sought. Whether or not Kemble's book played any role in England's stand has been debated, but there is no disputing Kemble's willingness to put forward her abolitionist feelings at great personal cost. Fan railed that she could never forgive her mother for this betrayal, and Sarah became entangled in the family feud.

Following Lee's surrender at Appomattox, the wounds of war were slow to heal—as was the breach between mother and daughter. Kemble traveled back and forth between her family in England and her daughters in America. She was deeply disappointed that Fan remained devoted to the Butler estates in Georgia, even following Pierce Butler's death in 1867.

Even after her marriage to British clergyman James Leigh in 1873, Fan Butler Leigh remained in the South and continued her struggle to restore the Butler estates to their former glory, despite the family tensions this caused. Labor difficulties, suspicious fires, natural disasters and failing health heaped troubles on the Leigh family during their struggles in the Sea Islands. Finally, in 1876 the Reverend Leigh and his wife decided to abandon Georgia and settle in England with their young daughter Alice, who had been born in Philadelphia in 1874.

Having been assured that the Wister family would make frequent visits, Fanny Kemble decided to leave America as well. She made her final transatlantic crossing in 1877. Once settled back in London, she decided to earn some money by publishing her memoirs.

With her autobiographical writings, Fanny Kemble once again earned international acclaim and yet another generation of fans. She had begun her memoirs with cavalier abandon, writing to editor William Dean Howells of the *Atlantic Monthly:* "You are welcome to abridge or even entirely suppress my 'Gossip' provided you do not abridge or suppress my payment for it."[5] She added more seriously that he was welcome to trim the text, but asked him not to alter her prose. Her series of articles, entitled "An Old Woman's Gossip," began in late 1875 and ran for twenty installments. Richard Bentley asked

---

5. Furnas, *Fanny Kemble,* pp. 423–424.

her to expand the series into a book; *Records of a Girlhood* was published in 1878 and enjoyed great success on both sides of the Atlantic.

During her sixties, Kemble befriended expatriate American Henry James, with whom she dined or visited weekly nearly until the end of her life. She published volumes of poetry, plays, literary criticism, Shakespearean commentary, and even her first novel at the age of eighty. She was a literary phenomenon in her own era, and her vivid writing provides us a rich legacy today. Fanny Kemble's autobiographical accounts have given generations of historians incomparable reports on everything from slave women's pregnancies to nineteenth-century Shakespearean performance style, from the wretchedness of berths on New York canal boats to the splendors of Italian hill towns. Her thoughts on the tempests of her own personal conflicts reveal her eccentric passions, her polemical views, and her intense restlessness. Her voice, so discordant within her own lifetime, strikes us today as modern, stirring, engaging—that of a woman ahead of her time.

Because of her fame, anything Kemble wrote, said, or did was a matter of public interest from her theater debut in 1829 onward. Her meteoric rise as a stage star catapulted her into the limelight—everything from her hairstyle to her offhand remarks was of interest to the public and therefore to the press. In 1832 when Kemble joked with a Washington gentleman about hiring his horse, her remarks were taken out of context and branded as an attack on America. This trivial exchange was blown up into a dispute over national honor. Members of Congress were besieged by citizens demanding an apology from this uppity British actress. The handbills and hoopla ultimately came to naught, but this scandal, as well as others, made Kemble realize that her fame made her fodder for tabloid journalism.

In her youth she inadvertently contributed to the scandal-mongering when she promised a publisher her journal observations made over the course of her first visit to the United States in 1832–33. By the time she submitted the manuscript for publication, Kemble was already a published author, having sold her first drama at the age of twenty. She believed that her talent and future lay not in acting, but in writing, and hoped that retirement from the stage would allow her to pursue her dream.

This first American project was not exactly what she had in mind, however, and Kemble had reservations about publishing what was meant to be kept private. She had only agreed to publish the diary to secure an income for her invalid Aunt Dall, her beloved chaperone and companion. When Dall died in the spring of 1834, Kemble's commitment faltered. However, the income from the book would still go to a worthy cause: the money was destined for Dall's heir, her spinster sister who was a governess and would be able to retire when she received this legacy.

Despite her husband's entreaties, Kemble refused to break her contract. She expressed her doubts to her close friend Harriet St. Leger: "You know what my Journal always was, and that no word of it was ever written with the fear of the printer's devil before my eyes . . . When I sold it, it was an excellent, good book, for I thought it would help to make a small independence for my dear Dall; now she is gone, and it is mere trash, but I have sold it."[6]

She kept her commitment to the publisher, although this stand enraged her husband, as he leaned over her shoulder, suggesting deletions, trying to prevent embarrassment to him and his family. When the *Journal of Frances Anne Kemble* finally appeared in the summer of 1835, hundreds of copies were sold the first week in New York City alone. Reaction was instantaneous and sensational. Journalists were outraged at Kemble's disdain for them. Her "rough," blunt language offended many; her acerbic sketches of social climbers and other unattractive types offended many more. Parlors up and down the East Coast were abuzz as readers reacted to Kemble's saucy assessments.

Kemble was taken aback by the sharp response to her book. Her Philadelphia relatives were livid, and her own parents were scandalized as well. Friends such as Catharine Sedgwick scolded Kemble for

6. Frances Anne Kemble, *Records of Later Life* (New York: Henry Holt, 1882), p. 11.

her candor and her disregard for what they saw as her new social obligations as Butler's wife. As a result of the critical reception, Kemble did not publish another piece of writing under her own name until after the breakup of her marriage over a decade later.[7]

Following her final separation from her husband in 1845, Kemble spent a year abroad in Italy. Strapped for funds, living apart from her husband and without his financial support, she decided to pen a travel book for money. She published her diary of her time in Italy as *A Year of Consolation* (1847). With this project, Kemble hoped to cash in on the vogue for travel books—and her own reputation. This was Kemble's only journal begun with publication in mind. Ironically, it is a much less satisfying read than her other volumes— perhaps because it has a more guarded quality. Yet several interesting observations sneak through: descriptions between Kemble and her sister; reflections on Italian politics versus American customs, with Kemble finding Italy wanting. But generally the book is simply a travelogue, full of colorful commentary catering to tourists' interests, but lacking the blunt, bracing tone evident in her other books. She disparaged her Italian project, noting, "I feel very strongly my own inability to give any fresh interest to a mere superficial description of things and places seen and known by everybody, and written about by all the world and his wife, for the last hundred years. Nevertheless, I have done it; because I could not possibly neglect any means whatever that were pointed out to me of helping myself, and relieving others from helping me."[8]

Since this volume was so obviously a bid for commercial success, critics took aim. One noted "what would have made her writing better, and would doubtless have made her life happier—something less of the predominance of self." This particular sharpshooter continued: "The journal is interspersed with poems of a personal nature, set forth too prominently not to invite attention; yet we can hardly give the

---

7. She did, however, publish some translations during this time in order to earn money for her dressmaking bills.

8. Kemble, *Records of Later Life*, p. 473.

reader better advice than to skip them all."[9] *A Year of Consolation* was neither a critical nor a commercial success, although it did offer Kemble some badly needed revenue.

Kemble's writing was much more compelling when she wrote passionately and took a personal tone, qualities generally missing in *A Year of Consolation*. Her direct, immediate prose style—prevalent in the *Journal of Frances Anne Kemble* and abundant in her *Journal of a Residence on a Georgian Plantation*—is much more engaging for readers today than is the style typically employed by Kemble's contemporaries. Her letters usually were more vivid than her diary entries, and both were more dynamic than the formal prose she adopted for essays, reviews, and criticism. Perhaps because Kemble began her literary career as a dramatist, her writing had a theatrical flair.[10]

Over the course of her long and fascinating life, Kemble kept detailed diaries and maintained a prolific correspondence with several close friends.[11] While still a teenager, she befriended a young Irish aristocrat, Harriet St. Leger. She wrote weekly letters to this confidante for almost half a century. When Harriet fell ill in the 1870s, she returned Kemble's letters. This running account of her life through personal correspondence became the foundation for Kemble's *Records of a Girlhood* (1878), *Records of Later Life* (1881), and *Further Records* (1890).

When Kemble opened the large trunk St. Leger had sent her, she confronted thousands of pages full of the past fifty years of her life. Poring over her old letters was stressful. Kemble found it almost too painful to relive her estrangement from her husband and her separation from her children, and she burned most of these letters after just

---

9. "Mrs. Butler's Year of Consolation," *Living Age* (1847), p. 472.

10. I am indebted to Lewis Perry for pointing this out to me in comments on a paper presented at the Southern Historical Association (Charleston, 1985).

11. Unfortunately, no original copies of any of Kemble's diaries exist today. The Folger Shakespeare Library in Washington, D.C., has a few handwritten pages of a youthful diary, but this text is not included in her published work. Kemble did copy a version of her *Journal*, now available at the Library of Congress. As of this writing, none of the original journals have surfaced and descendants claim that, as far as they know, none exist.

one reading, not wanting them to fall into the wrong hands.

Of her six published journals, the manuscript she sent to the printer is available for only the first, the *Journal of Frances Anne Kemble* (1835).[12] The manuscript for her *Journal of a Residence on a Georgian Plantation*, which circulated among abolitionists for twenty years before it was published, has never surfaced. Kemble might have simply discarded the originals once the journals were published. She apparently disposed of all the letters Harriet St. Leger sent her after she had sorted through them for publication.

Kemble's eleven volumes of memoir, published as six separate works, illuminate the sweep of the nineteenth century. They also tell a story, Kemble's own story, the way she wanted it told—or the way she way she felt forced to tell it. Because the spotlight shone so brightly on every aspect of her life and because she came from a celebrated family, Fanny Kemble was a public figure from an early age. She saw details of her life distorted and exploited by others, and consequently was moved to provide her own version of events.

Perhaps it was also in response to the public's assumption that, as a stage personality, she must be shallow or frivolous that made Kemble a serious intellectual. She read widely in French, German and Italian, and preferred classics to modern fiction. Her letters are full of erudite discussions of great philosophers; her journals overflow with classical and literary references. All who knew her knew Kemble to be intensely intellectual and, although sociable, intensely private.

The invasion of Kemble's privacy began as soon as her name appeared on playbills. Kemble became painfully aware of the unwanted consequences of fame through her stage celebrity. As an actress, even simply as a daughter of the first family of the British stage, she became the topic of unsavory gossip. Charles Kemble frequently threatened to sue some scoundrel or another for libel on his daughter's behalf. Fanny would discourage him, reminding her father pragmatically that

---

12. This manuscript, which includes Kemble's cuts and changes, is on deposit at the Library of Congress.

their life on the "highways" meant they would inevitably get splattered with mud.

When Kemble began to entertain suitors, especially during her tour of America, the gossip became even more of a nuisance. Her retirement from the stage and marriage to one of Philadelphia's most eligible bachelors did not quell the wagging tongues for long.

A guessing game began shortly after she wed as to how long the union might last. From the earliest days of her marriage, Kemble was not content to play the submissive wife. Further, her sense of being weighed on the scales by Philadelphia's social arbiters, of being under her in-laws' watchful—and often disapproving—gaze contributed to stress within the marriage. Her growing disillusionment with her husband, her outspokenness during marital wrangles, and the couple's violent battles over her writing made the Butlers' unhappy marriage a topic of gossip in parlors up and down the eastern seaboard.

When Kemble sailed with her daughter Sarah to visit her family in England in the fall of 1836 without her husband, a New York newspaper reported: "What with her playing, scribbling, riding, a marrying, she has been as much talked about as a comet! . . . From the silent manner of her departure, we fear there is a settled coolness between her and our republican publick."[13]

The disintegration of Kemble's relationship with her husband is chronicled in detail in her *Journal of a Residence on a Georgian Plantation* (1863), which covers events during the winter and spring of 1838–39. Shortly after Kemble wrote this journal, which took the form of letters to her friend Elizabeth Dwight Sedgwick, Harriet St. Leger asked if she would publish the letters. Kemble replied:

> *I think such a publication would be a breach of confidence, an advantage taken on my part of the situation of trust, which I held on the estate. As my condemnation of the whole system is unequivocal, and all my illustrations of its evils must be drawn from our own plantation, I do not think I have a right to exhibit the interior management and*

---

13. Quoted in Furnas, *Fanny Kemble*, p. 181.

economy of that property to the world at large, as a sample of Southern
slavery, especially as I did not go thither with any such purpose. This
winter I think I shall mention my desire upon the subject before going to
the South, and of course any such publication must then depend on the
acquiescence of the owners of the estate.[14]

Kemble, however, never went South again, and never received her husband's consent to publish the journal.

Shortly after she wrote it, she suggested that her Georgia manuscript was of no importance, and could not help the slaves on her husband's plantation. But by the time the Civil War erupted, conditions had seriously altered. Although she no longer cared about offending her husband, Kemble did not want to alienate her younger daughter, Fan. But, mourning Union defeats, Kemble eventually decided to unmask the evils of slaveholding by letting the public read her eyewitness account of life in the Georgia Sea Islands.

As she visited England during the American Civil War, Kemble was appalled by the political overtures of southern sympathizers and feared that Britain would recognize the Confederacy. So Kemble, nerved by right, released her journal for publication. She believed that her celebrity and her eyewitness account "should carry with it some authority." She knew her brutal portraits of the slaves' suffering would move an audience. Kemble's lengthy recitation of the "bare details" was a staple of abolitionist propaganda. In many ways, she let the slaves speak for themselves.

When it was first published in England in May 1863, Kemble's Georgia journal met with strongly favorable reviews. The *Athenaeum* asserted that "a more startling and fearful narrative on a well-worn subject was never laid before readers."[15] The Ladies' Emancipation Society of London reprinted selections from Kemble's journal and dis-

---

14. Kemble, *Records of Later Life*, p. 203.

15. Quoted in Malcolm Bell, *Major Butler's Legacy* (Athens: University of Georgia Press, 1987), p. 376.

tributed hundreds of thousands of pamphlets to drum up support for the Union to defeat the Confederacy.

An American edition of the volume appeared in June 1863, and the Yankee press embraced the book enthusiastically. Frederick Law Olmsted, writing under a pen name, endorsed Kemble's indictment, calling her observations "deep, thorough, detailed."[16] The *Atlantic Monthly* called the book "a permanent and most valuable chapter in our history."[17]

Journal of a Residence on a Georgian Plantation remains Kemble's most enduring literary contribution. Her searing indictment of slavery is rendered even more powerful as it is interlaced with her own struggles over her marriage, her future, and her fears for her children. She journeyed South with high hopes, believing the stories she was told: that her husband's human property enjoyed a privileged status among southern slaves, that they were better treated than most. She wanted to live among her husband's slaves, where she hoped to improve their conditions by her Christian example and charity. Almost as soon as she set foot on Butler's Island, however, Kemble discovered the naiveté of these hopes and the incredible hardships of blacks in bondage.

Kemble established a slave hospital and dictated improvements for the slave nursery. When female slaves brought forward applications for assistance, she pleaded their cases to her husband. Kemble, however, soon found her entreaties on behalf of the slaves unwelcome. The overseer retaliated with a whip when women went directly to the mistress to lodge their complaints. Fanny's husband eventually forbade her to listen to their laments—which accelerated the deterioration of their faltering union.

Although Kemble was prevented from acting on slave women's behalf, she heard their testimony and her heart went out to them. Kemble was devastated by their detailed chronicles of miscarriages, by

---

16. Ibid., p. 377.

17. Ibid., p. 378.

the number of babies who died, by the unhealthy horrors wrought by plantation life.

Kemble was riveted by slave women's testimony of sexual exploitation. She came to understand that black women could not resist white male aggression—that they were coerced and occasionally raped. She learned of the complicity of white women, and of slave mothers who were whipped because they had given birth and confirmed the identity of the white man who had fathered their child.

Over the course of the weeks Kemble spent on Butler's plantations, her opinion of Butler's slaveholding role changed radically. She went from finding him merely difficult to deriding him as a tyrant. At one point Kemble ran away, rowing a boat in the dead of night to a nearby wharf. A descendant has speculated that Kemble's flight may have been motivated by discovery of her husband's sexual exploitation of a slave woman. In any case, Kemble returned to Butler and her children, resigned to endure the remainder of her days in Georgia and to do what she could to make the slaves' lives more bearable. She handed out scraps of flannel and bits of meat, feeling defeated by her circumscribed role.

Kemble's volume was the first eyewitness testimony by a white woman, a plantation mistress, to condemn slavery as a system of institutionalized concubinage—as a system that not only allowed but did nothing to punish white sexual predators. This indictment was only one element of Kemble's comprehensive attack upon slavery—her dismantling of planters' paternalism.

In the journal she claimed that "almost every Southern planter has a family more or less numerous of illegitimate colored children." Although she discreetly included dashes to hide the identity of the guilty, she nevertheless, to southern readers and especially to her Georgian neighbors, had named names. This was something for which Lost Cause advocates never forgave her. Almost a century after Kemble's *Journal of a Residence* was published, campaigns were still engineered to discredit her views.

In the 1930s a descendant of Roswell King (the overseer who

Kemble alleged fathered several mixed-race children) wrote letters claiming that Kemble had written lies about her grandfather because Kemble was in love with him and King did not return her affections.[18] In the 1960s historian Margaret Davis Cate tried to persuade John Anthony Scott to abandon his project on Kemble, contending that "now, at a time when feelings between the races is at such a stage, to bring out another edition of Fanny Kemble's false statements about what she saw in the south will fan the flames of hatred."[19]

When Scott refused her entreaties, Cate wrote an article designed to discredit Kemble. Cate argued that Kemble had included deliberate errors in her journal—for example, that she had claimed she was on the island during a tragic duel between members of two prominent planter families. Cate proved that the duel took place before Kemble ever landed on St. Simons, and went on to question Kemble's integrity, suggesting that her entire volume should be dismissed as a result. Who could trust Kemble when she had rearranged facts to heighten her book's drama?[20]

For over a hundred years white apologists were angered by Kemble's attack on theories of racial inferiority. Kemble offered illustrations of slaves being entrepreneurial, demonstrating industry and talent when given the chance. She described many instances of slaves acting noble, clever, and courageous. In short, Kemble debunked several aspects of planters' "Sambo" stereotypes.

She systematically demolished racist arguments. Kemble believed that the slaveholders' ideology was riddled with contradiction: she noted, for example, "There is no law in the white man's nature which

---

18. Julia King to ———, 24 October 1930, Julia King Collection, Georgia Historical Society.

19. Margaret Davis Cate to John Anthony Scott, 2 April 1960, Margaret Davis Cate Collection, Georgia Historical Society.

20. Margaret Davis Cate, "Mistakes in Fanny Kemble's Georgia Journal," *Georgia Historical Quarterly* 44 (March 1960). Cate ordered five thousand reprints of this article for circulation, sending it out to prominent writers and reviewers to discredit Scott's new edition of Kemble's journal.

prevents him from making a colored woman the mother of his children, but there is a law on his statute-books forbidding him to make her his wife."[21] Her deadly aim at racial hypocrisy invited the slave-holders' wrath.

Kemble felt more keenly the wrath of her own daughter, whose fury toward her mother's decision to publish the Georgia journal receded only glacially after the war. Fan Butler discouraged her mother's literary efforts, even after her father's death in 1867. During 1873 and 1874, when Kemble prepared her articles for publication in the *Atlantic Monthly*, and later, when her *Records of a Girlhood* (1879) became a best-seller, her younger daughter was indifferent. But when Kemble decided to edit another installment of her memoir, this one to cover the years following her marriage, Fan Butler exploded. She wrote her mother a lengthy diatribe in May 1881 to try to prevent publication, complaining, "You have said over and over again that you thought people most unjustified in writing personal reminiscences of others which would be painful to their relations and friends." She continued, enraged, "Does being their mother give you the right to wound and distress them?" She reminded her mother of their troubled past: "I have never lost in the least degree . . . the feeling of bitterness I have always felt about the publication of your first southern book . . . nothing would ever induce me to have it in the house."[22] Kemble responded tersely that she would be the judge of what she should or should not write and that she would accept the consequences. She thus found herself in conflict with her daughter over the very same issues she had fought over with her husband nearly half a century earlier.

Fan Butler Leigh was so upset that she tried to enlist her sister's support, sniping that "the success of her first book [*Records of a Girlhood*] has so aroused her vanity and love of notoriety that the desire to

---

21. Frances Anne Kemble, *Journal of a Residence on a Georgian Plantation* (New York: Harper & Bros., 1863), p. 15.

22. Fanny Butler Leigh to Fanny Kemble, 1 May 1881, Wister Family Collection, Historical Society of Pennsylvania.

keep herself before the public is irresistible."[23] Sarah Wister was unwilling to referee or to interfere. Yet Fan's complaints did have an effect; Kemble reported to her good friend Henry James that she was cutting her forthcoming manuscript and including "only such portions as I thought would give less pain and offence to everyone."[24] But Kemble wanted her side of the story told after so many years of gossip and speculation. She felt her own journals were a way to set the record straight.

At the same time, she fought fiercely with her publisher, Richard Bentley, over "filling in the blanks," providing the names of those to whom she wrote and those she discussed. Kemble even balked at identifying the close friend to whom most of the letters were addressed: "I do not wish my friend Miss St. Leger's *name* inserted—it is clearly indicated by the place of her residence, etc."[25]

Protracted negotiations with her publisher indicate the level of ambivalence Kemble felt about this project; several times she threatened to return her advance and cancel the contract. Eventually, however, despite her reservations and over the strenuous objections of her daughter Fan, Kemble published *Records of Later Life* in 1881. This volume met with even more acclaim than had the earlier *Records of a Girlhood.*

Kemble had excised as much personal material as she felt she could in this latest volume, and had even, in some cases, masked identities. Perhaps Fan saw this as a concession; in any case, Fan did not break off relations with her mother as she had threatened. Two years later, however, Fan published her own memoir, *Ten Years on a Georgian Plantation* (1883), which she saw as a means of correcting some of the misleading impressions she felt were conveyed in her mother's Georgian journal. Leigh's volume did not garner anything like the reception of

---

23. Quoted in Bell, *Legacy,* p. 398.

24. Quoted in Dorothy Marshall, *Fanny Kemble* (London: Weidenfeld & Nicholson, 1977), p. 263.

25. Frances Anne Kemble to Richard Bentley, 5 February 1879, Bentley Collection, University of Illinois, Urbana.

any of her mother's journals, going virtually unheralded. A later critic commented that to compare Fan's book to her mother's was like comparing *The Swiss Family Robinson* to *Wuthering Heights*.[26]

Kemble undertook several formidable literary projects throughout the 1880s. She published her Shakespearean criticism, and was finishing a novel in 1889 when publisher Richard Bentley contacted her, begging for another installment of her memoirs. Kemble was indifferent to his repeated requests; but she allowed him to peruse a stack of collected letters to see if they might be suitable, adding, "Pray believe once and for all that your entire rejection of the Mss. will not cause me the slightest annoyance."[27]

The letters she had sent along were not enough for a complete volume; so, early in 1890, at Bentley's request, she forwarded some additional letters, telling him to print them "where you please and how you please." She was essentially signing off on the project. For this reason, Kemble's final work of memoir, *Further Records* (1890), is much inferior to the two previous installments, and is full of flaws and errors. Many dates are wrong, and the letters appear hodge-podge. Yet Bentley was right: the public had an insatiable appetite for Kemble's prose. Despite its shortcomings, her vivid voice and brilliant insights shine through in *Further Records*, the last installment of Fanny Kemble's remarkable memoirs.

When Kemble died in 1893, her friend Henry James asserted that she had created some of the finest autobiographical writing of her era. In the hundred-plus years since her death, her volumes of poems have gone out of print, her plays have fallen out of favor, and her novel is all but forgotten. Yet her journals have been mined by several generations of scholars. Kemble continues to be a favorite resource for southern historians.

As a writer and thinker, Fanny Kemble has been most warmly em-

---

26. Margaret Armstrong, *Fanny Kemble: A Passionate Victorian* (New York: Macmillan, 1938), p. 354.

27. Frances Anne Kemble to Richard Bentley, 15 October 1889, Bentley Collection, University of Illinois, Urbana.

braced by revisionist historians of slavery in the late twentieth century. Her compelling mix of evidence and analysis stirs each rising generation of readers into a better understanding of the conditions the slaves endured and the myths and realities that clashed every day on an antebellum slaveholder's estate. Kemble's writings on slavery remain riveting reading.

But Kemble was famous long before and long after her plantation journal and its publication. So for this reason *Fanny Kemble's Journals* includes excerpts from her other volumes of memoir. Here are Kemble's views on life in the theater, her comments on her role as wife and mother, and especially her views as a writer struggling to juggle the competing demands of gender and status. Kemble was a keen observer of her transatlantic world and offered perceptive comments on the conditions of workers in Europe and America, on women's education in England and the United States, on laws governing women's wages and the custody of children, and on many other issues debated during her day.

Yet the main body of excerpts concentrates on her confrontation with slavery. Here are her reactions to life among the slaves on Butler Island and St. Simons. The selections allow us to see the ways in which Kemble's plantation experiences permanently shaped her outlook and powerfully reveal issues of race and sex.

Kemble has in recent years been rediscovered by a new generation of feminist scholars interested in representations of voice, self, and gender. Reexamination of compelling texts from the past can lead to new directions for the future. Kemble's fresh, unvarnished opinions offer modern readers a stimulating portrait of a woman in struggle, a woman whose life spanned virtually the whole of a century and the transatlantic world.

Studying the journals to understand slavery or to appreciate women's lives in the nineteenth century can be a bracing exercise. But perhaps it is not as rewarding as just reading them. Above all, Fanny Kemble's writing is entertaining, informative, and full of memorable scenes: her first encounter with Niagara Falls, her rescue of a homeless boy in the streets of Hull, her impressions of a slave funeral. These and many more absorbing reminiscences draw us into her thrall and convince us of her wit, her compassion, and, above all, her talent as a writer.

The excerpts from Kemble's journals are given with a minimum of editorial apparatus, in order to present a chronological narrative of her life in her own words from when she was eighteen until she was in her seventies. At the end of each selection, in brackets, I cite the title of the publication from which the excerpt was taken, using the following abbreviations:

JA: *Journal of America* (1835).

YC: *A Year of Consolation* (1847).

GP: *Journal of a Residence on a Georgian Plantation* (1863).

RG: *Records of a Girlhood* (1878).

LL: *Records of Later Life* (1881).

FR: *Further Records* (1890).

Where appropriate, I have provided information about the subjects discussed in Kemble's entries and pertinent intervening events in her life, preceding or following entries and within the entries themselves (my comments within the entries appear in brackets). In addition, marginal notations have been inserted in order to highlight Kemble's subject matter.

Kemble's ellipses are indicated by the symbol ~~~. My deletions of text are indicated in the usual way, with three dots (. . .).

Kemble's own words are given throughout, complete with her idiosyncratic spelling, abbreviations, and use of language.

Life on the Stage
1828–1832

At the age of eighteen, while living in London with her family, Kemble contemplated a life on stage.

St. James Street, London
February 1828

Decision to go on stage

Dearest H [Harriet St. Leger (1795–1878), an Irish aristocrat and spinster who was Kemble's lifelong confidante],

In my last letter want of time and room prevented my enlarging on my hint about the stage, but as far as my own determination goes at present, I think it is the course that I shall most likely pursue. You know that independence of mind and body seems to me the great desideratum of life; I am not patient of restraint or submissive to authority, and my head and heart are engrossed with the idea of exercising and developing the literary talent which I think I possess. This is meat, drink, and sleep to me; my world, in which I live, and have my happiness; and, moreover, I hope, my means of fame (the prize for which I pray). To a certain degree it may be my means of procuring benefits of a more substantial nature, which I am by no means inclined to estimate at less than their worth. I do not think I am fit to marry, to make an obedient wife or affectionate mother; my imagination is paramount with me, and would disqualify me, I think, for the everyday, matter-of-fact cares and duties of the mistress of a household and the head of a family. I think I should be unhappy and the cause of unhappiness to others if I were to marry. I cannot swear I shall never fall in love, but if I do I will fall out of it again, for I do not think I shall ever so far lose sight of my best interest and happiness as to enter into a relation for which I feel so unfit. Now, if I do not marry, what is to become of me in the event of anything happening to my father? His property is almost all gone; I doubt if we shall ever to receive one pound from it. It is likely that, supposing I were willing to undergo the drudgery of writing for my bread, I could live by my wits and the produce of my brain; or is such an existence desirable?

Perhaps I might attain to the literary dignity of being the lioness of a season, asked to dinner parties "because I am so clever;" perhaps my writing faculty might become a useful auxiliary to some other less precarious dependence; but to write to eat,—to live, in short,—that seems to me to earn hard money after a very hard fashion. The stage is a profession that people who have a talent for it make lucrative, and which honourable conduct may make respectable; one which would place me at once beyond the fear of want, and that is closely allied in its nature to my beloved literary pursuits.

If I should (as my father and mother seem to think not unlikely) change my mind with respect to marrying, the stage need be no bar to that, and if I continue to write, the stage might both help me in and derive assistance from my exercise of the pursuit of dramatic authorship. And the mere mechanical labour of writing costs me so little, that the union of the two occupations does not seem to me a difficulty. My father said the other day, "There is a fine fortune to be made by any young woman, of even decent talent, on the stage now." A fine fortune is a fine thing; to be sure, there remains a rather material question to settle, that of "even decent talent." A passion for all beautiful poetry I am sure you will grant me; and you would perhaps be inclined to take my father and mother's word for my dramatic capacity. I spoke to them earnestly on this subject lately, and they both, with some reluctance, I think, answered me, to my questions, that they thought, as far as they could judge (and, unless partiality blinds them entirely, none can be better judges), I might succeed. In some respects, no girl intending herself for this profession can have had better opportunities of acquiring just notions on the subject of acting. I have constantly heard refined and thoughtful criticism on our greatest dramatic works, and on every various way of rendering them effective on the stage. I have been lately very frequently to the theatre, and seen and heard observingly, and exercised my own judgement and critical faculty to the best of my ability, according to these same canons of taste by which it has been formed. Nature has certainly not been as favourable to me as might have been wished, if I am to embrace a calling where personal beauty, if not indispensable, is so great an advantage. But if the informing spirit be mine, it shall go hard if, with a face and voice as obedient to my emotions as mine are, I do not in some measure make up for the want of good looks. My father is now proprietor and manager of the theatre, [Covent Garden] and those certainly are favourable circumstances for my entering on a career which is one of great labour and some exposure, at the best, to a woman, and where a young girl cannot be too prudent herself, nor her protectors too careful of her. I hope I have not taken up this notion hastily, and I have no fear of looking only on the bright side of the picture, for ours is a house where that is very seldom seen . . .

H[arriet], and if my going on the stage would nearly double that income, lessen my dear father's anxieties for us all, and the quantity of work which he latterly has often felt too much for him, and remove the many privations which my dear mother cheerfully endures, as well as the weight of her uncertainty about our future provision, would not this be a "consummation devoutly to be wished?". . . [RG]

St. James Street, London
Mardi 1828

My Dearest H[arriet]
I have been thinking what you have been thinking of my long silence, about which, however, perhaps you have not been thinking at all.

What you say in one of your last about my destroying your letters troubles me a good deal, dearest H[arriet]. I really cannot bear to think of it; why, those letters are one of my very few precious possessions. When I am unhappy (as I sometimes am), I read them over, and I feel strengthened and comforted; if it is your positive desire that I should burn them, of course I must do it; but if it is only a sort of "I think you had better," that you have about it, I shall keep them, and you must be satisfied with one of my old "I can't help it's." As for my own scrawls, I do *not* desire that you should keep them. I write, as I speak, on the impulse of the moment, and I should be sorry that the incoherent and often contradictory thoughts that I pour forth daily should be preserved against me by anybody.

My father is now in Edinburgh. He has been absent from London about a week. I had a conversation with him about the stage some time before he went, in which he allowed that, should our miserably uncertain circumstances finally settle unfavourably, the theatre might be an honourable and advantageous resource for me; but that at present he should be sorry to see me adopt that career. As he is the best and kindest father and friend to us all, such a decision on his part was conclusive, as you will easily believe; and I have forborne all further allusion to the subject, although on some accounts I regret being obliged to do so.

I was delighted with your long letter of criticisms; I am grateful to you for taking the trouble of telling me so minutely all you thought about my play. For myself, although at the time I wrote it I was rather puffed up and elated in spirit, and looked at it naturally in far too favourable a light, I assure you I have long since come to a much soberer frame of mind respecting it. I think it is quite unfit for the stage, where the little poetical merit it possesses would necessarily be lost; besides, its construction is wholly undramatic. The only satisfaction I now take in it is entirely one of hope; I am very young, and I cannot help feeling that it offers some promise for the future, which I trust may be fulfilled. Now even, already, I am sure I could do infinitely better; nor will it be long, I think, before I try my strength again. If you could see the multiplicity of subjects drawn up in my book under the head of "projected works," how you would shake your wise head, and perhaps your lean sides.   [*RG*]

St. James Street, London
August 22 [1829]

[My Dearest Harriet]

Planning stage debut

I have a great deal to tell you about our affairs, and the effect that their unhappy posture seems likely to produce upon my future plans and prospects. Do you remember a letter I wrote to you a long time ago about going on the stage? and another, some time before that, about my becoming a governess? The urgent necessity which I think now exists for exertion, in all those who are capable of it amongst us, has again turned my thoughts to these two considerations. My father's property, and all that we might ever have hoped to have derived from it, being utterly destroyed in the unfortunate issue of our affairs, his personal exertions are all that remain to him and us to look to. There are circumstances in which reflections that our minds would not admit at other times of necessity force themselves upon our consideration. Those talents and qualifications, both mental and physical, which have been so mercifully preserved to my dear father hitherto, cannot, in the natural course of things, all remain unimpaired for many more years. It is right then that those of us who have the power to do so should at once lighten his arms of all unnecessary burthen . . . [*RG*]

St. James Street, London
December 14 [1829]

[Dearest]

Theatrical debut

My trial is over, and, thank Heaven! most fortunately. Our most sanguine wishes could hardly have gone beyond the result, and at the same time I hail my success as a source of great happiness to my dear father and mother, I almost venture to hope that the interest which has been excited in the public may tend to revive once more the decaying dramatic art. You say it is a very fascinating occupation; perhaps it is, though it does not appear to me so, and I think it carries with it drawbacks enough to operate as an antidote to the vanity and love of admiration which it can hardly fail to foster. The mere embodying of the exquisite ideals of poetry is a great enjoyment, but after that, or rather for that, comes in ours, as in all arts, the mechanical process, the labour, the refining, the controlling the very feeling one has, in order to manifest it in the best way to the perception of others; and when that intense feeling and careful work can accomplish, is done, an actor must often see those points of his performance which are most worthy of approbation overlooked, and others, perhaps crude in taste or less true in feeling, commended; which must tend much, I think, to sober the mind as to the value of applause. Above all, the constant consciousness of the immeasurable distance between a fine conception and the best execution of it, must in acting, as in all art, be a powerful check to vanity and self-satisfaction.

As to the mere excitement proceeding from the public applause of a theatre, I am sure you will believe me when I say I do not think I shall ever experience it. But should I reckon too much upon my own steadiness, I have the incessant care and watchfulness of my dear mother to rely on, and I do rely on it as an invaluable safeguard, both to the purity and good taste of all that I may do on the stage, and the quiet and soberness of my mind under all this new excitement. She has borne all her anxieties wonderfully well, and I now hope she will reap some repayment for them. My dear father is very happy; indeed, we have all cause for heartfelt thankfulness when we think what a light has dawned upon our prospects, lately so dismal and overcast. My own motto in all this must be, as far as possible, "Beget a temperance in all things." I trust I shall be enabled to rule myself by it, and in the firm hope that my endeavour to do what is right will be favoured and assisted, I have committed myself, nothing doubting, to the stormy sea of life . . .   [RG]

St. James Street, London
March 9 [1830]

[Dearest Harriet]

. . . However, all went well with me till the last act, when my father's acting and my own previous state of nervousness combined to make my part of the tragedy anything but feigning; I sobbed so violently that I could hardly articulate my words, and at the last fell upon the dead body of Beverley with a hysterical cry that had all the merit of pure nature, if none other, to recommend it. Fortunately the curtain fell then, and I was carried to my dressing-room to finish my fit in private. The last act of that play gives me such pains in my arms and legs, with sheer nervous distress, that I am ready to drop down with exhaustion at the end of it; and this reminds me of the very difficult question which you expect me to answer, respecting the species of power which is called into play in the act, so called, of *acting* . . .

My dearest H[arriet], you express something of regret at my necessity (I can hardly call it choice) of a profession. There are many times when I myself cannot help wishing it might have been otherwise; but then came other thoughts: the talent which I possess for it was, I suppose, given to me for some good purpose, and to be used. Nevertheless, when I reflect that although hitherto my profession has not appeared to me attractive enough to engross my mind, yet admiration and applause, and the excitement springing therefrom, may become necessary to me, I resolve not only to watch but to pray against such a result. I have no desire to sell my soul for anything, least of all for sham fame, mere notoriety. Besides, my mind has such far deeper enjoyment in other pursuits; the *happiness* of reading Shakespeare's heavenly imaginations is so far beyond all the excitement of acting them (white satin, gas lights, applause, and all), that I cannot conceive a time when having him in my hand will not compensate for the absence of any amount of public popularity. While I can sit obliviously curled up in an armchair, and read what he says till my eyes are full of delicious, quiet tears, and my heart of blessed, good, quiet thoughts and feelings,

I shall not crave that which falls so far short of any real enjoyment, and hitherto certainly seems to me as remote as possible from any real happiness . . . [RG]

Great Russell Street, London
March 9, 1831

My Dear H[arriet],
Why are you not here to kiss and congratulate me? I am so proud and happy! Mr. Murray [John Murray (1809–1892), son and successor of eminent publisher of same name] has given me four hundred and fifty pounds for my play, alone! the other things he does not wish to publish with it. Only think of it—was there ever such publishing munificence! My father has the face to say *it is not enough!* but looks so proud and pleased that his face alone shows it is *too much* by a great deal; my mother is enchanted, and I am so happy, so thankful for this prosperous result of my work, so delighted at earning so, much, so surprised and charmed to think that what gave me nothing but pleasure in the doing has brought me such an after-harvest of profit; it is too good almost to be true and yet it is true . . . [RG]

Great Russell Street, London
April 25 [1831]

[Dearest Harriet]
Dall [Adelaide de Camp, Fanny's mother's sister, who lived with the Kembles] was saying that she thought in two years of hard work we might, that is, my father and myself, earn enough to enable us to live in the south of France. This monstrous theatre and its monstrous liabilities will banish us all as it did my uncle Kemble [John Philip Kemble, Charles's brother, whose financial difficulties forced him into exile]. But that I should be sorry to live so far out of the reach of H[arriet], I think the south of France would be a pleasant abode: a delicious climate, a quiet existence, a less artificial state of society and mode of life,

a picturesque nature round me, and my own dear ones and my scribbling with me,—I think with all these conditions I could be happy enough in the south of France or anywhere . . . [*RG*]

Great Russell Street, London
June 23 [1831]

[Dearest Harriet]

On marriage

We [Author Anna Jameson (1794–1860) and Kemble] talked of marriage, and a woman's chance of happiness in giving her life into another's keeping. I said I thought if one did not expect too much one might secure a reasonably fair amount of happiness, though of course the risk one ran was immense. I never shall forget the expression of her face; it was momentary, and passed away almost immediately, but it has haunted me ever since. [*RG*]

Great Russell Street, London
Thursday, July 7 [1831]

America

. . . At dinner, as we were talking about America, and I was expressing my disinclination ever to go thither, my father said: "If my cause (our Chancery suit) goes ill before the Lords, I think the best thing I can do will be to take ship from Liverpool and sail to the United States." [Charles Kemble had several legal cases pending, to maintain his claim on Covent Garden.] I choked a little at this, but presently found voice to say, "Ebben son pronta," but he replied, "No, that he should go alone." That you never should, my own dear father!∼∼∼But I do hate the very thought of America . . . [*RG*]

Great Russell Street, London
Friday, July 15 [1831]

Had a long talk this morning with dear Dall about my dislike to the stage. I do not think it is the acting itself that is so disagreeable to me, but the public personal exhibition, the violence done (as it seems to me) to womanly dignity and decorum in thus becoming the gaze of every eye and theme of every tongue . . . [RG]

Great Russell Street, London
Friday, July 22 [1831]

. . . "While you remain single," says she [Dall], "and choose to work, your fortune is an independent and ample one; as soon as you marry, there's no such thing. Your position in society," says she, "is both a pleasanter and more distinguished one than your birth or real station entitles you to; but that also is the result of your professional exertions, and might, and probably would, alter for the worse if you left the stage; for, after all, it is mere frivolous fashionable popularity." I ought to have got up and made her a curtsy for that. So that it seems I have fortune and fame (such as it is)—positive real advantages, which I cannot give with myself, and which I cease to own when I give myself away, which certainly makes my marrying any one or any one marrying me rather a solemn consideration; for I lose everything and my marryee gains nothing in a worldly point of view—says she—and it's incontrovertible and not pleasant. So I took up Dante, and read about the devils boiled in pitch, which refreshed my imagination and cheered my spirits very much . . . [RG]

Great Russell Street, London
Friday, August 5 [1831]

. . . We had a long discussion to-day as to the possibility of women being good dramatic writers. I think it is so impossible that I actually believe their I physical organization is against it; and, after all, it is great nonsense saying that intellect is of no sex. The brain is, of course, of the same sex as the rest of the creature; besides, the original feminine nature, the whole of our training and education, our inevitable ignorance of common life and general human nature, and the various experience of existence, from which we are debarred with the most sedulous care, is insuperably against it. Perhaps some of the manly, wicked

Women writers

Queens—Semiramis [celebrated ruler in Assyria who founded Baby-
lon and built great cities and aquaducts; when she was overthrown by
her son, tradition says she was changed into a dove and became a de-
ity], Cleopatra, could have written plays; but they lived their tragedies
instead of writing them.   [RG]

Southampton
August 19, 1831

My Dearest H[arriet],
I do not like to defer answering you any longer, though I am not very
fit to write, for I am half blind with crying, and have a torturing side-
ache, the results of bodily fatigue and nervous anxiety; but if I do not
write to you to-night I know not when I *shall* be able to do so, for I
shall have to rehearse every morning and to act every night, and I expect the intermediate hours will be spent on the road to and from
Bannisters, the Fitzhughs' place near here. [The Fitzhughes were close
friends of the Kembles; Emily Fitzhugh's mother was one of Sarah
Siddons's best friends.] I have been travelling ever since half-past eight
to-day, and have hardly been three hours out of the coach which
brought us from Weymouth, where we have been acting for the last
week. Your letter followed me from Plymouth, and right glad I was to
get it~~~I do not know what I can write you of if not myself, and I
dare say, after all, my thoughts are more amusing to you, or rather,
perhaps, more useful, in your processes of observing and studying human nature in general, through my individual case, than if I wrote you
word what plays we had been acting, etc., etc.~~~To meet pain, no
matter how severe, the mind girds up its loins, and finds a sort of
strength of resistance in its endurance, which is a species of activity. To
endure hopelessly prolonged suspense is another matter quite, and a
far heavier demand upon all patient power that is in one . . .   [RG]

Great Russell Street, London
Wednesday, December 21 [1831]

[Dearest Harriet]
I found a letter at home from Emily Fitzhugh; she writes me word she *Acting*
has been revising my aunt Siddons's letters; thence an endless discus- *genius*
sion as to the nature of genius, what it is. I suppose really nothing but
the creative power, and so it remains a question if the greatest actor
can properly be said to possess it. Again, how far does the masterly
filling out of an inferior conception by a superior execution of it, such
as really great actors frequently present, fall short of creative power,
properly so called? Is it a thing positive, of individual inherent quality,
or comparative, and composed of mere respective quantity? Can its
manifestation be partial, and restricted to one faculty, or must it be a
pervading influence, permeating the whole mind? Certainly Mrs.
Siddons was what we call a great dramatic genius, and off the stage
gave not the slightest indication of unusual intellectual capacity of any
sort. Kean [Edmund Kean, British actor renowned for his roles as
Richard III, Othello, Hamlet, and Lear], the only actor whose performances have ever realized to me my idea of the effect tragic acting
ought to produce, acted part of his parts rather than ever a whole
character, and a work of genius should at least show unity of conception. My father, whose fulfilling of a particular range of characters is as
nearly as possible perfect, wants depth and power, and power seem to
me the core, the very marrow, so to speak, of genius; and if it is not genius that gave incomparable majesty and terror to my aunt's Lady
Macbeth, and to Kean's Othello incomparable pathos and passion, and
to my father's Benedict incomparable spirit and grace, what is it? Mere
talent carried beyond a certain point? If so, where does the one begin
and the other end? Or is genius a precious, inconvertible, intellectual
metal, of which some people have a grain and a half, and some only
half a grain . . . [RG]

Great Russell Street, London
Wednesday, February 29 [1832]

[Dearest Harriet]

I rode with Henry [Kemble's younger brother (1814–1857)], and after I got home told my father that his horse was quite well, and would be fit for his use on Saturday. He replied sadly that his horse must be sold, for that from the first, though he had not liked to vex me by saying so, it was an expense he could not conscientiously afford. I had expected this, and certainly, when from day to day a man may be obliged to declare himself insolvent, keeping a horse does seem rather absurd. He then went on to speak about the ruin that is falling upon us; and dismal enough it is to stand under the crumbling fabric we have having and living, body, substance, and all but soul, to prop, and see it must inevitably fall and crush us presently. Yet from my earliest childhood I remember this has been hanging over us. I have heard it foretold I have known it expected, and there is no reason why it should now take any of us by surprise, or strike us with sudden dismay. Thank God, our means of existence lie within ourselves; while health and strength are vouchsafed to us there is no need to despond. It is very hard and sad to be come so far on in or rather so far into age, as my father is, without any hope of support for himself and my mother but toil, and that of the severest kind; but God is merciful. He has hitherto cared for us, as He cares for all His creatures, and He will not forsake us of we do not forsake Him or ourselves~~~My father and I need scarcely remain without engagements, either in London or the provinces~~~If our salaries are smaller, so must our expenses be. The house must go, the carriage must go, the horses must go, and yet we may be sufficiently comfortable and very happy—unless, indeed, we have to go to America, and that will be dreadful~~~We are yet all stout and strong, and we are yet altogether. It is pitiful to see how my father still clings to that theatre. Is it because the art he loves once had its noblest dwelling there? Is it because his own name and the names of his brother and sister are graven, as it were, on its very stones? Does he think he could not act in a smaller theatre? What can, in spite of his interest, make him so loath to leave that ponderous ruin? Even to-day, after summing up all the sorrow and care and toil and waste of life and fortune which that concern has cost his brother, himself, and all of us, he exclaimed, "Oh, if I had but £10,000, I could set it all right again, even now!" My mother and I actually stared at this infatuation. If I had twenty, or a hundred thousand pounds, not one farthing would I give to the redeeming of that fatal millstone, which cannot be raised, but will infallibly drag everything tied to it down to the level of its own destruction. The past is past, and for the future we must think and act as speedily as we may. If our salaries are half what they am now we need not starve; and, as long as God keeps us in health of body and mind, nothing need signify, provided we are not obliged to separate and go off to that dreadful America . . .   [RG]

Edinburgh
July 1, 1832

Dearest H[arriet],
We left London on Wednesday at eight o'clock. The parting between my mother and Dall . . . and myself and my dear little sister, was most bitter~~~John [Kemble's older brother (1807–1857)] came down to Greenwich with us but would not come on board the steamboat. He stood on the shore and I at the ship's side, looking at what I knew was him, though my eyes could distinguish none of his features from the distance. My poor mother stood crying by my side, and bade me send him away. I gave him one signal, which he returned, and then ran up the beach, and was gone!—gone for two years, perhaps more; perhaps gone from me for ever in this world!~~~

Departure for America

We should be in Liverpool on Monday morning, the 16th of July, and go to Radley's Hotel, where I hope we shall find you on our arrival. My father is pretty well, in spite of all the late anxieties and annoyances he has had to wade through. In the course of the day preceding our departure from London two arrests were served upon him by creditors of the theatre, who, I suppose, when he is gone the whole concern must collapse and fall to pieces, and I began to think some means would be devised to prevent our leaving England after our parting on Wednesday morning, was, as I told you, most miserable~~~My poor mother was braver than I had expected; but her parting from us, poor thing, is yet to come~~~. [RG]

Edinburgh
July 7 1832

Saturday, 7th.—Miserable day of parting! of tearing away and wrenching asunder!~~~At eleven we were obliged to go to rehearsal, and when we returned found my mother busy with her packing~~~When she was gone, I sat down beside my father with a book in my hand, not reading, but listening to his stifled sobbing; and every now and then, in spite of my determination not to do it, looking up to see how far the ship had moved. (Our windows looked over the Forth [river feeding into the harbor].) But the white column of steam was rising steadily from close under Newhaven, and for upwards of half an hour continued to do so. I had resolved not to raise my eyes again from my book, when a sudden exclamation from my father made me spring up, and I saw the steamer had left the shore, and was moving fast towards Inchkeith, the dark smoky wake that lingered behind it showing how far it had already gone from us, and warning us how soon it would be beyond the ken of our aching eyes~~~The carriage was announced, and with a heavy heart and aching head, I drove to the theatre~~~The play was "Francis I," for the first time. The house was very fine; I acted abominably, but that was not much to be wondered at. However, I always have acted this part of my own vilely; the language is not natural—mere stilted declamation from first to last, most fatiguing to the chest, and impossible for me to do anything with, as it excites no emotion in me whatever~~~   [RG]

Edinburgh
July 9, 1832

My Dearest H[arriet],
I had just left my father at the window that overlooks the Forth, watching my poor mother's ship sailing away to England, when I received your letter; and it is impossible to imagine a sorer, sadder heart than that which I greeted it~~~Thank you for the pains you are taking about your picture for me; crammed with occupation as my time is here, I would have done the same for you, but that I think in Lawrence's print [Kemble's portrait by Sir Thomas Lawrence] you have the best and likest thing you can have of me~~~I cannot tell you at what hour we shall reach Liverpool, but it will be very early on Monday morning~~~I am glad you have not deferred sitting for your picture till you came to Liverpool, for it would have encroached much upon our time together. I remember when I returned from abroad, a schoolgirl, I thought I had forgotten my mother's face. This copy of yours will save me from that nonsensical morbid feeling, and you will surely not forget mine~~~You bid me, if anything should go ill with me, summon you across the Atlantic. Alas! dear H[arriet], you forget that before a letter from that other world can reach this, more than a month must have elapsed, and the writer may no longer be in either. You say you hope I may return a renewed being; and I have no doubt my health will be benefited, and my spirits revived by change of external objects; but oh, how dreary it all is now! You bid me cheer my father when my mother shall have left us, without knowing that she is already gone. I make every exertion that duty and affection can prompt; but, you know, it is my nature rather to absorb the sorrow of others than to assist them in throwing it off; and when one's own heart is all but frozen, one knows not where to find warmth to impart to those who are shivering with misery beside one . . .   [RG]

Shipboard
August 1, 1832

Wednesday, August 1st—Another break in my journal, and here I am on board the *Pacific,* bound for America, having left home, and all the world behind.—Well!

I had a bunch of carnations in my hand, which I had snatched from our drawing-room chimney;—English flowers!—dear English flowers! they will be withered long before I again see land, but I will keep them until I once more stand upon the soil on which they grew . . . [*JA*]

Shipboard
August 20

Storm at sea

Monday, 20th—Calm—utter calm—a roasting August sun, a waveless sea, the sails flapping idly against the mast, and our black cradle rocking to and fro without progressing a step. They lowered the boat, and went out rowing—I wanted to go, but they would not let me! A brig was standing some four miles off us, which, by the by, I was the first to see, except our mate, in my morning watch, which began at five o'clock, when I saw the moon set and the sun rise, and feel more than ever convinced that absolute reality is away from the purpose of works of art. The sky this morning was as like the sea-shore, as ever sand and shingle were, the clouds lying along the horizon in pale dusky yellow layers, and higher up, floating in light brown ribbed masses, like the sands which grow wrinkled under the eternal smiling of the sea. Against the dim horizon, which blended with the violet-coloured sky, the mate then showed me, through the glass, the brig standing on the sea's edge, for all the world like one of the tiny birds who were wheeling and chirping round our ship's stern. I have done more in the shape of work to-day, than any since the two first I spent on board; translated a German fable without much trouble, read a canto in Dante, ending with a valuation of fame. "O spirio gentil" how lived fair wisdom in your soul—how, shines she in your lays!—Wrote journal, walked about, worked at my cap, in the evening danced merrily enough, quadrilles, country dances, la Boulangers and the monaco; fairly danced myself tired—came to bed. But oh! not to sleep—mercy what a night! The wind blowing like mad, the sea rolling, the ship pitching, bouncing, shuddering and reeling, like a thing possessed. I lay awake, listening to her creaking and groaning, till two o'clock, when, sick of my sleepless berth, I got up and was going up stairs, to see, at least, how near drowning we were, when D[all], who was lying awake too, implored me to lie down again. I did so for the hundred and eleventh time, conplaining bitterly that I should be stuffed down in a loathesome berth, cabined, cribbed, confined, while the sea was boiling below, and the wind bellowing above us. Lay till daylight, the gale increasing, furiously, boxes, chairs, beds and their contents, wooden valuables, and human invaluables, rolling about and clinging to one another in glorious confusion. At about eight o'clock, a tremendous sea took the ship in the waist, and rushing over the deck, banged against our sky-light, and bounced into our cabin. Three women were immediately apparent from their respective cribs and poor H [Harriet Hodgkinson, a British girl Fanny befriended] appeared in all her lengthy full-length, and came and took refuge with me. As I held her in my arms, and put my cloak round her, shook from head to foot, poor child!—I was not the least frightened, but rather excited by this invasion of Dan Neptune's; but I wish to goodness I had been on deck,— oh how I wish I had seen that spoonful of salt water flung from the sea's boiling bowl . . .   [JA]

Shipboard
September 2, 1832

Rose at half past six: the sun was shining brilliantly; woke H[arriet] and went on deck with her. The morning was glorious, the sun had risen two hours sky, the sea was cut by a strong breeze, and curled into ridges that came like emerald banks crowned with golden spray round our ship; she was going through the water at nine knots an hour. I sat

Sighting land

and watched the line of light lay like a fairy road to the east—towards my country, my dear, dear home.

Breakfasted at table for the first time since I've been on board the ship, I did hope, the last. After breakfast put my things to rights, tidied our cabin for prayers, and began looking out the lessons; while doing so, the joyful sound, "Land, land!" was heard aloft. I rushed on deck, and between the blue waveless sea, and the bright unclouded sky, lay the wished-for line of, darker element. 'Twas Long Island: through a glass I described the undulations of the coast, and even the trees that stood relieved against the sky. Hail, strange land! my heart greets you coldly and sadly! Oh how I thought of Columbus, as with eyes strained and on tip-toe our water-weary passengers, stood, after a summer's sail of thirty days, welcoming their mother earth. The day was heavenly, though intensely hot, the sky utterly cloudless, and by that same token, I do not love a cloudless sky. They tell me that this is their American weather almost till Christmas; that's nice, for those who like frying. Commend me to dear England's soft, rich, sad, harmonious skies and foliage, commend me to the misty curtain of silver vapour that hangs over her September woods at morning, and shrouds them at night:—in short, I am home-sick before touching land . . .   [JA]

America
1832–1833

New York City
September 3, 1832

The houses are almost all painted glaring white or red; the other favourite colours appear to be pale straw colour and grey. They have all
green venetian shutters, which give an idea of coolness, and almost
every house has a tree or trees in its vicinity, which looks pretty and
garden-like. We reached our inn,—the gentlemen were waiting for us,
and led us to our drawing-room. I had been choking for the last three
hours, and could endure no more, but sobbed like a wretch aloud.

There was a piano in the room, to which I flew with the appetite of
one who has lived on the music of the speaking-trumpet for a month;
that, and some iced lemonade and cake, presently restored my spirits. I
went on playing and singing till I was exhausted, and then sat down
and wrote journal. Mr. [William Hodgkinson, son of one of the Duke
of Norfolk's tenants who befriended the Kembles on his emigration to
Boston] went out and got me Sir Humphrey Davy's *Salmonia*, which I
had been desiring, and he had been speaking of, on board ship.

At five o'clock we all met once more together to dinner. Our drawing-room being large and pleasant, the table was laid in it. 'Tis curious

how an acquaintanceship of thirty days has contrived to bind together in one common feeling of kindness and good-fellowship persons who never met before, who may never meet again. Tomorrow we all separate to betake ourselves each to our several paths; and as if loath to part company, they all agreed to meet once more on the eve of doing so, probably for ever. How strongly this clinging principle is inherent in our natures! These men have no fine sympathies of artificial creation, and this exhibition of *adhesiveness* is in them a real, and heart-sprung feeling. It touched me—indeed it may well do so; for friends of thirty days are better than utter strangers, and when these my shipmates shall be scattered abroad, there will be no human being left near us whose face we know, or whose voice is familiar to us. Our dinner was a favourable specimen of eating as practised in this new world; everything good, only in too great a profusion, the wine drinkable, and the fruit beautiful to look at; in point of flavour it was infinitely inferior to English hot-house fruit, or even fine espalier fruit raised in a good aspect.

Everything was wrapped in ice, which is a most luxurious necessary in this hot climate; but the things were put on the table in a slovenly, outlandish fashion; fish, soup, and meat, at once, and puddings, and tarts, and cheese, at another once; no finger glasses, and a patched table-cloth,—in short, a want of that style and neatness which is found in every hotel in England. The waiters, too, reminded us of the half-savage highland lads that used to torment us under that denomination in Glasgow—only that they were wild Irish instead of wild Scotch. The day had cleared, and become intensely hot, towards evening softening and cooling under the serene influences of the loveliest moon imaginable. The streets were brilliantly lighted, the shops through the trees, and the people parading between them, reminded me very much of the Boulevards. We left the gentlemen, and went down stairs, where I played and sang for three hours. On opening the door, I found a junta of men sitting on the hall floor, round it, and smoking. Came up for coffee; most of the gentlemen were rather elated,—we sang, and danced, and talked, and seemed exceedingly loath to say good-by. I sat listening to the dear Doctor's theory of the nature of the soul, which savoured infinitely more of the spirituality of the bottle than of immaterial existences, I heard him descant very tipsily upon the vital principle, until my fatigue getting fairly the better of my affection for him, I bade our remaining guests good night, and came to bed.   [*JA*]

New York City
September 5, 1832

I have been in a sulky fit half the day, because people will keep walking in and out of our room without leave or license, which is coming a great deal too soon to Hope's idea of Heaven. I am delighted to see my friends, but I like to tell them so, and not that they should take it for granted . . .

Came home up Broadway, which is a long street of tolerable width, full of shops, in short the American Oxford road, where all people go to exhibit themselves, and examine others. The women that I have seen hitherto have all been very gaily dressed, with a pretension to French style, and a more than English exaggeration of it. They all appear to me to walk with a French shuffle, which, as their pavements are flat, I can only account for by their wearing shoes made in the French fashion, which are enough in themselves to make a waddler of the best walker that ever set foot to earth. Two or three were pretty girls, but the town being quite empty, these are probably bad specimens of the graces and charms that adorn Broadway in its season of shining . . . to the Theatre. Wallack [British actor and contemporary of John Kemble] was to act in *The Rent Day.* Mercy how strange I felt as I once more set foot in a theatre; the sound of the applause set my teeth on edge. The house is pretty though rather gloomy, well formed, about the size of the Haymarket, with plenty of gold carving, and red silk about it, looking rich and warm. The audience was considerable, but all men; scarce, I should think, twenty women in the dress circle, where, by the bye, as well as in the private boxes, I saw men sitting with their hats on . . . I cried most bitterly during the whole piece, for as in his very first scene Wallack asks his wife if she will go with him to

America, and she replies, "What, leave the farm?" I set off from thence and ceased no more . . .   [*JA*]

New York City
September 6, 1832

American democracy

These democrats are as title-sick as a banker's wife in England. My father told me to-day, that Mr. [Philip Hone, former mayor and prominent businessman], talking about the state of the country, spoke of the lower orders finding their level; now this enchants me, because a republic is a natural anomaly; there is nothing republican in the construction of the material universe; there be highlands and lowlands, lordly mountains as barren as any aristocracy, and lowly valleys, as productive as any labouring classes. The feeling of rank, of inequality, is inherent in us, a part of the veneration of our natures; and like most of our properties seldom finds its right channels—in place of which it has created artificial ones suited to the frame of society into which the civilized world has formed itself. I believe in my heart that a republic is the noblest, highest, and purest form of government; but I believe that according to the present disposition of human creatures, 'tis a mere beau ideal, totally incapable of realization. What the world may be fit for six hundred years hence, I cannot exactly perceive—but in the mean time, 'tis my conviction that America will be a monarchy before I am a skeleton.

One of the curses of living at an inn in this unceremonious land: Dr. [Charles Mifflin, a prominent physician] walked in this evening, accompanied by a gentleman, whom he forthwith introduced to us. I behaved very *ill,* as I always do on these occasions; but 'tis an impertinence, and I shall take good care to certify such to be my opinion of these free and easy proceedings. The man had a silly manner, but he may be a genius for all that. He abused General Jackson, and said the cholera was owing to his presidency; for that Clay had predicted, that when he came into power, battle, pestilence, and famine would come upon the land: which Prophecy finds its accomplishment thus: they have had a war with the Indians, the cholera has raged, and the people, flying from the infected cities to the country, have eaten half the farmers out of house and home. This hotel reminds me most extremely of our "iligant" and untidy apartments in dear nasty Dublin, at the Shelbourne. The paper in our bedroom is half peeling from the walls, our beds are without curtains, then to be sure there are pier looking-glasses, and one or two pieces of showy French furniture in it. 'Tis customary, too, here, I find, for men to sleep three or four in a room; conceive an Englishman shown into a dormitory for half-a-dozen! I can't think how they endure it; but, however, I have a fever at all those things . . . [JA]

New York City
September 9, 1832

After dinner, sat looking at the blacks parading up and down; most of them in the height of the fashion, with every colour in the rainbow about them. Several of the black women I saw pass had very fine figures; (the women here appear to me to be remarkably small, my own being, I should think, the average height): but the contrast of a bright blue, or pink crape bonnet, with the black face, white teeth, and glaring blue whites of the eyes, is beyond description grotesque. The carriages here are all, to my taste, very ugly; hung very high from the ground, and of all manner of ungainly, old-fashioned shapes. Now this is where, I think, the Americans are to be quarreled with: they are beginning, at a time, when all other nations are arrived at the highest point of perfection, in all matters conducive to the comfort and elegance of life; they go into these countries; into France, into our own dear little snuggery, from whence they might bring models of whatever was most excellent, and give them to their own manufacturers, to imitate or improve upon. When I see these awkward, uncomfortable vehicles, swinging through the streets, and think of the beauty, the comfort, the strength, and lightness of our English built carriages and cabs, I am much surprised at the want of emulation and enterprise, which can be satisfied with inferiority, when equality, if not superiority, would be so easy . . . [JA]

African Americans

America, 1832–1833

45

New York City
September 13, 1832

American
Indians

The destruction of the original inhabitants of a country by its discoverers, always attended, as it is, with injustice and cruelty, appears to me one of the most mysterious dispensations of Providence.

The chasing, enslaving, and destroying creatures, whose existence, however inferior, is as justly theirs, as that of the most refined European is his; who for the most part, too, receive their enemies with open-handed hospitality, until taught treachery by being betrayed, and cruelty by fear; the driving the child of the soil off it, or, what is fifty times worse, chaining him to till it; all the various forms of desolation which have ever followed the landing of civilized men upon uncivilized shores; in short, the theory and practice of discovery and conquest, as recorded in all history, is a very singular and painful subject of contemplation.

'Tis true, that cultivation and civilization, the arts and sciences that render life useful, the knowledge that ennobles, the adornments that refine existence, above all, the religion that is its most sacred trust and dear reward, all these, like pure sunshine and healthful airs following a hurricane, succeed the devastation of the invader; but the sufferings of those who are swept away are not the less, and though I believe that good alone is God's result, it seems a fearful proof of the evil wherewith this earth is cursed, that good cannot progress but over such a path. No one, beholding the prosperous and promising state of this fine country, could wish it again untenanted of its enterprising and industrious possessors; yet even while looking with admiration at all that they have achieved, with expectation amounting to certainty to all that they will yet accomplish; 'tis difficult to refrain from bestowing some thoughts of pity and of sadness upon those, whose homes have been overturned, whose language has past away, and whose feet are daily driven further from those territories of which they were once sole and sovereign lords. How strange it is to think, that less than one hundred years ago, these shores, resounding with the voice of populous cities—these waters, laden with the commerce of the wide world, were silent wildernesses, where sprang and fell the forest leaves, where ebbed and flowed the ocean tides from day to day, and from year to year in uninterrupted stillness; where the great sun, who looked on the vast empires of the east, its mouldering kingdoms, its lordly palaces, its ancient temples, its swarming cities, came and looked down upon the still dwelling of utter loneliness, where nature sat enthroned in everlasting beauty, undisturbed by the far off din of worlds "beyond the flood" . . .   [*JA*]

New York City
September 15, 1832

The women here, like those of most warm climates, ripen very early, and decay proportionately soon. They are, generally speaking, pretty, with good complexions, and an air of freshness and brilliancy, but this I am told is very evanescent; and whereas, in England, a woman is in the full bloom of health and beauty from twenty to five-and-thirty; here, they scarcely reach the first period without being faded, and looking old. They marry very young, and this is another reason why age comes prematurely upon them. There was a fair young thing at dinner today who did not look above seventeen, and she was a wife. As for their figures, like those of French women, they are too well dressed for one to judge exactly what they are really like: they are, for the most part, short and slight, with remarkably pretty feet and ancles; but there's too much pelerine and petticoat, and "de quoi" of every sort to guess anything more.   [*JA*]

American women

New York City
September 20, 1832

. . . By the bye, Essex [an African American whom they met on shipboard] called this morning to fetch away the captain's claret jug; he asked my father for an order [of theater tickets], adding, with some hesitation, "It must be for the gallery, if you please, sir, for people of colour are not allowed to go to the pit, or any other part of the house."

Segregation

I believe I turned black myself, I was so indignant. Here's aristocracy with a vengeance! . . .   [JA]

New York City
September 21, 1832

Reviews . . . My own opinion of poor Mr. Keppel [Romeo to her Juliet] is that no power on earth or in heaven can make him act decently; however, of course, I did not object to his trying again; he did not swamp me the first night, so I don't suppose he will the fifth. We dined at five; just before dinner received a most delicious bouquet, which gladdened my very heart with its sweet smell and lovely colours: some of the flowers were strangers to me. After dinner, Colonel [Sibell, otherwise unidentified] called, and began pulling out heaps of newspapers, and telling us a long story about Mr. Keppel, who it seems has been writing to the papers to convince them and the public that he is a good actor, at the same time throwing out sundry hints which seem aimed our way, of injustice, oppression, hard usage, and the rest on't . . . Came to bed in a tremendous dudgeon. The few critiques that I have seen upon our acting have been, upon the whole, laudatory. One was sent to me from a paper called the Mirror, which pleased me very much; not because the praise in it was excessive, and far beyond my deserts, but that it was written with great taste and feeling, and was evidently not the produce of a common press hack . . .   [JA]

New York City
September 22, 1832

American manners Went into a shop to order a pair of shoes. The shopkeepers in this place with whom I have hitherto had to deal, are either condescendingly familiar, or insolently indifferent in their manner. Your washerwoman sits down before you, while you are *standing* speaking to her; and a shop boy bringing things for inspection, not only sits down, but keeps his hat on in your drawing-room. The worthy man to whom I went for my shoes was so amazingly ungracious, that at first I thought I would go out of the shop; but recollecting that I should probably only go farther and fare worse, I gulped, sat down, and was measured. All this is bad: it has its origin in a vulgar misapprehension, which confounds ill breeding with independence, and leads people to fancy that they elevate themselves above their condition by discharging its duties and obligations discourteously . . .   [JA]

New York City
September 24, 1832

At the end of the play, the clever New Yorkians actually called for Mr. Keppel! and this most worthless clapping of hands, most worthless bestowed upon such a worthless object, is what, by the nature of my craft, I am bound to care for; I spit at it from the bottom of my soul! Talking of applause, the man who acted Bedamar to-night thought fit to be two hours dragging me off the stage, in consequence of which I had to scream, "Jaffier, Jaffier," till I thought I should have broken a blood-vessel; on my remonstrating with him upon this, he said, "Well, you are rewarded, listen:" the people were clapping and shouting vehemently; this is the whole history of acting and actors. We came home tired, and thoroughly disgusted, and found no supper. The cooks, who do not live in the house, but come and do their work, and depart home whenever it suits their convenience, had not thought proper to stay to prepare any supper for us: so we had to wait for the readiest things that could be procured out of doors for us—this was pleasant—very! At last appeared a cold, boiled fowl, and some monstrous oysters, that looked for all the world like an antediluvian race of oysters, "for in those days there were giants." Six mouthfuls each; they were well-flavoured, but their size displeased my eye, and I swallowed but one, and came to bed . . .   [JA]

Philadelphia
October 9, 1832

To-day, on board the boat, it was a perfect shower of saliva all the time; and I longed to be released from my fellowship with these very obnoxious chewers of tobacco.* (*It has happened to me after a few hour's travelling in a steamboat to find the white dress put on fresh in the morning, covered with yellow tobacco stains; nor is this very offensive habit confined to the lower orders alone. I have seen *gentlemen* spit upon the carpet of the room where they were sitting, in the company of women, without the slightest remorse; and I remember once seeing a gentleman, who was travelling with us, very deliberately void his tobacco juice into the bottom of the coach, instead of through the windows, to my inexpressible disgust.) . . . At about four o'clock, we reached Philadelphia, having performed the journey between that and New York (a distance of a hundred miles) in less than ten hours, in spite of bogs, ruts, and all other impediments. The manager came to look after us and our goods, and we were presently stowed into a coach which conveyed us to the Mansion House, the best reputed inn in Philadelphia. On asking for our bed-rooms, they showed D[all] and myself into a double-bedded room; on my remonstrating against this, the chamber maid replied that they were not accustomed to allow lodgers so *much* room as a room a piece. However, upon my insisting, they gave me a little nest, just big enough to turn about in, but where, at least, I can be by myself. Dressed, and dined at five; after dinner, wrote journal till tea time, and then came to bed . . . We passed another larger building, also a bank, in the Corinthian style, which did not please me so much. The shops here are much better looking than those at New York; the windows are larger, and more advantageously constructed for the display of goods; and there did not appear to be the same anomalous mixture of vendibles, as in the New York shops. The streets were very full of men hurrying to the town house, to give their votes. It is election time, and much excitement subsists with regard to the choice of the future President. The democrats or radicals are for the re-election of General Jackson, but the aristocratic party, which here at all events is the strongest, are in favour of Henry Clay. Here is the usual quantity of shouting and breaking windows that we are accustomed to on these occasions. I saw a caricature of Jackson and Van Buren, his chief supporter, which was entitled "the king and his minister." Van Buren held a crown in his hand, and the devil was approaching Jackson with a sceptre. Came in at half past four, dressed for dinner: they gave us an excellent one. The master of this house was, it seems, once a man of independent fortune and a great bon vivant. He has retained from thence a fellow-feeling for his guests, and does by them as he would be done by. After dinner worked till tea-time; after tea wrote journal, and now I'll go to bed. We are attended here by a fat old lively negro, by name Henry; who canters about in our behalf with great alacrity, and seems wrapt in much wonderment at many of our proceedings. By the bye, the black who protected our baggage from the steam-boat was ycleped Oliver Cromwell. I have begun Grahame's *History of America,* and like it "mainly," as the old plays say . . .

They [her theater audience] were very, attentive certainly, but how they did make me work! 'Tis amazing how much an audience loses by this species of hanging back, even where the silence proceeds from unwillingness to interrupt a good performance; though in reality it is the greatest compliment an actor can receive, yet he is deprived by that very stillness of half his power. Excitement is reciprocal between the performer and the audience; he creates it in them, and receives it back again from them and in that last scene in *Fazio,* half the effect that I produce is derived from the applause which I receive, the very noise and tumult of which tends to heighten the nervous energy which the scene itself begets. I know that my aunt Siddons has frequently said the same thing. And besides the above reason for applause, the physical powers of an actor require, after any tremendous exertion, the rest and regathering of breath and strength, which the interruption of the audience affords him; moreover, as 'tis the conventionai of expressing approbation in the theatre, it is chilling and uncomfortable to go toiling on, without knowing whether, as the maid-servants say, "one gives satisfaction or no." They made noise enough, however, at the end of the play. Came home, supped, and to bed: weary to death, and with a voice like a cracked bagpipe . . . [JA]

Philadelphia
October 13, 1832

Gentleman caller

He [Pierce Butler, her future husband] was a pretty-spoken, genteel youth enough; he drank tea with us, and offered to ride with me. He is, it seems, a great fortune; consequently, I suppose, in spite of his inches, a great man. Now, I'll go to bed; my cough's enough to kill a horse . . . [JA]

Philadelphia
October 16, 1832

Just as I had finished dinner, a most beautiful, fragrant, and delicious nosegay was brought to me, with a very laconic note from a Philadelphia *"friend"* dashed under, as though from a Quaker. [Pierce Butler had signed the note as "friend."] Whoever 'tis from, Jew or Gentile, Puritan or Pagan, he, she, or it, hath my most unbounded gratitude. Spent an ecstatic half hour, in arranging my flowers in glasses . . . The dignified and graceful influence which married women, among us, exercise over the tone of our manners, uniting the duties of home to the charms of social life; and bearing, at once, like the orange-tree, the fair fruits of maturity with the blossoms of their spring, is utterly unknown here. Married women are either house-drudges and nursery-maids, or, if they appear in society, comparative cyphers; and the retiring, modest, youthful bearing, which among us distinguishes girls of fifteen or sixteen, is equally unknown. Society is entirely led by chits, who in England would be sitting behind a pianoforte; the consequence is, that it has neither the elegance, refinement, the propriety *which* belongs to ours; but is a noisy, racketty, vulgar congregation of flirting boys and girls, alike without style or decorum . . . [JA]

New York City
December 1, 1832

First day of the last month of the year—go it old fellow! I'm sick of the road, and would be at my journey's end. Got two hundred dollars from my father, and immediately after breakfast sallied forth: paid bills and visits, and came home. Found my father sitting with our kinsman, Mr. [Gouveneur Kemble, who owned an estate in the Hudson Valley], busily discussing the family origin, root, branches, and all. We are an old family, they say, but the direct line is lost after Charles the Second's reign. Our kinsman is a nice man, with a remarkably fine face, with which I was greatly struck. When he was gone, persuaded my father to come down and take a breathing on the Battery with me. And a breathing it was with a vengeance. The wind blew tempestuously, the waters, all troubled and rough, were of a yellow green colour, breaking into short, strong, angry waves, whose glittering white crests the wind carried away, as they sank to the level surface again. The shores were all cold, distinct, sharp-cut, and wintry-looking, the sky was black and gloomy, with now and then a watery wan sunlight running through it. The wind was so powerful, we could scarcely keep our legs. My sleeves and skirts fluttered in the blast, my bonnet was turned front behind, my nose was blue, my cheeks were crimson, my hair was all tangled, my breath was gone, my blood was in a glow: what a walk! . . . The keen cutting wind whizzed along the streets; huge masses of dark clouds, with soft brown edges lay on the pale delicate blue of the evening sky. The moon was up, clear, cold, and radiant; the crowd had ebbed away from the busy thoroughfare, and only a few men in great coats buttoned up to their chins, and women wrapped in cloaks, were scudding along in the dim twilight and the bitter wind towards their several destinations, with a frozen shuddering look that made me laugh I had got perished in the coach, and seeing that the darkness covered me, determined to walk home, and bade the coach follow me. How pleasant it was: I walked tremendously fast, enjoying the fresh breath of the north, and looking at the glittering moon, as she rode high in the evening sky. How I do like, walking alone—being alone; for this alone I wish I were a man . . .   [JA]

Philadelphia
December 3, 1832

Rose at half past four. The sky was black as death, but in the night winter, had dropped his mantle on the earth, and there it lay, cold, and purely white, against the inky sky. Dressed: crammed away all the gleanings of the packing, and in thaw, and sleet, and rain, drove down to the steamboat. Went directly to the cabin. On my way thither, managed to fall down half a dozen steep steps, and give myself as many bruises. I was picked up and led to a bed, where I slept profoundly till breakfast time. Our kinsman, Mr. [Governeur Kemble], was our fellow-passenger: I like him mainly. After breakfast returned to my crib. As I was removing *Contarini Fleming* [a novel by Disraeli], in order to lie down, a lady said to me, "Let me look at one of those books," and without further word of question or acknowledgement, took it from my hand, and began reading. I was a *little surprised*, but said nothing, and went to sleep. Presently I was roused by a pull on the shoulder, and another lady, rather more civil and particularly considerate, asked me to do her the favour of lending her the other. I said by all manner of means, wished her at the devil, and turned round to sleep once more. Arrived at Amboy, we disembarked and bundled ourselves into our coach, ourselves, our namesake, and a pretty quiet lady, who was going, in much heaviness of heart, to see a sick child. The roads were unspeakable; the day most delightfully disagreeable. My bruises made the saltatory movements of our crazy conveyance doubly torturing; in short, all things were the perfection of misery. I attempted to read, but found it utterly impossible to do so. Arrived at the Delaware, we took boat again; and, as I was sitting very quietly reading *Contarini Fleming*, with the second volume lying on the stool at my feet, the same unceremonious lady who had *borrowed* it before, snatched it up without addressing a single syllable to me, read as long as she pleased, and threw it down again in the same style when she went to dinner. Now I know that half the people here, if they were to read that in Trollope, would say, "Oh, but you know she could not have been a lady; not fair to judge of our manners by the vulgar specimens of American society which a steamboat may afford." Very true: but granting that she was *not* a lady, (which she certainly was not,) supposing her to have been a housemaid, or anything else of equal pretensions to good breeding, the way to judge is by comparing her, not with ladies in other countries, but with housemaids, persons in her own condition of life, and 'tis most certain that no person whatsoever, however ignorant, low, or vulgar, in England, would have done such a thing as that. But the mixture of the republican feeling of equality peculiar to this country, and the usual want of refinement common to lower classes of most countries, forms a singularly felicitous union of impudence and vulgarity to be met with no where but in America. Arrived at the Mansion House, which I was quite glad to again. Installed myself in a room, and while they brought in the packages, finished *Contarini Fleming*. It reminded me of Combe's [George Combe, Scottish phrenologist] book: I wonder whether he is turning phrenologist at all? those physiological principles were the bosom friends of the Combe's phrenological ones. Stowed away my things, made a delicious huge wood fire, dressed myself, and went down to dinner. Our kinsman dined with us. Mr. [Pierce Butler] came in while we were at dinner. After dinner came up to my room, continued unpacking and putting away my things till near nine o'clock. When we went down to tea, my father was lying on the sofa asleep, and a man was sitting with his back to the door, reading the newspaper. He looked up as we came in; it was [Mr. Staley, otherwise unidentified] whom I greatly rejoiced to see again. During tea, he told us all the Philadelphia gossip. So the ladies are all getting up upon horses, and wearing the "*Kemble* cap," as they call Lady [Frances Egerton]'s device. How she would laugh if she could hear it; how I did laugh when I did hear it. The Kemble cap, forsooth! thus it is that great originators too often lose the fame of their inventions, and that the glory of a *new idea* passes by the head that conceived it, to encircle, as with a halo, that of some mere imitator; thus it is that this very big world comes to be called America . . . [JA]

America, 1832–1833

Philadelphia
December 5, 1832

In the last scene of the play, I was so mad with the mode in which all the preceding ones had been perpetrated, that, lying over Mr. ———— [unidentified actor]'s corpse, and fumbling for his dagger, which I could not find, I, Juliet, thus apostrophized—Romeo being dead— "Why, where the devil *is* your dagger, Mr. ————?" What a disgusting travesty. On my return home I expressed my entire determination to my father to perform the farce of Romeo and Juliet no more. Why, it's an absolute shame that one of Shakespeare's plays should be thus turned into a mockery. I received a note from young Mr. [Edward Biddle, son of the wealthy banker, Nicholas Biddle] accompanied by a very curious nosegay in shells; a poor substitute for the breathing, fresh, rosy flowers he used to furnish me with, when I was last here. [JA]

Philadelphia
December 7, 1832

Secessionist politics Carolina is in a state of convulsion. Reports have arrived that the Nullifiers and Unionists have had a fight in Charleston, and that lives have been lost. "Bide a wee," as the Scotchman says, we talk a good deal on the other side the water of matters that are far enough off; but as for America, the problem is not yet solved—and this very crisis, (a more important one than has yet occurred in the political existence of this country,) is threatening to slacken the bonds of brotherhood between the states, and shake the Union to its centre. The interests of the northern states are totally different from, and in some respects opposite to those of the southern ones . . .

The tariff question is the point in debate; and the Carolinians have, it seems, threatened to secede from the Union in consequence of the policy pursued with regard to that. I was horrified at Dr. ————'s account of the state of negroes in the south. To teach a slave to read or write is to incur a penalty either of fine or imprisonment. They form the larger proportion of the population, by far; and so great is the dread of insurrection on the part of the white inhabitants, that they are kept in the most brutish ignorance, and too often treated with the most brutal barbarity, in order to insure their subjection. Oh! what a breaking asunder of old manacles there will be, some of these fine days; what a fearful rising of the black flood; what a sweeping away, as by a torrent, of oppressions and tyrannies; what a fierce and horrible retaliation and revenge for wrong so long endured—so wickedly inflicted . . .

So "Old Hickory" [Andrew Jackson] means to lick the refractory southerns: why they are coming to a civil war! However, the grumblers haven't the means of fighting without emancipating and arming their slaves. That they will not and dare not do; the consequences will be, I suppose, that they will swallow the affront, and submit . . .   [JA]

Philadelphia
December 28, 1832

She [unidentified] amuses me much by her intense anxiety that I should be married. First, she wishes [Pierce Butler] would propose to me,—then she thinks Mr. [Shelton, otherwise unidentified]'s estates in Cuba would be highly acceptable; in short, my single blessedness seems greatly to annoy her, and I believe she attributes everything evil in life to that same . . . We went to the theatre at half past five. Play, *Hunchback;* after it Katharine and Petruchio. I thought I should have died of the side ache—I was in perfect agony. The people here are more civil and considerate than can be imagined. I sent, yesterday evening, for some water-ice: the confectioner had none; when, lo! tonight he brings me some he has made on purpose for me, which he entreats my acceptance of. I admired a very pretty fan Mrs. ——— [unidentified] had in her hand; and at the end of the play, she had it sent to my dressing-room;—and these sort of things are done by me, not once, but ten times every day. Nothing can exceed the kindness and attention which has encountered us every where since we have been in this country. I am sure I am bound to remember America and

Suitors

Americans thankfully; for, whatever I may think of their ways, manners, or peculiarities, to me they have shown unmingled good will, and cordial, real kindness. Remained up, packing, till two o'clock . . . [JA]

Philadelphia
December 29, 1832

Dramatic
arts

We had a long discussion about the stage,—the dramatic art; which, as Helen says, "is none," for, "no art but taketh time and pains to learn." Now I am a living and breathing witness that a person may be accounted a good actor, and to a certain degree deserve the title, without time or pains of any sort being expended upon the acquisition of the reputation. But on other grounds, acting has always appeared to me to be the very lowest of the arts, admitting it deserves to be classed among them at all, which I am not sure it does. In the first place, it originates nothing; it lacks, therefore, the grand faculty which all other arts possess—creation. An actor is at the best but the filler up of the outline designed by another,—the expounder, as it were, of things which another has set down; and a fine piece of acting is at best, in my opinion, a fine translation. Moreover, it is not alone to charm the senses that the nobler powers of mind were given to man; 'tis not alone to enchant the eye that the gorgeous pallet of the painter, and the fine chisel of the statuary, have become through heavenly inspiration, magical wands, summoning to life images of loveliness, of majesty, and grace; 'tis not alone to soothe the ear that music has possessed, as it were, certain men with the spirit of sweet sounds; 'tis not alone to delight the fancy that the poet's great and glorious power was given him, by which, as by spell, he peoples all space, and all time, with undying witnesses of his own existence; 'tis not alone to minister to our senses that these most beautiful capabilities were sown in the soil of our souls. But 'tis that through them all that is most refined, most excellent and noble, in our mental and moral nature, may be led through their loveliness, as through a glorious archway, to the source of all beauty, and all goodness. It is that by them our perceptions of truth may be made more vivid, our love of loveliness increased, our intellect refined and elevated, our nature softened, our memory stored with images of brightness, which, like glorious reflections, falling again upon our souls, may tend to keep alive in them, the knowledge of, and the desire after what is true, and fair, and noble. But, that art may have this effect, it must be to a certain degree enduring. It must not be a transient vision, which fades and leaves but a recollection of what it was, which will fade too. It must not be for an hour, a day, or a year, but biding, inasmuch as anything earthly may abide, to charm the sense and cheer the soul of generation after generation. And here it is that miserable deficiency of acting is most apparent. Whilst the poems, the sculptures of the old Grecian time yet remain to witness to these latter ages of enduring life of truth and beauty,—whilst the poets of Rome surviving the trophies of her thousand victories, are yet familiar in our mouths as household words,—whilst Dante, Boccaccio, that giant, Michael Angelo, yet live and breathe, and have their being amongst us, through the rich legacy their genius has bequeathed to time,—whilst the wild music of Salvator Rosa, solemn and sublime as his painting, yet rings in our ears, and the souls of Shakespeare, Milton, Raphael, and Titian, are yet shedding into our souls divinest influences from the very fountains of inspiration—where are the pageants that night after night, during the best era of dramatic excellence, riveted the gaze of thousands, and drew forth their acclamations?—gone, like rosy sunset clouds;—fair painted vapours, lovely to the sight, but vanishing as dreams, leaving no trace in heaven, no token of their ever having been there. Where are the labours of Garrick, of Macklin, of Cooke, of Kemble, of Mrs. Siddons?—chronicled in the dim memories of some few of their surviving spectators; who speak of them with an enthusiasm which we who never saw them, fancy the offspring of that feeling which makes the old look back to the time of their youth, as the only days when the sun knew how to shine. What have these great actors left either to delight the sense, or elevate the soul, but barren names, unwedded to a single lasting evidence of greatness. If, then, acting be alike without the creating power, and the enduring property, which are at once the highest faculty of art, and its most beneficial purpose, what becomes of it when ranked with efforts displaying both in the highest degree. To me it seems no art, but merely a highly rational, interesting, and exciting amusement; and I think men may as well, much better, perhaps, spend three hours in a theatre, than in a billiard or bar-room,—and this is the extent of my approbation and admiration of my art . . .

On my way home, met young [Butler], with his head so completely in the clouds, that I had bowed to him, and was driving on, when he just perceived me, and fell into a confusion of bows, which he continued long after the coach had passed him. Found the usual token of his having been at our house—a most beautiful nosegay; roses, hyacinths, and myrtle . . .   [JA]

Philadelphia
December 30, 1832

Spent my Sunday morning on my knees, indeed, but packing, not praying. The horses did not come till half past twelve; so that instead of avoiding, we encountered the pious multitude. I'm sure when we mounted, there were not less than a hundred and fifty beholders round the Mansion House. Rode out to Laurel Hill. The cross road was muddy, so we took the turnpike, which was clean and short, and would have been pleasant enough but for my brute of a horse. Upon my word, these American horses are most unsafe to ride. I never mount one but I recommend myself to the care of heaven, for I expect to have every bone in my body broken before I dismount again. At Laurel Hill we lunched. While D[all] put up her hair, [Butler] and I ran down to the water side. The ice had melted from the river, in whose still waters the shores and trees and bridge lay mirrored with beautiful and fairy-like distinctness. The long icicles under the rocky brow beneath which we stood had not melted away, though the warm sun was shining brilliantly on them, and making the granite slab on which we stood sparkle like a pavement of diamonds. I called to the echo, and sang to it scales up, and scales down, and every manner of muscial discourse I could think of, during which interesting amusement I as nearly as possible slipped from my footing into the river, which caused both [Butler] and myself to gulp. We left our pleasant sunny stand at last, to rejoin D[all] and the lunch, and having eaten and drunken, we remounted and proceeded on . . . We reached Philadelphia at half past four, and had again to canter down Chestnut Street just as the folks were all coming from church, which caused no little staring, and turning of heads.   [JA]

Baltimore
December 31, 1832

This boat—the *Charles Carroll*—is one of the finest they have. 'Tis *Steamboat travel* neither so swift nor so large, I think, as some of the North river boats, but it is a beautiful vessel, roomy and comfortable in its arrangements. I went below for a few minutes, but found, as usual, the atmosphere of the cabin perfectly intolerable. The ladies' cabin, in winter, on board one of these large steamers, is a right curious sight. 'Tis generally crammed to suffocation with women, strewn in every direction. The greater number cuddle round a stove, the heat of which alone would make the atmosphere unbreathable. Others sit lazily in a species of rocking-chair,—which is found wherever Americans sit down,—cradling themselves backwards and forwards, with a lazy, lounging, sleepy air, that makes me long to make them get up and walk. Others again manage, even upon fresh water, to be very sick. There are generally a dozen young human beings, some naughty, sick, and squalling, others happy, romping, and riotous; and what with the vibratory motion of the rocking-chairs and their contents, the women's shrill jabber, the children's shriller wailing and shouting, the heat and closeness of the air, a ladies' cabin on board an American steamboat is one of the most overpowering things to sense and soul that can well be imagined. There was a poor sick woman with three children, among our company, two of which were noisy, unruly boys, of from eight to ten years old. One of them set up a howl as soon as he came on board, which he prolonged, to our utter dismay, for upwards of half an hour sans intermission, except to draw breath. I bore it as long as I could; but threats, entreaties, and bribes having been resorted to in vain, by all the women in the cabin, to silence him, I at length very composedly took him up in my arms, and deposited him on his back in one of the upper berths; whereupon his brother flew at his mother, kicking, thumping, screaming and yelling. The cabin was in an uproar; the little wretch I held in my arms struggled like a young giant, and though I succeeded in lodging him upon the upper shelf, presently slid down from it like an eel. However, this effort had a salutary effect, for it obtained silence,—the crying gave way to terror, which produced silence, of which I availed myself to sleep till dinner time.   [JA]

Baltimore
January 6, 1833

Southern race relations Mrs. [Caton, daughter of Maryland statesman Charles Carroll] amused me very much by her account of the slaves on their estates, whom, she said, she found the best and most faithful servants in the world. Being born upon the land, there exists among them somthing of the spirit of clanship, and "our house," "our family," are the terms by which they designate their owners. In the south there are no servants but blacks; for the greater proportion of domestics being slaves, all species of servitude whatever is looked upon as a degradation; and the slaves themselves entertain the very highest contempt for white servants, whom they designate as "poor white trash" . . .   [JA]

Washington, D.C.
January 14, 1833

Washington We walked up to the Capitol: the day was most beautifully bright and sunny and the mass of white building, with its terraces and columns, stood out in fine relief against the cloudless blue sky. We went first into the senate, or upper house, because Webster [Daniel Webster, famous orator] was speaking, whom I especially wished to hear. The room itself is neither large nor lofty; the senators sit in two semi-circular rows, turned towards the president, in comfortable arm-chairs. On the same ground, and literally sitting among the senators, were a whole regiment of ladies, whispering, talking, laughing, and fidgeting. A gallery, level with the floor, and only divided by a low partition from the main room, ran round the apartment: this, too, was filled with pink, and blue, and yellow bonnets; and every now and then, while the business of the house was going on, and Webster was speaking, a tremendous bustle, and waving of feathers, and rustling of silks would be heard . . . [*JA*]

Washington, D.C.
January 15, 1833

At eleven o'clock Mr. [Edward Everett, distinguished orator and statesman] called. Went with him to see the original of the Declaration of Independence, also a few medals, for the most part modern ones, and neither of much beauty or curiousity. Afterwards went to the War Office, where we saw sundry Indian properties,—bows and arrows, canoes, smoking pipes, and what interested me much more, the pictures of a great many savage chiefs, and one or two Indian women. The latter were rather pretty: the men were not any of them handsome; scorn round the mouth, and cunning in the eyes seemed to be the general characteristic of all their faces. There was a portrait of Red Jacket, which gave me a most unpoetical, low-life impression of that great palaverer. The names of many of them delighted me, as, the *Everawake;* the *Man that Stands and Strikes;* the *North Wind.* One of the women's names amused me a great deal, *the Woman that spoke first,*—which title occasioned infinite surmise among us as to the occasion on which she earned it. After we had done seeing what was to be seen, we went on to the president's house, which is a comfortless, handsome-looking building, with a withered grass-plot enclosed in wooden palings in front, and a desolate reach of uncultivated ground down to the river behind. Mr. [Everett] gave us a most entertaining account of the levees, or rather public days, at the president's house. Every human being has a right to present himself there; the consequence is that great numbers of the very commonest sort of people used to rush in, and follow about the servants who carried refreshments, seizing upon whatever they could get, and staring and pushing about, to the infinite discomfiture of the more respectable and better-behaved part of the assembly. Indeed, the nuisance became so great, that they discontinued the eatables, and in great measure got rid of the crowd. Mr. [Bancroft, the British charges d'affaires] assured me that on one of these occasions, two *ladies* had themselves lifted up and seated on the chimney-piece, in order to have a better view of the select congregation beneath them . . .   [JA]

Washington, D.C.
January 16, 1833

Acting

We had a discussion as to how far real feeling enters into our scenic performances. 'Tis hard to say: the general question it would be impossible to answer, for acting is altogether a monstrous anomaly. John Kemble and Mrs. Siddons were always in earnest in what they were about; Miss O'Neill [Irish actress with great success on the British stage 1814–1819] used to cry bitterly in all her tragedy parts; whilst Garrick could be making faces and playing tricks in the middle of his finest points, and Kean would talk gibberish while the people were in an uproar of applause at his. In my own individual instance, I know that sometimes I could turn every word I am saying into burlesque, (*never* Shakespeare, by the bye,) and at others my heart aches, and I cry real, bitter, warm tears, as earnestly as if I was in earnest.   [JA]

Washington, D.C.
January 17, 1833

Andrew
Jackson

His excellency Andrew Jackson, is very tall and thin, but erect and dignified in his carriage—a good specimen of a fine old well-battered soldier. His hair very thick and grey: his manners are perfectly simple and quiet, therefore very good; so are those of his niece, Mrs. [Emily Donelson, Jackson's niece and White House hostess], who is a very pretty person, and lady of the house, Mrs. Jackson having been dead some time. He talked about South Carolina, and entered his protest against scribbling ladies, assuring us that the whole of the present southern disturbances [the Nullification Controversy, when South Carolina attempted to assert states' rights and defy the federal government] had their origin in no larger a source than the nib of the pen of a lady. Truly, if this be true, the lady must have scribbled to some purpose. We sat a little more than a quarter of an hour . . .

Habited, and at about one o'clock Mr. [Adams] called for me. On going to the door, I found him and his horse, and a strange, tall, grey horse for me, and young gentlemen of the name of [Fulton, nephew of the inventor of the steamboat] to whom I understood it belonged, and whom Mr. [Adams] introduced to me as very anxious to join my party. I was a little startled at this, as I did not quite think Mr. [Adams] ought to have brought any body to ride with me without my leave. However, as I was riding his horse, I was not just as well pleased that he was by, for I don't like having the responsibility of such valuable property as a private gentleman's horse to take care of. I told him this, alleging it as a reason for my preferring to ride an indifferent hack horse, about which I had no such anxiety. He replied that I need have none about his. I told him laughingly that I would give him two dollars for the hire of it, and then I should feel quite happy; all which nonsense passed as nonsense should, without a comment. He is a son of [Fulton]: I thought him tolerably pleasant and well informed.   [JA]

Washington, D.C.
January 19, 1833

"Fanny," quoth my father, "something particularly disagreeable has occurred, pray, can you call to mind anything you said during the course of your Thursday's ride which was likely to be offensive to Mr. [Fulton], or anything abusive of this country?" As I have already had sundry specimens of great talent there is for tattle in the exclusive coteries of this gossiping new world, I merely untied my bonnet, and replied that I did not at that moment recollect a word that I had said during my whole ride, and should certainly not give myself any trou-

Scandal

ble to do so. "Now my dear," said my father, his own eyes flashing with indignation, "don't put yourself into a passion; compose yourself and recollect. Here is a letter I have just received." He proceeded to read it, and the contents were to this effect—that during my ride with Mr. [Fulton] I had said I did not choose to ride an American gentleman's horse, and *had offered him two dollars for the hire of his,*—that moreover, I had spoken most derogatorily of America and Americans; in consequence of all which, if my father did not give some explanation, or make some apology to the public, I should certainly be hissed off the stage, as soon as I appeared on it that evening. This was pleasant. I stated the conversation as it had passed, adding, that as to any sentiments a person might express on any subject; liberty of opinion and liberty of speech were alike rights which belonged to every body, and that, with a due regard to good feeling, and good breeding, they were riots which nobody ought, and I never would forego. Mr. [Featherstone, otherwise unidentified] opened his eyes. I longed to add that any conversation between me and any other person was nobody's business but mine, and his or hers, and that the whole thing was on the part of the young gentleman concerned, the greatest piece of blackguardism, and on that of the old gentleman concerned, the greatest piece of twaddle that it had ever been my good fortune to hear of. "For," said Mr. [Featherstone], "not less than fifty members of Congress have already mentioned the matter to me." Fifty old gossiping women! why the whole thing is for all the world like a village tattle in England, among half a dozen old wives round their tea-pots. All Washington was in dismay; and my evil deeds and evil words were the town talk,—fields, gaps, marshes, and all, rang with them. This is an agreeable circumstance, and a display of national character highly entertaining and curious. It gave me at the time, however, a dreadful side-ache, and nervous cough. I went to the theatre, dressed, and came on the stage in the full expectation of being hissed off it, which is a pleasant sensation, very, and made my heart full of bitterness to think I should stand,—as no woman ought to stand,—the mark of public insult. However, no such thing occurred,—I went on and came off without any such trial of my courage; but I had been so much annoyed, and was still so indignant, that I passed the intervals between my scenes crying,—which, of course, added greatly to the mirth and spirit of my performance of Beatrice . . .

When I came on in my fine dress, at the beginning of the second act, the people hailed me with such a tremendous burst of applause, and prolonged it so much, that I was greatly puzzled to imagine what on earth possessed them. I concluded they were pleased with my dress, but could not help being rather amused at their vehement and continued clapping, considering they had seen it several times before. However, they ceased at last, and I thought no more about it. Towards the time for the beginning of the third act, which opens with my being discovered waiting for Fazio's return, as I was sitting in my dressing-room working, D[all] suddenly exclaimed, "Hark!—what is that?" [Dall] opened the door, and we heard a tremendous noise of shouts and of applause. "They are waiting for you, certainly," said D[all]. She ran out, and returned, saying, "the stage is certainly waiting for you, Fanny, for the curtain is up." I rushed out of the room, but on opening the door leading to the stage, I distinctly heard my father's voice addressing the audience. I turned sick with a sort of indefinite apprehension, and on inquiry found that at the beginning of the play a number of hand-bills had been thrown into the pit, professing to quote my conversation with Mr. [Fulton] at Washington, and calling upon the people to resent my conduct in the grossest and most vulgar terms. This precious document had, it seems, been brought round by somebody to my father, who immediately went on with it in his hand, and assured the audience that the whole thing was a falsehood. I scarce heard what he said, though I stood at the side scene: I was crying dreadfully with fright and indignation. How I wished I was a caterpillar under a green gooseberry-bush!

Oh, how I did wince to think of going on again after this scene, though the feeling of the audience was most evident; for all the applause I had fancied they bestowed upon my dress, was, in fact, an unsolicited testimony of their disbelief in the accusation brought against me. They received my father's words with acclamations; and when the curtain drew up, and I was discovered, the pit rose and waved their hats, and the applause was tremendous. I was crying dreadfully, could hardly speak; however, I mastered myself and went on with my part,—though, what with the dreadful exertion that it is in itself, and the painful excitement I had just undergone, I thought I should have fainted before I got through with it . . .   [JA]

Washington, D.C.
February 4, 1833

The play was the Merchant of Venice, and Katharine and Petruchio for the farce;—my father's benefit: the house was crammed from floor to ceiling as full as it could hold: so much for the success of the hand-bills. Indeed, as somebody suggested, I think if we could find the author of that placard out, we are bound to give him a handsome re-ward, for he certainly has given us two of the finest benefits that ever were seen. I heard that a man said the other day that he should not be surprised if my *father had got the whole of this up* himself. Oh, day and night! that such thoughts should come into any human being's head. At the end, the people shouted and shrieked for us. He went on, and made them a speech, and I went on and made them a courtesy; and certainly they do deserve the civillest of speeches, and lowest of cour-tesies from us, for they behaved most kindly and courteously to us, and for mine own good part, I love the whole city of Philadelphia from this time forth, for ever more . . .   [JA]

New York City
February 23 1833

Women and religion

On our way, discussing the difference between religion as felt by men and women, [Butler] agreed with me, that hardly one man out of five thousand held any distinct and definite religious belief. He said that religion was a sentiment, and that as regarded all creeds, there was no midway with them; that entire faith, or utter disbelief were the only al-ternatives, for that displacing one jot of any of them made the whole totter,—which last is, in some measure, true, but I do not think it is true that religion is only a sentiment. There are many reasons why women are more religious than men. Our minds are not generally naturally analytical—our educations tend to render them still less so: 'tis seldom in a woman's desire, (because seldom in her capacity,) to investigate the abstract bearings of any metaphysical subject. Our imaginations are exceedingly sensitive, our subservience to early impressions, and exterior forms, proportionate; and our habits of thought, little enlarged by experience, observation, or proper culture, render us utterly incapable of almost any logical train of reasonings. With us, I think therefore, faith is the only secure hold; for disbelief acting upon mental constructions so faulty and weak, would probably engender insanity, or a thousand species of vague, wild, and mischievous enthusiasms. I believe, too, that women are more religious than men because they have warmer and deeper affections. There is nothing surely on earth that can satisfy and utterly fulfill the capacity for loving which exists in every woman's nature. Even when her situation in life is such as to call forth and constantly keep in exercise the best affections of her heart, as a wife, and a mother, it still seems to me as if more would be wanting to fill the measure of yearning tenderness, which, like an eternal fountain, gushes up in every woman's heart; therefore I think it is that we turn, in the plenitude of our affections, to that belief which is a religion of love, and where the broadest channel is open to receive the devotedness, the clinging, the confiding trustfulness, which are idolatry when spent upon creatures like ourselves, but become a holy worship when offered to heaven. Nor is it only from the abundance and overflowing of our affections that we are devout; 'tis not only from our capacity of loving, but also from our capacity of suffering that our piety springs. Woman's physical existence, compared with that of man, is one of incessant endurance. This in itself begets a necessity for patience, a seeking after strength, a holding forth of the hands for support; thus, the fragile frame, the loving heart, and the ignorant mind, are in us sources of religious faith. But it often happens that those affections, so strong, so deep, so making up the sum and substance of female existence, instead of being happily employed, as I have supposed above, are converted into springs of acute suffering. These wells of feeling hidden in the soul, upon whose surface the slightest smile of affection falls like sunlight, but whose very depths are stirred by the breath of unkindness, are too often unvisited by the kindly influence of kindred sympathies, and go wearing their own channels deeper, in silence and in secrecy, and in infinite bitterness,—undermining health, happiness, the joy of life, and making existence one succession of burden-bearing days, and toilsome, aching, heavy hours. It is in this species of blight, which falls upon many women, that any religious faith becomes a refuge and a consolation, more especially that merciful and compassionate faith whose words are, "Come unto me, all ye that labour and are heavy laden, and I will give you rest." To that rest betakes itself the wearied spirit, the wounded heart; and it becomes a blessing beyond all other blessings; a source of patience, of fortitude, of hope, of strength, of endurance; a shelter in the scorching land,—a spring of water in the wilderness.   [*JA*]

Boston, Massachusetts
April 15, 1833

Mount Auburn cemetery

We rode out to *Cambridge*, the University of Massachusetts [Harvard University], about three miles distant from Boston. The village round it, with its white cottages, and meeting roads, and the green lawns and trees round the college reminded me of England. We rode on to a place called Mount Auburn, a burial-ground which the Bostonians take great pride in, and which is one of the lions of the place. The entrance is a fine, solid, granite gateway, in a species of Egyptian style, with this inscription engraved over it: "Then shall the dust return to the earth as it was, and the spirit shall return unto God, who gave it." The whole place is at present in an unfinished state, its capabilities are very great, and, as far as it has progressed, they have been taken advantage of. The enclosure is of considerable extent, about one hundred acres,—and contains several high hills and deep ravines, in the bottom of which are dark, still, melancholy looking meres. The whole is cut with much skill and good taste, by roads for carriages, and small, narrow footpaths. The various avenues are distinguished by the names of trees, Linden walk, Pine walk, Beech walk; and already two or three white monuments are seen glimmering palely through the woods, reminding one of the solemn use to which this ground is consecrated, which, for its beauty, might seem a pleasure-garden instead of a place of graves . . .   [JA]

Boston, Massachusetts
April 17, 1833

It is quite comical to see the people in the morning at the box office: our window is opposite to it, and 'tis a matter of the greatest amusement to me to watch them. They collect in crowds for upwards of an hour before. The doors open, and when the bolts are withdrawn, there is a yelling and shouting as though the town were on fire. In they rush, thumping and pummeling one another, and not one comes out without rubbing his head, or his back, or showing a piteous rent in his clothes. I was surprised to see men of a very low order pressing foremost to obtain boxes, but I find that they sell them again at an enormous increase to others who have not been able to obtain any; and the better to carry on their traffic, these worthies smear their clothes with molasses, and sugar, etc., in order to prevent any person of more decent appearance, or whose clothes are worth a cent, from coming near the box office: this is ingenious, and deserves a reward . . .   [JA]

Scalping tickets

Boston, Massachusetts
April 20, 1833

At about twelve we [Kemble and Butler] rode to Mount Auburn. The few days of sunshine since we were last there, have clothed the whole earth with delicate purple and white blossom, a little resembling the wood anemone, but growing close to the soil, and making one think of violets with their pale purple colour: they have no fragrance whatever. We afterwards rode on to a beautiful little lake called Fresh Pond . . . [JA]

Schenectady, New York
July 10, 1833

*Canal
boats*

The only nuisances are the bridges over the canal, which are so very low, that one is obliged to prostrate oneself, on the deck of the boat, to avoid being scraped off it; and this humiliation occurs, upon an average, once every quarter of an hour. Mr. [Edward Trelawny, writer and friend of Byron and Shelley] read Don Quixote to us: he reads very peculiarly; slowly, and with very marked emphasis. He has a strong feeling of humour, as well as of poetry; in fact they belong to each other, for Humour is but Fancy laughing, and Poetry but Fancy sad . . .

The valley of the Mohawk, through which we crept the whole sunshining day, is beautiful from beginning to end; fertile, soft, rich, and occasionally approaching sublimity and grandeur, in its rocks and hanging woods. We had a lovely day, and a soft blessed sunset, which, just as we came to a point where the canal crosses the river, and where the curved and wooded shores on either side recede, leaving a broad smooth basin, threw one of the most exquisite effects of light and colour I ever remember to have seen, over the water, and through the sky. The sun had scarce been down ten minutes from the horizon, when the deck was perfectly wet with the heaviest dew possible, which drove us down to the cabin. Here I fell fast asleep, till awakening by the cabin girl's putting her arms affectionately round me, and telling me that I might come and have the first choice of a berth for the night, in the horrible hencoop allotted to the female passengers. I was too sleepy to acknowledge or avail myself of the courtesy, but the girl's manner was singularly gentle and kind. We sat in the men's cabin until they began making preparations for bed, and then withdrew into a room about twelve feet square, where a whole tribe of women were getting into their beds. Some half undressed, some brushing, some curling, some washing, some already asleep in their narrow cribs, but all within a quarter inch of each other: it made one shudder. As I stood cowering in a corner, half asleep, half crying, the cabin girl came to me again and entreated me to let her make a bed for me; however, upon my refusing to undress before so much good company, or lie down in such narrow neighbourhood, she put D[all] and myself in a small closet, where were four empty berths, where I presently fell asleep, where she established herself for the night, and where D[all], wrapped up in a shawl, sat till morning under the half open hatchway, breathing damp starlight . . .   [JA]

Trenton Falls, New York
July 12, 1833

We crossed a small wood immediately adjoining the house, and de- *Waterfalls* scending several flights of steps, connected by paths in the rocky bank, we presently stood on the brink of the channel, where the water was boiling along, deep and black, and passing away like time. We followed along the rocky edge: the path is not more than a foot wide, and is worn into all manner of unevenesses, and cavities, and slippery with the eternal falling of the spray. [Butler] walked before me: we dared not turn our heads for fear of tumbling into the black whirlpool be- low. We walked on steadily, warning each other at every step, and pres- ently we arrived at the first fall, where the rest of our party were halt- ing. I can't describe it: I don't know either its heighth or width; I only know it was extremely beautiful, and came pouring down like a great rolling heap of amber. The rocks around are high to the heavens, scooped, and singularly regular; and the sides of the torrent are, every now and then, paved with large, smooth layers of rock, as even and regular in their proportions as if the fairies had done the work. After standing before the tumbling mass of water for a length of time, we climbed to the brink above, and went on. Mr. [Trelawny] flung himself down under a roof of rock by the waterfall. My father, D[all], and the guide went on, out of sight; and [Butler] and I loitered by the rapid waters, flipping light branches and flowers upon the blood-coloured torrent, that whirled, and dragged, and tossed them down to the plunge beneath. When we came to the beautiful circular fall, we crept down to a narrow ridge, and sat with our feet hanging over the black cauldron, just opposite a vivid rainbow, that was clasping the waterfall. We sat here till I began to grow dizzy with the sound and motion of the churning darkness beneath us, and begged to move, which we did very cautiously. I was in an agony lest we should slip from the narrow, dripping ledges along which we crawled. We wandered on, and stopped again, at another fall, upon a rocky shelf overhanging the torrent, beside the blasted and prostrate trunk of a large tree. I was tired with walking; and [Butler] was lifting me up to seat me on the fallen tree, when we saw Mr. [Trelawny] coming slowly towards us. He stopped and spoke to us, and presently passed on; we remained behind talking and dipping our hands into the fresh water. At length we rejoined the whole party, sitting by a narrow channel, where the water looked like ink. Beyond this our guide saw it was impossible to go. I was for ascertaining this by myself; but my father forbade me to attempt the passage further. I was thirsty; and the guide having given me a beautiful strawberry and pale bluebell that he had found, like a couple of jewels, in some dark crevice of the rocks, I devoured the one, and then going down to the black water's edge, we dipped the fairy cup in, and drank the cold clear water, with which abundant draught I relieved my father's thirst also . . .   [JA]

On the Road to Niagara Falls
July 16, 1833

Carriage accident

Just as we were nearing the inn at this same place, our driver took it into his head to give us a taste of his quality. We were all earnestly engaged in a discussion, when suddenly I felt a tremendous sort of stunning blow, and as soon as I opened my eyes, found that the coach was overturned, lying completely on its side. I was very comfortably curled up under my father, who by heaven's mercy did not suffocate me; opposite sat D[all], as white as a ghost, with her forehead cut open, and an awful-looking stream of blood falling from it; by her stood Mr. [Trelawny], also as pale as ashes; [Butler] was perched like a bird above us all on the edge of the door-way, which was open. The first thing I did was to cry as loud as ever I could "I'm not hurt! I'm not hurt!" which assurance I shouted sufficiently lustily to remove all anxiety from their minds. The next thing was to get my father up, in accomplishing which he trampled upon me most cruelly. As soon as I was relieved from his mountainous pressure, I got up, and saw to my dismay two men carrying Mr. [Trelawny] into the house. We were all convinced that some of his limbs were broken. I ran after as quickly as I could, and presently the house was like an hospital. They carried him into an upper room, and laid him on a bed: here too they brought D[all], all white and bleeding. Our hand-baskets and bags were ransacked for salts and eau de cologne; cold water, hot water, towels, and pocket handkerchiefs were called into requisition; and I with my clothes all torn and one shoulder all bruised and cut, went from the one to the other in utter dismay. Presently, to my great relief, Mr. [Trelawny] revived and gave ample testimony of having the use of his limbs, by getting up, and in the most skillful manner plastering poor D[all]'s broken brow up. [Butler] went in quest of my father, who had received a violent blow on his leg, and was halting about, looking after the baggage, and the driver, who had escaped unhurt. The chief cause of our misfortune was the economy with which the stage-coaches are constructed in this thrifty land, that is, they have but one door, and of course are obliged to be turned round much oftener than if they had two. In wheeling us therefore rapidly up to the inn, and turning the coach with the side that had a door towards the house, we swung over and fell. While the coach was being repaired, and the horses changed, we, bound up, bruised, and aching but still very merry, sat down to breakfast. Mr. [Trelawny], who had been merely stunned, seized on the milk and honey, and stuffed away with great zeal; poor D[all] was the most deplorable of the party, with a bloody handkerchief bound over one half her face; I only ached a little; and I believe [Butler] escaped with a scratch on his finger; so, seeing it was no worse, we thanked God, and devoured. After breakfast, we packed ourselves again in our vehicle, and progressed.   [JA]

Niagara Falls, New York
July 17, 1833

Niagara Arrived on the other side, i.e., Canada, there was a second pause as to how we were to get conveyed to the falls . . . My mind was eagerly dwelling on what we were going to see: that sight which [Trelawny] said was the only one in the world which had not disappointed him. I felt absolutely nervous with expectation. The sound of the cataract is, they say, heard within fifteen miles when the wind sets favourably: to-day however there was no wind: the whole air was breathless with the heat of mid-summer, and though we stopped our wagon once or twice to listen as we approached, all was profoundest silence. There was no motion in the leaves of the trees, not a cloud sailing in the sky, every-thing was as though in a bright warm death. When we were within about three miles of the falls, just before entering the village of Niag-ara, [Trelawny] stopped the wagon, and then we heard distinctly, though far off, the voice of the mighty cataract. Looking over the woods which appeared to overhang the course of the river, we beheld one silver cloud rising slowly into the sky—the everlasting incense of the waters. A perfect frenzy of impatience seized upon me. I could have set off and run the whole way, and when at length the carriage stopped at the door of the Niagara House, waiting neither for my fa-ther, D[all], nor [Butler], I rushed through the hall, and the garden, down the steep foot-path cut in the rocks. I heard steps behind me, [Trelawny] was following me; down, down I sprang, and along the narrow foot-path, divided only by a thicket from the tumultuous rap-ids, I saw through the boughs the white glimmer of the sea of foam— "Go on, go on, don't stop," shouted [Trelawny], and in another minute the thicket was passed. I stood upon Table Rock. [Trelawny] seized me by the arm, and without speaking a word, dragged me to the edge of the rapids, to the brink of the abyss. I saw Niagara—Oh God! who can describe that sight!!!   [JA]

Marriage and Motherhood
1834–1838

*Kemble married Pierce Butler on June 7, 1834, in Philadelphia and re-
tired from the stage soon after.*

Philadelphia
October 26, 1834

Dearest Mrs. Jameson [Anna Jameson, British writer],
However stoutly your incredulity may have held out hitherto against
the various "authentic" reports of my marriage, I beg you will, upon
receipt of [*sic*] immediately believe that I was married on the 7th of
June last, and have now been a wife nearly five mortal months. You
know that in leaving the stage I left nothing that I regretted; but the utter separation from my family consequent upon settling in this country is a serious source of pain to me.?~~With regard to what you say,
about the first year of one's marriage not being as happy as the second,
I know not how that may be. I had pictured myself no fairyland of en-
chantments within the mysterious precincts of matrimony; I expected
from it rest, quiet, leisure to study, to think, and to work, and legitimate channels for the affections of my nature~~~

In the closest and dearest friendship, shades of character, and the precise depth and power of the various qualities of mind and heart, never approximate to such a degree, as to preclude all possibility of occasional misunderstandings.

> Not e'en the nearest heart, and most our own
> Knows half the reasons why we smile or sigh.

It is impossible that it should be otherwise: for no two human beings were fashioned absolutely alike, even in their gross outward bodily form and lineaments, and how should the fine and infinite spirit admit of such similarity with another? But the broad and firm principles upon which all honorable and enduring sympathy is founded, the love of truth, the reverence for right, the abhorrence of all that is base and unworthy, admit of no difference or misunderstanding; and where these exist in the relations of two people united for life, it seems to me that love and happiness, as perfect as this imperfect existence affords, may be realized.~~~

Of course, kindred, if not absolutely similar, minds do exist; but they do not often meet, I think, and hardly ever unite. Indeed, though the enjoyment of intercourse with those who resemble us may be very great, I suppose the influence of those who differ from us is more wholesome; for in mere unison of thought and feeling there could be no exercise for forbearance, toleration, self-examination by comparison with another nature, or the sifting of one's own opinions and feelings, and testing their accuracy and value, by contact and contrast with opposite feelings and opinions. A fellowship of mere accord, approaching to identity in the nature of its members, would lose much of the uses of human intercourse and its worth in the discipline of life, and, moreover, render the separation of death intolerable. But I am writing you a disquisition, and no one needs it less.~~~

What can I tell you of myself? My life, and all its occupations, are of a sober neutral tint. I am busy preparing my Journal [*Journal of America*] for the press. I read little, and that of old-fashioned kinds. I have never read much, and am disgracefully ignorant: I am looking forward with delight to hours of quiet study, and the mental hoards in store for me. I am busy preparing to leave town; I am at present, and have been ever since my marriage, staying in the house of my brother-in-law, and feel not a little anxious to be in a home of my own. But painters, and carpenters, and upholsterers are dirty divinities of a lower order, not to be moved, or hastened, by human invocations (or even imprecations), and we must e'en bide their time.

I please myself much in the fancying of furniture, and fitting up of the house; and I look forward to a garden, green-house, and dairy, among my future interests, to each of which I intend to addict myself zealously.

My pets are a horse, a bird, and a black squirrel, and I do not see exactly what more a reasonable woman could desire. Human companionship, indeed, at present, I have not much of; but as like will to like, I do not despair of attracting towards me, by-and-by, some of my own kind, with whom I may enjoy pleasant intercourse; but you can form no idea—none—none—of the intellectual dearth and drought in which I am existing at present . . . [LL]

Philadelphia
November 27, 1834

My Dear H[arriet]
You half fly into a rage with me all across the Atlantic, because I tell you that I hope ere long to see you; really that was not quite the return I expected for what I thought would be agreeable news to you; however, hear further~~~If I am alive next summer, I hope to spend three months in England: one with my own family and Emily Fitzhugh: one in Scotland; and one with you, if you and Mrs. Taylor [unidentified] please~~~I have been obliged to give up riding, for some time ago my horse fell with me, and though I was not at all hurt, I was badly frightened; so I trot about on my feet, and drive to and from town and the farm in a little four-wheeled machine called here a wagon.

The other day, for the first time, I explored my small future domain, which is bounded, on the right, by the high-road; on the left, by a not unromantic little mill-stream, with bits of rock, and cedar-bushes, and dams, and, I am sorry to say, a very picturesque, half-tumbled-down factory; on the north, by fields and orchards of our neighbors, and another road; and on the south, by a pretty, deep, shady lane, running from the high-road to the above-mentioned factory~~~I think the extent of our estate is about three hundred acres. A small portion of it, perhaps some seventy acres, lies on the other side of the high-road. Except a kitchen-garden, there is none deserves the name: no flower beds, no shrubberies, no gravel-walks. A large field, now planted with maize, or Indian corn, is on one side of an avenue of maple-trees leads to the house; on the other is an apple-orchard. There is nothing can call itself a lawn, though coarse grass grows all round the house. There are four pretty pasture meadows, and a very pretty piece of woodland, which, coasting the stream and mill-dam, will, I foresee, become a favorite haunt of mine. There is a farm-yard, a cider-press, a pond, a dairy, and out-houses, and adjuncts innumerable.

I have succeeded, after difficulties and disasters manifold, in engaging an apparently tolerably decent staff of servants; the house is freshly painted and clean, the furniture being finished with all expedition, the carpets ready to lay down; next week I hope to send our household out, and the week after I sincerely hope we shall transfer ourselves thither, and I shall be in a home of my own.

Miss Martineau [Harriet Martineau, British author] is just now in Philadelphia: I have seen and conversed with her, and I think, were her stay long enough to admit of so agreeable a conclusion, we might become good friends. It is not presumptuous for me to say that, dear H[arriet], because, you know, a very close degree of friendship may exist where there is great disparity of intellect. Her deafness is a serious bar to her enjoyment of society, and some drawback to the pleasure of conversing with her, for, as a man observed to me last night, "One feels so like a fool, saying, 'How do you do?' through a speaking-trumpet in the middle of a drawing-room;" and unshoutable commonplaces form the staple of drawing-room conversation. They are giving literary parties to her, and balls to one of their own townswomen who has just returned from abroad, which makes Philadelphia rather gayer than usual; and I have had so long a fast from dissipation that I find myself quite excited at the idea of going to a dance again.

I toil on, copying my Journal [*Journal of America*], and one volume of it is already printed; but now that the object of its publication is gone, I feel rather disgusted at the idea of publishing it at all. You know what my Journal always was, and that no word of it was ever written with the fear of the printer's devil before my eyes, and now that I have become careless as to its money value, it seems to me a mere mass of trivial egotism~~~When I sold it, it was an excellent, good book, for I thought it would help to make a small independence for my dear Dall; now she is gone [Dall had died in April 1834], and it is mere trash, but I have sold it~~~

My country life will, I hope, be one of study, and I pray and believe, of quiet happiness. I drove out to the farm yesterday, and walked nearly four miles, through meadows and lanes and by-roads, and over plowed fields, found mill-stream and bits of picturesque rock, and pretty paths to be explored at further length on horseback hereafter, I have one very great pleasure almost: in contemplation; I think it probable that my friend, Miss Sedgwick [Catharine Sedgwick, writer], will visit Philadelphia this winter. If she does I am sure she will remain a short time here, which will be a great delight to me.~~~   [*LL*]

Branchtown
May 27, 1835

[My Dearest Harriet]
You ask me if I do not love the country as I used to do. Indeed for, like all best good things, it seems the lovelier for near and intimate acquaintance. Yet the country here, and this place in particular, is not to me as it might be, and will be yet. This place is not ours, and during the life of old Miss B. [Pierce's aunt, Frances Butler, the executor of Major Butler's estate] not belong to us; this, of course, keeps my spirit of improvement in check, and indeed, even if it were made over to us, with signing and sealing and all due legal ceremonies, I should still feel some delicacy in making wholesale alterations in a place which an el-

American country life

derly person, to whom it has belonged, remembers such as it is for many years.

The absolute absence of all taste in matters of ornamental cultivation is lamentably evident in the country dwellings of rich and poor alike, as far as I have yet seen in this neighborhood. No natural beauty seems to be perceived and taken advantage of, no defect hidden or adorned; proximity to the road for obvious purposes of mere convenience seems to have been the one idea in the selection of building sites; and straight, ungraveled paths, straight rows of trees, straight strips of coarse grass, straight box borders, dividing straight narrow flower-beds, the prevailing idea of a garden; together with a deplorable dearth of flowers, shrubberies, ornamental trees, and everything that really deserves the name. [*LL*]

Kemble gave birth to her first child, Sarah, on May 28, 1835.

Branchtown
[June] 1835

[Dear Mrs. Jameson]
I think, however, it will please you to hear that I am well and happy, and that my whole state of life and being has assumed a placid, tranquil, serene, and even course, which, after the violent excitements of my last few years, is both agreeable and wholesome. I should think, ever since my coming out on the stage, I must have lived pretty much at the rate of three years in every one—I mean in point of physical exertion and exhaustion. The season of my repose is, however, arrived, and it seems almost difficult to imagine that, after beginning life in such a tumult of action and excitement, the remainder of my years is lying stretched before me like a level, peaceful landscape, through which I shall saunter leisurely towards my grave. This is the pleasant probable future, God only knows what changes and chances may sweep across the smiling prospect, but at present, according to the calculations of mere human foresight, none are likely to arise.

As I write these words, I do bethink me of one quarter from which our present prosperous and peaceful existence might receive a shock—the South. The family into which I have married are large slaveholders; our present and future fortune depend greatly upon extensive plantations in Georgia. But the experience of every day, besides our faith in the great justice of God, forbids dependence on the duration of the mighty abuse by which one race of men is held in abject physical and mental slavery by another. As for me, though the toilsome earning of my daily bread were to be my lot again to-morrow, I should rejoice with unspeakable thankfulness that we had not to answer for what I consider so grievous a sin against humanity.

I believe many years will not pass before this cry ceases to go up from earth to heaven. The power of opinion is working silently and strongly in the hearts of men; the majority of people in the North of this country are opposed to the theory of slavery, though they tolerate its practice in the South; and though the natural selfishness with which men cling to their interests is only at present increasing the vigilance of the planters in guarding their property and securing their prey, it is a property which is crumbling under their feet, and a prey which is escaping from their grasp; and perhaps, before many years are gone by, the black population of the South will be free, and we comparatively poor people.—Amen! with all my heart~~~I had hoped to revisit England before the winter,~~~but this cannot be, and I shall certainly not see England this year, if ever again~~~I think women in England are gradually being done justice to, and many sources of goodness, usefulness, and happiness, that have hitherto been sealed, are opened to them now, by a truer and more generous public feeling, and more enlightened views of education.

I saw a good deal of Harriet Martineau, and liked her very much indeed, in spite of her radicalism. She is gone to the South, where I think she cannot fail to do some good, if only in giving another impulse to the stone that already topples on the brink—I mean in that miserable matter of slavery. [*LL*]

Branchtown
June 27, 1835

[My Dearest Harriet]
I have resumed my riding, and am beginning to feel once more like my
unmarried self. I may have told you that I had some time ago a pretty,
thoroughbred mare, spirited and good tempered too; but she turned
out such an inveterate *stumbler* that I have been obliged to give up riding her, as, of course, my neck is worth more to me even than my
health. So, this morning I have been taking a most delectable eight
miles trot upon a huge, high, heavy carriage-horse, who all but shakes
my soul out of my body, but who is steady upon his legs, and which I
shall therefore patronize till I can be more *genteelly* mounted with
safety.

You bid me study Natural Philosophy~~~and ask me what I
read; but since my baby has made her entrance into the world, I neither read, write, nor cast up accounts, but am as idle, though not
nearly as well dressed, as the lilies of the field; my reading, if ever I take
to such an occupation again, is like, I fear, to be, as it always has been,
rambling, desultory and unprofitable~~~

Reading   Come, I will take as a sample of my studies, the books just now lying on my table, all of which I have been reading lately: Alfieri's *Life,* by
himself, a curious and interesting work; Washington Irving's last book,
A Tour on the Prairies, rather an ordinary book, upon a not ordinary
subject, but not without sufficiently interesting matter in it too; Dr.
Combe's *Principles of Physiology;* and a volume of Marlowe's plays,
containing *Dr. Faustus.* I have just finished Hayward's Translation of
Goethe's *Faust,* and wanted to see the old English treatment of the
subject. I have read Marlowe's play with more curiosity than pleasure.
This is, after all, but a small sample of what I read, but if you remember the complexion of my studies when I was a girl at Heath Farm, and
read Jeremy Taylor and Byron together, I can only say they are still apt
to be of the same heterogeneous quality. But my brain is kept in a certain state of activity by them, and that, I suppose, is one of the desirable results of reading. As for writing anything, or things—good gra-

cious! no, I should think not indeed! It is true, if you allude to the mechanical process of calligraphy, here is close to my elbow a big book, in which I enter all passages I meet with in my various readings tending to elucidate obscure parts of the Bible: I do not mean disputed points of theology, mysteries, or significations more or less mystical, but simply any notices whatever which I meet with relating to the customs of the Jews, their history, their language, the natural features of their country; and so bearing upon my reading of passages in the Old Testament. I read my Bible diligently every day, and every day wish more and more earnestly that I understood what I was reading . . . I mean this with regard to the Old Testament only, however. The life of Christ is that portion of the New alone vitally important to me, and that, thank God, is comparatively comprehensible.

I have just finished writing a long and vehement treatise against negro slavery, which I wanted to publish with my Journal, but was obliged to refrain from doing so, lest our fellow-citizens should tear our house down, and make a bonfire of our furniture—a favorite mode of remonstrance in these parts with those who advocate the rights of the unhappy blacks. *Antislavery writing*

You know that the famous Declaration of Independence, which is to all Americans what Moses commanded God's law to be to the Israelites, begins thus: "Whereas all men are born free and equal." Somebody, one day, asked Jefferson how he reconciled that composition of his to the existence of slavery in this country; he was completely surprised for a moment by the question, and then very candidly replied, "By God! I never thought of that before" . . .

These are some of my occupations: then I do a little housekeeping; then I do, as the French say, a little music; then I waste a deal of time in feeding and cleaning a large cageful of canary-birds, of which, as the pleasure is mine, I do not choose to give the rather disgustful trouble to any one else; strolling round the garden, watching my bee-hives, which are full of honey just now; every chink and cranny of the day between all this desultoriness, is filled with "the baby"; and study, of every sort (but that most prodigious study of any sort, i.e., "the baby") seems further off from me than ever~~~

Marriage and Motherhood, 1834–1838

Dear H[arriet], I shall surely see you, if I live, in less than a year, when we shall have so much to say to each other that we shall not know where to begin, and had better not begin, perhaps; for we shall know still less where to stop~~~   [*LL*]

Branchtown
October 31, 1835

My Dearest H[arriet],

Childbirth   I wonder where this will find you, and how long it will be before it does so. I have been away from home nearly a month, and on my return found a long letter from you waiting for me~~~I cannot believe that women were intended to suffer as much as they do, and be as helpless as they are, in child-bearing. In spite of the third chapter of Genesis, I cannot believe (the beneficent action of ether had not yet mitigated the female portion of the primeval curse) that all the agony and debility attendant upon the entrance of a new creature into life were ordained; but rather that both are the consequences of our many and various abuses of our constitutions, and infractions of God's natural laws. The mere item of tight stays, tight garters, tight shoes, tight waist-bands, tight arm-holes, and tight bodices,—of which we are accustomed to think little or nothing, and under the bad effects of which most young women's figures are suffered to attain their growth, both here and in civilized Europe,—must have a tendency to injure irreparably the compressed parts, to impede circulation and respiration, and in many ways which we are not aware of, as well as by the more obvious evils which they have been proved to produce, destroy the health of the system, affect disastrously all its functions, and must aggravate the pains and perils of child-bearing~~~Many women here, when they become mothers, seem to lose looks, health, and strength and are mere wrecks, libels upon the great Creator's most wonderful contrivance, the human frame, which, in their instance, appears utterly unfit for the most important purpose for which, He designed it.

Pitiable women! comparatively without enjoyment or utility in existence. Of course, this result is attributable to many various causes, and admits of plenty of individual exceptions, but I believe tight-lacing, want of exercise, and a perpetual inhaling of over-heated atmosphere, to be among the former~~~They pinch their pretty little feet cruelly, which certainly need no such embellishment, and, of course, cannot walk; and if they did, in the state of compression to which they submit for their beauty's sake, would suffer too much inconvenience, if not pain, to derive any benefit from exercise under such conditions~~~

When one thinks of the tragical consequences of all this folly, one is tempted to wish that the legislature would interfere in these matters, and prevent the desperate injury which is thus done to the race. The climate, which is the general cause assigned for the want of health of the American women, seems to me to receive more than its due share of blame. The Indian women, the squaws, are, I believe, remarkable for the ease with which they bear their children, the little pain they suffer comparatively, and the rapidity with which they regain their strength; but I think in matters of diet, dress, exercise, regularity in eating, and due ventilation of their houses, the Americans have little or no regard for the laws of health; and all these causes have their share in rendering the women physically incapable of their natural work, and unequal to their natural burdens . . . I am sorry to find that my physical courage has been very much shaken by my confinement. Whereas formerly I scarcely knew the sensation of fear, I have grown almost cowardly on horseback or in a carriage. I do not think anybody would ever suspect that to be the case, but I know it in my secret soul, and am much disgusted with myself in consequence~~~Our horses ran away with the carriage the other day, and broke the traces, and threatened us with some frightful catastrophe. I had the child with me, and though I did not lose my wits at all, and neither uttered sound nor gave sign of my terror, after getting her safely out of the carriage and alighting myself I shook from head to foot, for the first time in my life, with fear; and so have only just attained my full womanhood: for what says Shakespeare?—

Marriage and Motherhood, 1834–1838

God bless you, dearest friend.   [*LL*]

Branchtown
[November] 1835

Dear Mrs. Jameson,

It is so very long since I have written to you that I almost fear my handwriting and signature may be strange to your eyes and memory alike . . . What should a woman write about, whose sole occupations are eating, drinking, and sleeping; whose pleasures consist in nursing her baby, and playing with a brace of puppies; and her miseries in attempting to manage six republican servants—a task quite enough to make any "Quaker kick his mother," a grotesque illustration of demented desperation, which I have just learned, and which is peculiarly appropriate in these parts? Can I find it in my conscience, or even in the nib of my pen, to write to you all across the great waters that my child has invented two teeth, or how many pounds of tea, sugar, flour, etc., etc., I distribute weekly to the above-mentioned household of unmanageables? To write, as to speak, one should have some thing to say, and I have literally nothing, except that I am well in mind, body, and estate, and hope you are so too.

Our summer has been detestable; if America had the grace to have fairies (but they don't cross the Atlantic), I should think the little Yankee Oberon and Titania had been by the ears together: such wintry squalls! such torrents of rain! The autumn, however, has been fine, and we spent part of it in one of the most charming regions imaginable.

Shakers   A "Happy Valley" indeed!—the Valley of the Housatonic, locked in by walls of every shape and size, from grassy knolls to bold basaltic cliffs. A beautiful little river wanders singing from side to side in this secluded Paradise, and from every mountain cleft come running crystal springs to join it; it looks only fit for people to be baptized in (though I believe the water is used for cooking and washing purposes).

In one part of this romantic hill-region exists the strangest worship that ever the craving need of religious excitement suggested to the imagination of human beings.

I do not know whether you have ever heard of a religious sect called the Shakers; I never did till I came into their neighborhood: and all that was told me before seeing them fell short of the extraordinary effect of the reality. Seven hundred men and women, whose profession of religion has for one of its principal objects the extinguishing of the human race and the end of the world, by devoting themselves and persuading others to celibacy and the strictest chastity. They live all together in one community, and own a village and a considerable tract of land in the beautiful hill country of Berkshire.

They are perfectly moral and exemplary in their lives and conduct, wonderfully industrious, miraculously clean and neat and incredibly shrewd . . . thrifty and money-making. Their dress is hideous, and their worship, to which they admit spectators, consists of a fearful species of dancing, in which the whole number of them engage in going round and round their vast ball or temple of prayer, shaking their hands like the paws of a dog sitting up to beg, and singing in a deplorable psalm-tune in brisk jig time. The men without their coats, in their shirt-sleeves, with their lank hair hanging on their shoulders, and a sort of loose knee-breeches—knickerbockers—have a grotesque air of stage Swiss peasantry. The women without a single hair escaping from beneath their hideous caps, mounted upon very high-heeled shoes, and every one of them with a white handkerchief folded napkin-fashion and hanging over her arm. In summer they all dress in white and what with their pale, immovable countenances, their ghost-like figures, and ghastly, mad spiritual dance, they looked like the nuns in *Robert the Devil*, condemned, for their sins in the flesh, to post-mortem decency and asceticism, to look ugly, and to dance like ill-taught bears.

The whole exhibition was at once so frightful and so ludicrous, that I very nearly went off into hysterics, when I first saw them. We shall be in London, I hope, in the beginning of May next year, when I trust you will be there also, when I will edify you with all my new experiences of life, in this "other world," and teach you how to dance like a Shaker . . .   [*LL*]

Branchtown
December 2, 1835

Female education

Dearest Dorothy [Dorothy Wilson, Harriet St. Leger's companion],
I was at first a little disappointed that my baby was not a man-child, for the lot of woman is seldom happy, owing principally, I think, to the many serious mistakes which have obtained universal sway in female education. I do not believe that the just Creator intended one part of his creatures to lead the sort of lives that many women do~~~In this country the difficulty of giving a girl a good education is even greater, I am afraid, than with us, in some respects. I do not think even accomplishments are well taught here; at least, they seem to me for the most part very flimsy, frivolous, and superficial, poor alike both in quality and quantity. More solid acquirements do not abound among my female acquaintance either, and the species of ignorance one encounters occasionally—is so absolute and profound as to be almost amusing, and quite curious . . .   [*LL*]

Branchtown
October 5 [1836]

Southern slavery

My Dearest H[arriet],
It is a great disappointment to me that I am not going to the South this winter. There is no house, it seem, on the plantation but a small cottage, inhabited by the overseer, where the two gentlemen proprietors can be accommodated, but where there is no room for me, my baby, and her nurse, without unhousing the poor overseer and his family altogether. The nearest town to the estate, Brunswick, is fifteen miles off, and a wretched hole, where I am assured it will be impossible to obtain a decent lodging for me, so that it has been determined to leave me and baby behind, and the owner will go with his brother, but without

us, on his expedition to Negroland. As far as the child is concerned, I am well satisfied~~~but I would undergo much myself to be able to go among those people. I know that my hands would be in a great measure tied. I certainly could not—free them, nor could I even pay them for their labor, or try to instruct them, even to the poor degree of teaching them to read. But mere personal influence has a great efficiency; moral revolutions of the world have been wrought by those who neither wrote books nor read them; the Divinest Power was that of One Character, One Example; that Character and Example which we profess to call our Rule of life. The power of individual personal qualities is really the great power, for good or evil, of the world; and it is upon this ground that I feel convinced that, in spite of all the cunningly devised laws by which the negroes are walled up in a mental and moral prison, from which there is apparently no issue, the personal character and daily influence of a few Christian men and women living among them would put an end to slavery, more speedily and effectually than any other means whatever. You do not know how profoundly this subject interests me, and engrosses my thoughts: it is not alone the cause of humanity that so powerfully affects my mind; it is, above all, the deep responsibility in which we are involved, and which makes it a matter of such vital paramount importance with me~~~It seem to me that we are possessed of power and opportunity to do a great work; how can I not feel the keenest anxiety as to the use we make of this talent which God had entrusted us with? We dispose of the physical, mental, and moral condition of some hundreds of our fellow-creatures. How can I bear to think that this great occasion of doing good, of dealing justly, of setting a noble example to others, may be wasted or neglected by us? How can I bear to think that the day will come, as come it surely must, when we shall say: We once had it in our power to lift this burden from four hundred heads and hearts, and stirred no finger to do it; but carelessly and indolently, or selfishly and cowardly, turned our back upon so great a duty and so great a privilege.

I cannot utter what I feel upon this subject, but I pray to God to pour His light into our hearts, and enable us to do that which is right.

Marriage and Motherhood, 1834–1838

In every point of view, I feel that we ought to embrace the cause of these poor people. They will be free assuredly, and that before many years; why not make friends of them instead of deadly enemies? Why not give them at once the wages of their labor? Is it to be supposed that a man will work more for fear of the lash than he will for the sake of an adequate reward? As a matter of policy, and to escape personal violence, or the destruction of one's property, it were well not to urge them—ignorant, savage, and slavish, as they are—into rebellion. As a mere matter of worldly interest, it would be wise to make it worth their while to work with zeal and energy for hire, instead of listlessly dragging their reluctant limbs under a driver's whip.

Oh, how I wish I was a man! How I wish I owned these slaves! instead of being supported (disgracefully, as it seems to me) by their unpaid labor~~~.   [LL]

Park Place, London
December 28, 1836

. . . Nevertheless, and in spite of all your doubts, and notwithstanding all the improbabilities and all the impossibilities, here I am, dearest H[arriet], in very deed in England, and in London, once again. And shall it be that I have crossed that terrible sea, and am to pass some time here, and to return without *seeing* you? I cannot well fancy that. Surely, now that the Atlantic is no longer between us, though the Alps may be, we shall meet once more before I go back to my dwelling-place beyond the uttermost parts of the sea.

My absolute impossibility of taking the baby to the South determined the arrangements that were made; and as I was at any rate to be alone all the winter, I obtained leave to pass it in England, whither I am come, alone with my chick, through tempestous turbulence of winds and waves, and where I expect to remain peaceably with my own people, until such time as I am fetched away. When this may be, however, neither I nor any one else can tell, as it depends upon the meeting and sitting of a certain Convention, summoned for the revising of the constitution of the State of Pennsylvania; and there is at present an uncertainty as to the time of its opening. It was at first appointed to convene on the 1st of May, and it was then resolved that I should return early in March, so as to be in America by that time; but my last news is that the meeting of the Convention may take place in February, and my stay in England will probably be prolonged for several months in consequence~~~

Your various propositions, regarding negro slavery in America, I will answer when we meet, which I hope will be ere long~~~I wish to heaven I could have gone down to Georgia this winter!~~~

My father took his farewell of the stage last Friday. How much I could say upon that circumstance alone! The house was immensely full, the feeling of regret and good-will universal, and our own excitement, as you may suppose, very great. My father bore it far better than I had anticipated, and his spirits do not appear to have suffered since; I know not whether the reaction may not make itself felt hereafter . . .
[LL]

In September 1837 Kemble was joined by her husband in England. They then returned to Philadelphia, where Kemble gave birth to their second child, Frances, on May 28, 1838.

Philadelphia
May 27 [1838]

My Dear Mrs. Jameson,
I have received within the last few days your second letter from London; the date, however, is rather a puzzle, it being *August the 10th*, instead (I presume) of April . . .

In spite of the admirable forethought which prompted the beginning of this letter, my dear Mrs. Jameson, it is now exactly a fortnight since I wrote the above lines; and here I am at my writing-table, in my drawing room, having in the interim perpetrated another baby girl~~~My new child was born in the same day of the month that her sister was, and within an hour of the same time, which I think shows an orderly, systematic, and methodical mode of proceeding in such matters, which is creditable to me~~~ [LL]

Philadelphia
July 23, 1838

[My Dear Mrs. Jameson]

Abolitionist riots The friends of good order, in this excellent city of brotherly love, have been burning down a large new building erected for *purposes of free discussion*, because Abolition meetings were being held in it; and the Southern steamer [the *Pulaski*] has been wrecked with dreadful loss of life [death toll of 160], owing to the exceeding small esteem in which its officers appear to have held that "quintessence of dust, Man." The vessel was laden with Southerners coming north for the summer; and I suppose there is scarcely a family from Virginia to Florida that is not in some way touched by this dreadful and wanton waste of life . . . [LL]

Begun at Lenox,
Ended at Philadelphia
October 29–November 3, 1838

Dearest Harriet,
Since the receipt of your last letter, one from Emily has reached me, bringing me the intelligence of my mother's death!~~~ There is something so deplorable in perceiving (what one only fully perceives as they are ceasing forever) all the blessed uses of which these mysterious human relations are capable, all their preciousness, all their sweetness, all their holiness, alas! alas!~~~

Cecilia [Sarah Siddons's daughter, Kemble's cousin] and Mr. Combe [George Combe, the phrenologist, and Cecilia's husband] arrived in this country by the *Great Western* about a fortnight ago. On their road from New York to Boston they passed a night within six miles of Lenox, and neither came to see nor sent me word that they were so near, which was being rather more phrenological and philosophically phlegmatical than I should have expected of them. For my heart had warmed to Cecilia in this pilgrimage of hers to a foreign land, where I alone was of kin to her; and I felt as if I both knew and loved her more than I really do~~~

I understand Mr. Combe has parceled out both his whereabouts and whatabouts to the very inch and minute, for every day in the next two years to come, which he intends to devote to the phrenological regeneration of this country. I am afraid that he may meet with some disappointment in the result of his labors: not indeed in Boston, where considerable curiosity exists upon that subject, and a general proneness to intellectual exercises of every description~~~

Throughout New England, his book on the *Constitution of Man*, and his brother's, on the treatment of that constitution, are read and valued, and their name is held in esteem by the whole reading community of the North. But I doubt his doing more than exciting a mere temporary curiosity in New York and in Philadelphia; and further south I should think he would not be listened to at all, unless he comes prepared to demonstrate phrenologically that the colored population of the Southern States is (or are), by the conformation of their skulls, the legitimate slaves of the whites.

Can anything be stranger than to think of Cecilia trotting over the length and breadth of North America at the heels of a lecturing philosopher? When I think of her in her mother's drawing room in London, in the midst of surroundings and society so different, I find no end to my wonderment. She must have extraordinary adaptability to circumstances in her composition.

I have just finished the play of which you read the beginning in England—my *English Tragedy* [Kemble's third play]—and am, as usual, in high delight just now with my own performance. I wish that agreeable sentiment could last; it is so pleasant while it does! I think I will send it over to Macready [William Macready, leading Shakespearean interpreter], to try if he will bring it out at Covent Garden. I think it might succeed, perhaps; unless, indeed, the story is too objectionable for anything—but reality.

Perhaps I have had my share of health. I am sure I have had enough to be most grateful for, if I should lie on a sick-bed for the rest of my days~~~   [*LL*]

Philadelphia
Tuesday, November 13, 1838

. . . The sad news of my poor mother's death, my dear Mrs. Jameson, reached me while I was staying up at Lenox, among those whom my good fortune has raised up in this strange country to fill for me the place of the kindred and friends from whom I am so widely sundered~~~

That the winter in Georgia, whither we are going immediately, may be beneficial to the invalid member of our party is the only pleasant anticipation with which I set my face towards a part of the country where the whole manner of existence is repugnant to my feelings, and where the common comforts of life are so little known, that we are obliged to ship a freight of necessary articles of food for our use while we are on the plantation.

Wheaten bread is unknown, meal made of the Indian corn being alone used there: and though the provision Nature has furnished, in the shape of game, abounds, the only meat, properly so called, which can be procured there, is shipped in barrels (salted, of course) from the North.

Society, or the shadow of it, is not to be dreamt of; and our residence, as far as I can learn, is to be a half-furnished house in the midst of rice-swamps, where our habitual company will be our slaves, and our occasional visitors an alligator or two from the Altamaha . . .

We shall find, no doubt, our former animal friends, from the fleas up to the alligators: the first, swarming in the filthy negroes' huts; the last, expatiating in the muddy waters of the Altamaha. I trust they will none of them have forgotten us. Did I tell you before of those charming creatures, the moccasin snakes, which, I have just been informed, abound in every part of the southern plantations? Rattlesnakes I know by sight: but the moccasin creature, though I may have seen him, I do not feel acquainted, or at any rate familiar, with. Our nearest civilized town, you know, is Savannah, and that is sixty miles off. I cannot say the expedition is in any way charming to me, but the alternative is remaining alone here; and, as it is possible to live on the plantation with the children, I am going. Margery [O'Brien, the children's nurse], of course, comes with me~~~

Did I tell you, my dear Irishwoman, that we had no potatoes on the plantation, and that Indian meal holds the place of wheaten flour, bread baked of the latter being utterly unknown? Do not be surprised if I dwell upon these small items of privation, even now that I am about to go among these people the amelioration of whose condition I have considered as one of my special duties. With regard to this, however, I have, alas! no longer the faintest shadow of hope~~~   [*LL*]

On the Plantation
1838–1839

While she was in Georgia, Kemble kept a journal in the form of a series of letters written for her good friend Elizabeth Dwight Sedgwick.

Butler's Island
Near Darien, Georgia
December 1838

Island life . . . There are four settlements or villages (or, as the negroes call them, camps) on the island, consisting of from ten to twenty houses, and to each settlement is annexed a cook's shop with capacious caldrons, and the oldest wife of the settlement for officiating priestess. Pursuing my walk along the river's bank, upon an artificial dike, sufficiently high and broad to protect the fields from inundation by the ordinary rising of the tide—for the whole island is below high-water mark—I passed the blacksmith's and cooper's shops. At the first all the common iron implements of husbandry or household use for the estate are made, and at the latter all the rice barrels necessary for the crop, besides tubs and buckets, large and small, for the use of the people, and cedar tubs, of noble dimensions and exceedingly neat workmanship, for our own household purposes. The fragrance of these when they are first made, as well as their ample size, renders them preferable as dressing-room furniture, in my opinion, to all the china foot-tubs that ever came out of Staffordshire. After this I got out of the vicinity of the settlement, and I pursued my way along a narrow dike—the river on the one hand, and, on the other, a slimy, poisonous-looking swamp, all rattling with sedges of enormous height, in which one might lose one's way as effectually as in a forest of oaks. Beyond this, the low rice-fields, all clothed in their rugged stubble, divided by dikes into monotonous squares, a species of prospect by no means beautiful to the mere lover of the picturesque. The only thing that I met with to attract my attention was a most beautiful species of ivy, the leaf longer and more graceful than that of the common English creeper, glittering with the highest varnish, delicately veined, and of a rich brown-green, growing in profuse garlands from branch to branch of some stunted evergreen bushes which border the dike, and which the people call salt-water bush. My walks are rather circumscribed, inasmuch as the dikes are the only promenades. On all sides of these lie either the marshy rice-fields, the brimming river, or the swampy patches of yet unreclaimed forest, where the huge cypress-trees and exquisite evergreen under-growth spring up from a stagnant sweltering pool, that effectually forbids the foot of the explorer . . .

Now, E[lizabeth], I have no intention of telling you a one-sided story, or concealing from you what are cited as the advantages which these poor people possess; you, who know that no indulgence is worth simple justice, either to him who gives or him who receives, will not thence conclude that their situation thus mitigated is, therefore, what it should be. On this matter of the sixty dollars earned by Mr. [Butler]'s two men much stress was laid by him and his overseer. I look at it thus: If these men were industrious enough, out of their scanty leisure, to earn sixty dollars, how much more of remuneration, of comfort, of improvement might they not have achieved were the price of their daily labor duly paid them, instead of being unjustly withheld to support an idle young man and his idle family—*i.e.*, myself and my children . . .

I mentioned to you just now that two of the carpenters had made a boat in their leisure time. I must explain this to you, and this will in-

Slave house servants

volve the mention of another of Miss Martineau's [Harriet Martineau, British author] mistakes with regard to slave labor, at least in many parts of the Southern States. She mentions that on one estate of which she knew, the proprietor had made the experiment, and very successfully, of appointing to each of his slaves a certain task to be performed in the day, which once accomplished, no matter haw early, the rest of the four-and-twenty hours were allowed to the laborer to employ as he pleased. She mentions this as a single experiment, and rejoices over it as a decided amelioration in the condition of the slave, and one deserving of general adoption. But in the part of Georgia where this estate is situated, the custom of task labor is universal, and it prevails, I believe, throughout Georgia, South Carolina, and parts of North Carolina; in other parts of the latter state, however—as I was informed by our overseer, who is a native of that state—the estates are small, rather deserving the name of farms, and the laborers are much upon the same footing as the laboring men at the North, working from sunrise to sunset in the fields with the farmer and his sons, and coming in with them to their meals, which they take immediately after the rest of the family. In Louisiana and the new south-western slave states, I believe, task labor does not prevail; but it is in those that the condition of the poor human cattle is most deplorable, as you know it was there that the humane calculation was not only made, but openly and unhesitatingly avowed, that the planters found it, upon the whole, their most profitable plan to work off (kill with labor) their whole number of slaves about once in seven years, and renew the whole stock. By-the-bye, the Jewish institution of slavery is much insisted upon by the Southern upholders of the system; perhaps this is their nation of the Jewish jubilee, when the slaves were by Moses' strict enactment to be all set free. Well, this task system is pursued on this estate; and thus it is that the two carpenters were enabled to make the boat they sold for sixty dollars. These tasks, of course, profess to be graduated according to the sex, age, and strength of the laborer; but in many instances this is not the case, as I think you will agree when I tell you that on Mr. [Butler]'s first visit to his estates he found that the men and the women who labored in the fields had the same task to perform. This was a noble admission of female equality, was it not?—and thus it had been on the estate for many years past. Mr. [Butler], of course, altered the distribution of the work, diminishing the quantity done by the women.

I had a most ludicrous visit this morning from the midwife of the estate—rather an important personage both to master and slave, as to her unassisted skill and science the ushering of all the young negroes into their existence of bondage is intrusted. I heard a great deal of conversation in the dressing-room adjoining mine while performing my own toilet, and presently Mr. [Butler] opened my room door, ushering in a dirty, fat, good-humored looking old negress, saying, "The midwife, Rose, wants to make your acquaintance." "Oh massa!" shrieked out the old creature, in a paroxysm of admiration, "where you get this lilly alabaster baby!" For a moment I looked round to see if she was speaking of my baby; but no, my dear, this superlative apostrophe was elicited by the fairness of my skin: so much for degrees of comparison. Now I suppose that if I chose to walk arm in arm with the dingiest mulatto through the streets of Philadelphia, nobody could possibly tell by my complexion that I was not his sister, so that the mere quality of mistress must have had a most miraculous effect upon my skin in the eyes of poor Rose. But this species of outrageous flattery is as usual with these people as with the low Irish, and arises from the ignorant desire, common to both the races, of propitiating at all costs the fellow-creature who is to them as a Providence—or rather, I should say, a fate—for 'tis a heathen and no Christian relationship. Soon after this visit, I was summoned into the wooden porch or piazza of the house, to see a poor woman who desired to speak to me. This was none other than the tall, emaciated-looking negress who, on the day of our arrival, had embraced me and my nurse with such irresistible zeal. She appeared very ill to-day, and presently unfolded to me a most distressing history of bodily afflictions. She was the mother of a very large family, and complained to me that, what with childbearing and hard field labor, her back was almost broken in two. With an almost savage vehemence of gesticulation, she suddenly tore up her scanty clothing, and exhibited a spectacle with which I was inconceivably shocked and sickened. The facts, without any of her corroborating statements, bore tolerable witness to the hardships of her existence. I promised to attend to her ailments and give her proper remedies; but these are natural results, inevitable and irremediable ones, of improper treatment of the female frame; and, though there may be alleviation, there can not be any cure when once the beautiful and wonderful structure has been thus made the victim of ignorance, folly, and wickedness.

Slave infirmary

After the departure of this poor woman, I walked down the settlement toward the infirmary or hospital, calling in at one or two of the houses along the row. These cabins consist of one room, about twelve feet by fifteen, with a couple of closets smaller and closer than the state-rooms of a ship, divided off from the main room and each other by rough wooden partitions, in which the inhabitants sleep. They have almost all of them a rude bedstead, with the grey moss of the forests for mattress, and filthy, pestilential-looking blankets for covering. Two families (sometimes eight and ten in number) reside in one of these huts,—which are mere wooden frames—pinned as it were, to the earth by a brick chimney outside, whose enormous aperture within pours down a flood of air, but little counteracted by the miserable spark of fire which hardly sends an attenuated thread of lingering smoke up its huge throat. A wide ditch runs immediately at the back of these dwellings, which is filled and emptied daily by the tide. Attached to each hovel is a small scrap of ground for a garden, which, however, is for the most part untended and uncultivated. Such of these dwellings as I visited to-day were filthy and wretched in the extreme, and exhibited that most deplorable consequence of ignorance and an abject condition, the inability of the inhabitants to secure and improve even such pitiful comfort as might yet be achieved by them. Instead of the order, neatness, and ingenuity which might convert even these miserable hovels into tolerable residencies, there was the careless, reckless, filthy indolence which even the brutes do not exhibit in their lairs and nests, and which seemed incapable of applying to the uses of existence the few miserable means of comfort yet within their reach. Firewood and shavings lay littered about the floors, while the half-naked children were cowering round two or three smouldering cinders. The moss with which the chinks and crannies of their ill-protecting dwellings might have been stuffed was trailing in dirt and dust about the ground, while the back door of the huts, opening upon a most unsightly ditch, was left wide open for the fowls and ducks, which they are allowed to raise, to travel in and out, increasing the filth of the cabin by what they brought and left in every direction. In the midst of the floor, or squatting round the cold hearth, would be four or five little children from four to ten years old, the latter all with babies in their arms, the care of the infants being taken from the mothers (who are driven afield as soon as they recover from child labor), and developed upon these poor little nurses, as they are called, whose business it is to watch the infant, and carry it to its mother whenever it may require nourishment. To these hardly human little beings I addressed my remonstrances about the filth, cold, and unnecessary wretchedness of their room, bidding the elder boys and girls kindle up the fire, sweep the floor, and expel the poultry. For a long time my very words seemed unintelligible to them, till, when I began to sweep and make up the fire, etc., they first fell to laughing, and then imitating me. The incrustations of dirt on their hands, feet, and faces were my next object of attack, and the stupid negro practice (by-the-bye, but a short time since nearly universal in enlightened Europe) of keeping the babies with their feet bare, and their heads, already well capped by nature with their woolly hair wrapped in half a dozen hot, filthy coverings. Thus I traveled down the "street," in every dwelling endeavoring to awaken a new perception, that of cleanliness, sighing, as I went, over the futility of my own exertions, for how can slaves be improved? Natheless, thought I, let what can be done; for it may be that, the two being incompatible, improvement may yet expel slavery; and so it might, and surely would, if, instead of beginning at the end, I could but begin at the beginning of my task. If the mind and soul were awakened, instead of mere physical good attempted, the physical good would result, and the great curse vanish away; but my hands are tied fast, and this corner of the work is all that I may do. Yet it can not be but, from my words and actions, some revelations should reach these poor people; and going in and out among them perpetually, I shall

On the Plantation, 1838–1839

teach, and they learn involuntarily a thousand things of deepest import. They must learn, and who can tell the fruit of that knowledge are beings in the world, even with skins of a different color from their own, who have sympathy for their misfortunes, love for their virtues, and respect for their common nature—but oh! my heart is full almost to bursting as I walk among these most poor creatures.

The infirmary is a large two-story building, terminating the broad orange-planted space between the two rows of houses which form the first settlement; it is built of whitewashed wood, and contains four large-sized rooms. But how shall I describe to you the spectacle which was presented to me on entering the first of these? But half the casements, of which there were six, were glazed, and these were obscured with dirt, almost as much as the other windowless ones were darkened by the dingy shutters, which the shivering inmates had fastened to in order to protect themselves from the cold. In the enormous chimney glimmered the powerless embers, of a few sticks of wood, round which, however, as many of the sick women as could approach were cowering, some on wooden settles, most of them on the ground, excluding those who were too ill to rise; and these last poor wretches lay prostrate on the floor, without bed, mattress, or pillow, buried in tattered and filthy blankets, which, huddled round them as they lay strewed about, left hardly space to move upon the floor. And here, in their hour of sickness and suffering, lay those whose health and strength are spent in unrequited labor for us—those who, perhaps even yesterday, were being urged on to their unpaid task—those whose husbands, fathers, brothers, and sons were even at that hour sweating over the earth, whose produce was to buy for us all the luxuries which health can revel in, all the comforts which can alleviate sickness. I stood in the midst of them, perfectly unable to speak, the tears pouring from my eyes at this sad spectacle of their misery, myself and my emotion alike strange and incomprehensible to them . . .

Here lay women expecting every hour the terrors and agonies of childbirth, others who had just brought their doomed offspring into the world, others who were groaning over the anguish and bitter disappointment of miscarriages—here lay some burning with fever, others chilled with cold and aching with rheumatism, upon the hard cold ground, the draughts and dampness of the atmosphere increasing their sufferings, and dirt, noise, and stench, and every aggravation of which sickness is capable, combined in their condition—here they lay like brute beasts, absorbed in physical suffering; unvisited by any of those Divine influences which may ennoble the dispensations of pain and illness, forsaken, as it seemed to me, of all good; and yet, O God, Thou surely hadst not forsaken them! Now pray take notice that this is the hospital of an estate where the owners are supposed to be humane, the overseer efficient and kind, and the Negroes remarkably well cared for and comfortable.

As soon as I recovered from my dismay, I addressed old Rose the midwife, who had charge of this room, bidding her open the shutters of such windows as were glazed, and let in the light. I next proceeded to make up the fire; but, upon my lifting a log for that purpose, there was one universal outcry of horror, and old Rose, attempting to snatch it from me, exclaimed: "Let alone, missis—let be; what for you lift wood? you have nigger enough, missis, to do it!" I hereupon had to explain to them my view of the purposes for which hands and arms were appended to our bodies, and forthwith began making Rose tidy up the miserable apartment, removing all the filth and rubbish from the floor that could be removed, folding up in piles the blankets of the patients who were not using them, and placing, in rather more sheltered and comfortable positions, those who were unable to rise. It was all that I could do, and having enforced upon them all my earnest desire that they should keep their room swept, and as tidy as possible, I passed on to the other room on the ground floor, and to the two above, one of which is appropriated to the use of the men who are ill. They were all in the same deplorable condition, the upper rooms being rather the more miserable, inasmuch as none of the windows were glazed at all, and they had, therefore, only the alternative of utter darkness, or killing draughts of air from the unsheltered casements. In all, filth, disorder, and misery abounded; the floor was the only bed, and scanty begrimed rags of blankets the only covering. I left this refuge for Mr. [Butler]'s sick dependents with my clothes covered with dust, and full of vermin, and with a heart heavy enough, as you will well believe. My morning's work had fatigued me not a little, and I was glad to return to the house, where I gave vent to my indignation and regret at the scene I had just witnessed to Mr. [Butler] and his overseer, who, here, is a member of our family. The latter told me that the condition of the hospital had appeared to him, from his first entering upon his situation (only within the last year), to require a reform, and that he had proposed it to the former manager, Mr. K[ing], and Mr. [Butler]'s brother, who is part proprietor of the estate, but, receiving no encouragement from them, had supposed that it was a matter of indifference to the owners, and had left it in the condition in which he had found it, in which condition it has been for the last nineteen years and upward.

Overseer   This new overseer of ours [Mr. Oden] has lived fourteen years with an old Scotch gentleman, who owns an estate adjoining Mr. [Butler]'s, on the island of St. Simons, upon which estate, from everything I can gather, and from what I know of the proprietor's character, the slaves are probably treated with as much humanity as is consistent with slavery at all, and where the management and comfort of the hospital in particular had been most carefully and judiciously attended to. With regard to the indifference of our former manager upon the subject of the accommodation for the sick, he was an excellent overseer, the estate returned a full income under his management, and such men have nothing to do with sick slaves: they are tools, to be mended only if they can be made available again; if not, to be flung by as useless, without further expense of money, time, or trouble.

I am learning to row here, for circumscribed, as my walks necessarily are, impossible as it is to resort to my favorite exercise on horseback upon these narrow dikes, I must do something to prevent my blood from stagnating; and this broad brimming river, and the beautiful light canoes which lie moored at the steps, are very inviting persuaders to this species of exercise. My first attempt was confined to pulling an oar across the stream, for which I rejoiced in sundry aches and pains altogether novel, letting alone a delightful row of blisters on each of my hands.

...tle of what those see who are standing [upon] a pinnacle
far above the vapour that folds us in —
November 27th 1881 — My mother began talking about herself
dear dear Hall. but my mother is not the person to grasp
thoughts being the least in the world — no oh no tis not a
healthy mind — far, far from it — but yet too most highly
intellectual. Hal reminds me of Hamlet very much, their
thoughts are of the same colour — there is that vague & dreaming
restless wh seems aimless & objectless, that deep & earnest
& constant reflection tending to no result, the same melancholy
perception, or rather sensation of life — I feel every now & then
she is possessed of great power — but they seem to me only to add
by contrast to the morbid nothingness of all her thoughts &
feelings — I know no other way of expressing the sense of
vagueness she gives to me but by saying her mind is of no
colour, a species of gloomy neutral tint, & over this world of
colourless outlines, the Spirit of Doubting in some shape or
other for ever holds mastery — she doubts herself, she doubts
others — she doubts the very life she lives, she doubts that beyond
it — she doubts that wh she saw & touches, she doubts that
wh her senses cannot perceive — she doubts as she prays, the
..........she doubts as she fears, she doubts as she
hopes — I believe she sometimes must doubt her own identity
& tis the doubt that this doubting is evil that oppresses &
disturbs her — Oh this is very like Hamlet — dear dear Hall
I love her entirely & admire her much & pity her more —
no, rash as her mental powers compared to my own, I
wd not possess them — they are too wide — they have no
distinct boundary — her thoughts dwell over too large
an extent, they wander beyond her jurisdiction &
bring her back but faint & fearful histories of their
explorings into forbidden land

Page from Fanny Kemble's diary (*Courtesy Folger Shakespeare Library, Washington, D.C.*)

Fanny Kemble as Juliet *(Courtesy Folger Shakespeare Library, Washington, D.C.)*

Pierce Butler *(Courtesy Lenox Library Association)*

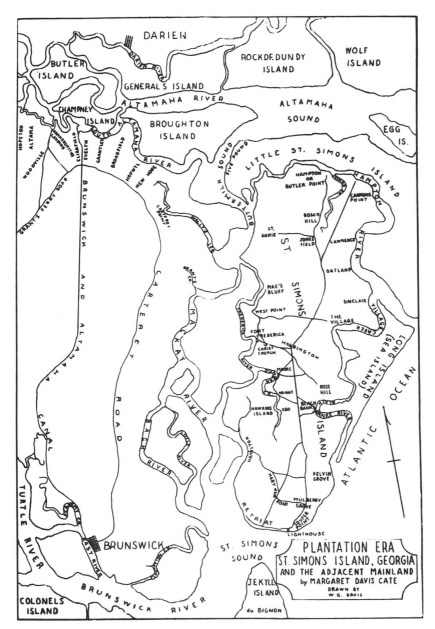

Map of St. Simons Island *(Courtesy Georgia Historical Quarterly)*

St. Simons Island *(Courtesy Georgia Historical Society, Savannah)*

Butler slave cabin *(Courtesy Georgia Historical Society, Savannah)*

Sarah and Fan Butler *(Courtesy Coastal Georgia Historical Society)*

Harriet St. Leger *(Courtesy Folger Shakespeare Library, Washington, D.C.)*

Elizabeth Dwight Sedgwick *(Courtesy Lenox Library Association)*

Fanny Kemble in later life

I forgot to tell you that in the hospital were several sick babies, whose mothers were permitted to suspend their field labor in order to nurse them. Upon addressing some remonstrances to one of these, who, besides having a sick child, was ill herself, about the horribly dirty condition of her baby, she assured me that it was impossible for them to keep their children clean; that they went out to work at daybreak, and did not get their tasks done till evening, and that then they were too tired and worn out to do anything but throw themselves down and sleep. This statement of hers I mentioned on my return from the hospital, and the overseer appeared extremely annoyed by it, and assured me repeatedly that it was not true.

In the evening Mr. [Butler], who had been over to Darien, mentioned that one of the storekeepers there had told him that, in the course of a few years, he had paid the Negroes of this estate several thousand dollars for moss, which is a very profitable article of traffic with them: they collect it from the trees, dry and pick it, and then sell it to the people in Darien for mattresses, sofas, and all sorts of stuffing purposes, which, in my opinion, it answers better than any other material whatever that I am acquainted with, being as light as horsehair, as springy and elastic, and a great deal less harsh and rigid. It is now bedtime, dear E[lizabeth], and I doubt not it has been sleepy time with you over this letter long ere you came thus far. There is a preliminary to my repose, however, in this agreeable residence, which I rather dread, namely, the hunting for, or discovering without hunting, in fine relief upon the white-washed walls of my bedroom, a most hideous and detestable species of *reptile* called centipedes, which come out of the cracks and crevices of the walls, and fill my very heart with dismay. They are from an inch to two inches long, and appear to have not a hundred, but a thousand legs. I cannot ascertain very certainly from the Negroes whether they sting or not, but they look exceedingly as if they might, and I visit my babies every night in fear and trembling, lest I should find one or more of these hateful creatures mounting guard over them. Good night; you are well to be free from centipedes— better to be free from slaves.   [GP]

Dear E[lizabeth],

This morning I paid my second visit to the infirmary, and found there had been some faint attempt at sweeping and cleaning, in compliance with my entreaties. The poor woman Harriet, however, whose statement with regard to the impossibility of their attending properly to their children had been so vehemently denied by the overseer, was crying bitterly. I asked her what ailed her, when, more by signs and dumb show than words, she and old Rose informed me that Mr. O[den] had flogged her that morning for having told me that the women had not time to keep their children clean. It is part of the regular duty of every overseer to visit the infirmary at least once a day, which he generally does in the morning, and Mr. O[den]'s visit had preceded mine but a short time only, or I might have been edified by seeing a man horsewhip a woman. I again and again made her repeat her story, and she again and again affirmed that she had been flogged for what she told me, none of the whole company in the room denying it or contradicting her. I left the room because I was so disgusted and indignant that I could hardly restrain my feelings, and to express them could have produced no single good result. In the next ward, stretched upon the ground, apparently either asleep or so overcome with sickness as to be incapable of moving, lay an immense woman; her stature, as she cumbered the earth, must have been, I should think, five feet seven or eight, and her bulk enormous. She was wrapped in filthy rags, and lay with her face on the floor. As I approached, and stooped to see what ailed her, she suddenly threw out her arms, and, seized with violent convulsions, rolled over and over upon the floor, beating her head violently upon the ground, and throwing her enormous limbs about in a horrible manner. Immediately upon the occurrence of this fit, four or five women threw themselves literally upon her, and held her down by main force; they even proceeded to bind her legs and arms together, to prevent her dashing herself about; but this violent coercion and tight bandaging seemed to me, in my profound ignorance, more likely to increase her illness by impeding her breathing and the circulation of her blood, and I bade them desist, and unfasten all the strings and ligatures not only that they had put round her limbs, but which, by tightening her clothes round her body, caused any obstruction. How much I wished that, instead of music, and dancing, and such stuff, I had learned something of sickness and health, of the conditions and liabilities of the human body, that I might have known how to assist this poor creature, and to direct her ignorant and helpless nurses! The fit presently subsided, and was succeeded by the most deplorable prostration and weakness of nerves, the tears streaming down the poor woman's cheeks in showers, without, however, her uttering a single word, though she moaned incessantly. After bathing her forehead, hands, and chest with vinegar, we raised her up, and I sent to the house for a chair with a back (there was no such thing in the hospital), and we contrived to place her in it. I have seldom seen finer women than this poor creature and her younger sister, an immense strapping lass called Chloe—tall, straight, and extremely well made—who was assisting her sister, and whom I had remarked, for the extreme delight and merriment which my cleansing propensities seemed to give her, on my last visit to the hospital. She was here taking care of a sick baby, and helping to nurse her sister Molly, who, it seems, is subject to those fits, about which I spoke to our physician [Dr. James Holmes] here—an intelligent man residing in Darien, who visits the estate whenever medical assistance is required. He seemed to attribute them to nervous disorder, brought on by frequent childbearing. This woman is young, I suppose at the outside not thirty, and her sister informed me that she had had ten children—ten children, E[lizabeth]! Fits and hard labor in the fields, unpaid labor, labor exacted with stripes—how do you fancy that? I wonder if my mere narration can make your blood boil as the facts did mine? . . .

I have ingeniously contrived to introduce bribery, corruption, and pauperism, all in a breath, upon this island, which, until my advent, was as innocent of these pollutions, I suppose, as Prospero's isle of refuge. Wishing, however, to appeal to some perception, perhaps a little less dim in their minds than the abstract loveliness of cleanliness, I have proclaimed to all the little baby nurses that I will give a cent to every little boy or girl whose baby's face shall be clean, and one to every individual with clean face and hands of their own. My appeal was fully comprehended by the majority, it seems, for this morning I was surrounded, as soon as I came out, by a swarm of children carrying their little charges on their backs and in their arms, the shining, and, in many instances, wet faces and hands of the latter bearing ample testimony to the ablutions which had been inflicted upon them. How they will curse me and the copper cause of all their woes in their baby bosoms!

Slaves'
faces

Do you know that, little as grown Negroes are admirable for their personal beauty (in my opinion, at least), the black babies of a year or two old are very pretty; they have, for the most part, beautiful eyes and eyelashes, the pearly perfect teeth, which they retain after their other juvenile graces have left them; their skins are all (I mean of blacks generally) infinitely finer and softer than the skins of white people.

Perhaps you are not aware that among the white race the *finest grained* skins generally belong to persons of dark complexion. This, as a characteristic of the black race, I think might be accepted as some compensation for the coarse woolly hair. The nose and mouth, which are so peculiarly displeasing in their conformation in the face of a Negro man or woman, being the features least developed in a baby's countenance, do not at first present the ugliness which they assume as they become more marked; and when the very unusual operation of washing has been performed, the blood shines through the fine texture of the skin, giving life and richness to the dingy color, and displaying a species of beauty which I think scarcely anybody who observed it would fail to acknowledge. I have seen many babies on this plantation who were quite as pretty as white children, and this very day stooped to kiss a little sleeping creature that lay on its mother's knees in the infirmary—as beautiful a specimen of a sleeping infant as I ever saw. The caress excited the irrepressible delight of all the women present—poor creatures! who seemed to forget that I was a woman, and had children myself, and bore a woman's and a mother's heart toward them and theirs . . .

While I am speaking of the Negro countenance, there is another beauty which is not at all infrequent among those I see here—a finely-shaped oval face—and those who know (as all painters and sculptors, all who understand beauty do) how much expression there is in the outline of the head, and how very rare it is to see a well-formed face, will be apt to consider this a higher matter than any coloring, of which, indeed, the red and white one so often admired is by no means the most rich, picturesque, or expressive. At first the dark color confounded all features to my eye, and I could hardly tell one face from another. Becoming, however, accustomed to the complexion, I now perceive all the variety among these black countenances that there is among our own race, and as much difference in features and in expression as among the same number of whites. There is another peculiarity which I have remarked on the women here—very considerable beauty in the make of hands; their feet are very generally ill-made, which must be a natural, and not an acquired defect, as they seldom injure their feet by wearing shoes. The figures of some of the women are handsome, and their carriage, from the absence of any confining or tightening clothing, and the habit they have of balancing great weights on their heads, erect and good . . .

I told Mr. [Butler], with much indignation, of poor Harriet's flogging, and represented that if the people were to be chastised for anything they said to me, I must leave the place, as I could not but hear their complaints, and endeavor, by all my miserable limited means, to better their condition while I was here. He said he would ask Mr. O[den] about it, assuring me, at the same time, that it was impossible to believe a single word any of these people said. At dinner, accordingly, the inquiry was made as to the cause of her punishment, and Mr. O[den] then said it was not at all for what she had told me that he had flogged her, but for having answered him impertinently; that he had ordered her into the field, whereupon she had said she was ill and could not work; that he retorted he knew better, and bade her get up and go to work; she replied: "Very well, I'll go, but I shall just come back again!" meaning that when in the field she would be unable to work, and obliged to return to the hospital.

"For this reply," Mr. O[den] said, "I gave her a good lashing; it was

On the Plantation, 1838–1839

her business to have gone into the field without answering me, and then we should have soon seen whether she could work or not; I gave it to Chloe too for some such impudence."

I give you the words of the conversation, which was prolonged to a great length, the overseer complaining of the sham sicknesses of the slaves, and detailing the most disgusting struggle which is going on the whole time, on the one hand to inflict, and on the other to evade oppression and injustice. With this sauce I ate my dinner, and truly it tasted bitter . . .

At the upper end of the row of houses, and nearest to our overseer's residence, is the hut of the head driver. Let me explain, by the way, his office. The negroes, as I before told you, are divided into troops or gangs as they are called; at the head of each gang is a driver, who stands over them, whip in hand, while they perform their daily task, who renders an account of each individual slave and his work every evening to the overseer, and receives from him directions for their next day's tasks. Each driver is allowed to inflict a dozen lashes upon any refractory slave in the field, and at the time of the offense; they may not, however, extend the chastisement, and if it is found ineffectual, their remedy lies in reporting the unmanageable individual either to the head driver or the overseer, the former of whom has power to inflict three dozen lashes at his own discretion, and the latter as many as he himself sees fit, within the number of fifty; which limit, however, I must tell you, is an arbitrary one on this plantation, appointed by the founder of the estate, Major [Butler], Mr. [Butler]'s grandfather, many of whose regulations, indeed I believe most of them, are still observed in the government of the plantation. Limits of this sort, however, to the power of either driver, head driver, or overseer, may or may not exist elsewhere; they are, to a certain degree, a check upon the power of these individuals; but in the absence of the master, the overseer may confine himself within the limit or not, as he chooses; and as for the master himself, where is his limit? He may, if he likes, flog a slave to death, for the laws which pretend that he may not are a mere pretense, inasmuch as the testimony of a black is never taken against a white; and upon this plantation of ours, and a thousand more, the overseer is the only white man, so whence should come the testimony to any crime of his? With regard to the oft-repeated statement that it is not the owner's interest to destroy his human property, it answers nothing; the instances in which men, to gratify the immediate impulse of passion, sacrifice not only their eternal, but their evident, palpable positive worldly interest, are infinite. Nothing is commoner than for a man under the transient influence of anger to disregard his worldly advantage; and the black slave, whose preservation is indeed supposed to be his owner's interest, may be, will be and is occasionally sacrificed to the blind impulse of passion . . .

I had a conversation that interested me a good deal, during my walk to-day, with my peculiar slave Jack. This lad, whom Mr. [Butler] has appointed to attend me in my roamings about the island, and rowing expeditions on the river, is the son of the last head driver, a man of very extraordinary intelligence and faithfulness—such, at least, is the account given of him by his employers (in the burial ground of the negroes is a stone dedicated to his memory, a mark of distinction accorded by his masters, which his son never failed to point out to me when we passed that way). Jack appears to inherit his quickness of apprehension; his questions, like those of an intelligent child, are absolutely inexhaustible; his curiosity about all things beyond this island [Butler], the prison-house of his existence, is perfectly intense; his countenance is very pleasing, mild, and not otherwise than thoughtful; he is, in common with the rest of them, a stupendous flatterer, and, like the rest of them, also seems devoid of physical and moral courage. To-day, in the midst of his torrent of inquiries about places and things, I suddenly asked him if he would like to be free. A gleam of light absolutely shot over his whole countenance, like the vivid and instantaneous lightning; he stammered, hesitated, became excessively confused, and at length replied, "Free, missis! what for me wish to be free? Oh no, missis, me no wish to be free, if massa only let me keep pig!" The fear of offending by uttering that forbidden wish—the dread of admitting, by its expression, the slightest discontent with his present situation—the desire to conciliate my favor even at the expense of strangling the intense natural longing that absolutely glowed in his

Slaves' desire for freedom

On the Plantation, 1838–1839

every feature—it was a sad spectacle, and I repented my question. As for the pitiful request, which he reiterated several times, adding, "No, missis, me no want to be free; me work till me die for missis and massa," with increased emphasis; it amounted only to this, that negroes once were, but no longer are, permitted to keep pigs. The increase of filth and foul smells consequent upon their being raised is, of course, very great; and, moreover, Mr. [Butler] told me, when I preferred poor Jack's request to him, that their allowance was no more than would suffice their own necessity, and that they had not the means of feeding the animals. With a little good management they might very easily obtain them, however; their little "kail-yard" [cabbage patch] alone would suffice to it, and the pork and bacon would prove a most welcome addition to their farinaceous diet. You perceive at once (or, if you could have seen the boy's face, you would have perceived at once) that his situation was no mystery to him; that his value to Mr. [Butler], and, as he supposed, to me, was perfectly well known to him, and that he comprehended immediately that his expressing even the desire to be free might be construed by me into an offense, sought, by eager protestations of his delighted acquiescence in slavery, to conceal his soul's natural yearning, lest I should resent it. 'Twas a sad passage between us, and sent me home full of the most painful thoughts . . .

River scenery

The whole course of this most noble river is full of shoals, banks, mud, sand-bars, and the navigation, which is difficult to those who know it well, is utterly baffling to the inexperienced. The fact is, that the two elements are so fused hereabouts that there are hardly such things as earth or water proper; that which styles itself to the former is a fat, muddy, slimy sponge, floating half under the turgid river, looks yet saturated with the thick waves which every now and then reclaim their late dominion, and cover it almost entirely; the water, again, cloudy and yellow, like pea-soup, seems but a solution of such islands, rolling turgid and thick with alluvium, which it gathers and deposits as it sweeps along with a swollen, smooth rapidity, that almost deceives the eye. Amphibious creatures, alligators, serpents, and wild-fowl haunt these yet but half-formed regions, where land and water are of the consistency of hasty-pudding—the one seeming too unstable to walk on, the other almost too thick to float in. But then the sky—if no human chisel ever yet cut breath, neither did any human pen ever write light; if it did, mine should spread out before you the unspeakable glories of these Southern heavens, the saffron brightness of morning, the blue intense brilliancy of noon, the golden splendor and the rosy softness of sunset. Italy and Claude Lorrain may go hang themselves together! Heaven itself does not seem brighter or more beautiful to the imagination than these surpassing pageants of fiery rays, and piled-up beds of orange, golden clouds, with edges too bright to look on, scattered wreaths of faintest rosy bloom, amber streaks and pale green lakes between, and amid sky all mingled blue and rose tints, a spectacle to make one fall over the side of the boat, with one's head broken off with looking adoringly upward, but which, on paper, means nothing! . . .

Slaves' clothing allowance

This request for summer clothing, by-the-bye, I think a very reasonable one. The allowance of clothes made yearly to each slave by the present regulations of the estate is a certain number of yards of flannel, and as much more of what they call plains—an extremely stout, thick, heavy woolen cloth, of a dark grey or blue color, which resembles the species of carpet we call drugget. This, and two pair of shoes, is the regular ration of clothing; but these plains would be intolerable to any but negroes, even in winter, in this climate, and are intolerable to them in the summer. A far better arrangement, in my opinion, would be to increase their allowance of flannel and under clothing, and to give them dark chintzes instead of these thick carpets, which are very often the only covering they wear at all. I did not impart all of this to my petitioners, but, disengaging myself from them, for they held my hands and clothes, I conjured them to offer us some encouragement to better their condition by bettering it as much as they could themselves—enforced the virtue of washing themselves and all belonging to them, and at length made good my retreat . . .

Religion

You have heard, of course, many and contradictory statements as to the degree of religious instruction afforded to the negroes of the South, and their opportunities of worship, etc. Until the late abolition movement, the spiritual interests of the slaves were about as little regarded as their physical necessities. The outcry which has been raised with threefold force within the last few years against the whole system has induced its upholders and defenders to adopt, as measures of personal extenuation, some appearance of religious instruction (such as it is), and some pretense at physical indulgences (such as they are), bestowed apparently voluntarily upon their dependents. At Darien a church is appropriated to the especial use of slaves, who are almost all of them Baptists here; and a gentlemen officiates in it (of course white), who, I understand, is very zealous in the cause of their spiritual well-being. He, like most Southern men, clergy or others, jump the present life in their charities to the slaves, and go on to furnish them with all requisite conveniences for the next. There were a short time ago two free black preachers in this neighborhood, but they have lately been ejected from the place. I could not clearly learn, but one may possibly imagine, upon what grounds—

Whites among slaves

I do not think that a residence on a slave plantation is likely to be peculiarly advantageous to a child like my eldest. I was observing her to-day among her swarthy worshipers, for they follow her as such, and saw, with dismay, the universal eagerness with which they sprang to obey her little gestures of command. She said something about a swing, and in less than five minutes head man Frank had erected it for her, and a dozen young slaves were ready to swing little "Missus." [Elizabeth], think of learning to rule despotically your fellow-creatures before the first lesson of self-government has been well spelt over! It makes me tremble; but I shall find a remedy, or remove myself and the child from this misery and ruin . . .

Slave parents

The relation [between slave parents and their children] indeed resembles, as far as circumstances can possibly make it do so, the short-lived connection between the animal and its young. The father, having neither authority, power, responsibility or charge in his children, is of course, as among brutes, the least attached to his offspring; the mother, by the natural law which renders the infant dependent on her for its first year's nourishment, is more so; but as neither of them is bound to educate or to support their children, all the unspeakable tenderness and solemnity, all the rational, and all the spiritual grace and glory of the connection, is lost, and it becomes mere breeding, bearing, suckling, and then an end. But it is not only the absence of the conditions which God has affixed to the relation which tends to encourage reckless increase of the race; they enjoy, by means of numerous children, certain positive advantages. In the first place, every woman who is pregnant, as soon as she chooses to make the fact known to the overseer, is relieved of a certain portion of her work in the field, which lightening of labor continues, of course, as long as she is so burdened. On the birth of a child certain additions of clothing and an additional weekly ration are bestowed on the family; and these matters, small as they may seem, act as powerful inducements to creatures who have none of the restraining influences actuating them which belong to the parental relation among all other people, whether civilized or savage. Moreover, they have all of them a most distant and perfect knowledge of their value to their owners as property; and a woman thinks, and not much amiss, that the more frequently she adds to the number of her master's live-stock by bringing new slaves into the world, the more claims she will have upon his consideration and good-will. This was perfectly evident to me from the meritorious air with which the women always made haste to inform me of the number of children they had borne, and the frequent occasions on which the older slaves would direct my attention to their children, exclaiming, "Look, missis! little niggers, for you and massa; plenty little niggers for you and little missis!" A very agreeable apostrophe to me indeed, as you will believe . . .

I went again today to the infirmary, and was happy to perceive that there really was an evident desire to conform to my instructions, and keep the place in a better condition than formerly. Among the sick I found a poor woman suffering dreadfully from the earache. She had done nothing to alleviate her pain but apply some leaves, of what tree or plant I could not ascertain, and tie up her head in a variety of dirty cloths, till it was as large as her whole body. I removed all these, and found one side of her face and neck very much swollen, but so begrimed with filth that it was really no very agreeable task to examine it.

Slave medicine

The first process, of course, was washing, which, however, appeared to her so very unusual an operation, that I had to perform it for her myself. Sweet oil and laudanum, and raw cotton, being then applied to her ear and neck, she professed herself much relieved, but I believe in my heart that the warm-water sponging had done her more good than anything else. I was sorry not to ascertain what leaves she had applied to her ear. These simple remedies resorted to by savages, and people as ignorant, are generally approved by experience, and sometimes condescendingly adopted by science. I remember once, when Mr. [Butler] was suffering from a severe attack of inflammatory rheumatism, Dr. [Chapman, of Philadelphia] desired him to bind round his knee the leaves of the tulip tree—poplar I believe you call it—saying that he had learned that remedy from the Negroes in Virginia, and found it a most effectual one.

Slave baby bundling

My next agreeable office in the infirmary this morning was superintending the washing of two little babies, whose mothers were nursing them with quite as much ignorance as zeal. Having ordered a large tub of water, I desired Rose to undress the little creatures and give them a warm bath; the mothers looked on in unutterable dismay; and one of them, just as her child was going to be put into the tub, threw into it all the clothes she had just taken off it, as she said, to break the unusual shock of the warm water. I immediately rescued them; not but what they were quite as much in want of washing as the baby, but it appeared, upon inquiry, that the woman had none others to dress the child in when it should have taken its bath; they were immediately wrung and hung by the fire to dry; and the poor little patients, having undergone this novel operation, were taken out and given to their mothers. Anything, however, much more helpless and inefficient than these poor ignorant creatures you cannot conceive; they actually seemed incapable of drying or dressing their own babies, and I had to finish their toilet myself. As it is only a very few years since the most absurd and disgusting customs have become exploded among ourselves, you will not, of course, wonder that these poor people pin up the lower part of their infants, bodies, legs, and all, in red flannel as soon as they are born, and keep them in the selfsame envelope till it literally falls off.

In the next room I found a woman lying on the floor in a fit of epilepsy, barking most violently. She seemed to excite no particular attention or compassion; the women said she was subject to these fits, and took little or no notice of her, as she lay barking like some enraged animal on the ground. Again I stood in profound ignorance, sickening with the sight of suffering which I knew not how to alleviate, and which seemed to excite no commiseration merely from the sad fact of its frequent occurrence. Returning to the house, I passed up the "street." It was between eleven o'clock and noon, and the people were taking their first meal in the day.

By-the-by E[lizabeth], how do you think Berkshire county farmers would relish laboring hard all day upon two meals of Indian corn or hominy? Such is the regulation on this plantation, however, and I beg you to bear in mind that the Negroes on Mr. [Butler]'s estate are generally considered well off. They go to the fields at daybreak, carrying with them their allowance of food for the day, which toward noon, and not till then, they eat, cooking it over a fire, which they kindle as best they can, where they are working. Their second meal in the day is at night, after their labor is over, having worked, at the very least, six hours without intermission of rest or refreshment since their noonday meal (properly so called, for it is meal, and nothing else). Those that I passed today, sitting on their doorsteps, or on the ground round them eating, were the people employed at the mill and threshing floor. As these are near to the settlement, they had time to get their food from the cookshop. Chairs, tables, plates, knives, forks, they had none; they sat, as I before said, on the earth or doorsteps, and ate either out of their little cedar tubs or an iron pot, some few with broken iron spoons, more with pieces of wood, and all the children with their fingers. A more complete sample of savage feeding I never beheld.

At one of the doors I saw three young girls standing, who might be between sixteen and seventeen years old; they had evidently done eating, and were rudely playing and romping with each other, laughing

Slave diet and conditions

and shouting like wild things. I went into the house, and such another spectacle of filthy disorder I never beheld. I then addressed the girls most solemnly, showing them that they were wasting in idle riot the time in which they might be rendering their abode decent, and told them that it was a shame for any woman to live in so dirty a place and so beastly a condition. They said they had seen buckree (white) women's houses just as dirty, and they could not be expected to be cleaner than white women. I then told them that the only difference between themselves and buckree women was, that the latter were generally better informed, and, for that reason alone, it was more disgraceful to them to be disorderly and dirty. They seemed to listen to me attentively, and one of them exclaimed, with great satisfaction, that they saw I made no difference between them and white girls, and that they never had been so treated before. I do not know anything which strikes me as a more melancholy illustration of the degradation of these people than the animal nature of their recreations in their short seasons of respite from labor. You see them, boys and girls, from the youngest age to seventeen and eighteen, rolling, tumbling, kicking, and wallowing in the dust, regardless alike of decency, and incapable of any more rational amusement; or lolling, with half-closed eyes, like so many cats and dogs, against a wall, or upon a bank in the sun, dozing away their short leisure hour, until called to resume their labors in the field or the mill.

After this description of the meals of our laborers, you will, perhaps, be curious to know how it fares with our house servants in this respect. Precisely in the same manner, as far as regards allowance, with the exception of what is left from our table, but, if possible, with even less comfort, in one respect, inasmuch as no time whatever is set apart for their meals, which they snatch at any hour, and in any way that they can—generally, however, standing, or squatting on their hams round the kitchen fire. They have no sleeping rooms in the house, but when their work is over, retire, like the rest, to their hovels, the discomfort of which has to them all the addition of comparison with our mode of living. Now, in all establishments whatever, of course some disparity exists between the comforts of the drawing room and best bedrooms, and the servants' hall and attics, but here it is no longer a matter of degree. The young woman who performs the office of lady's maid, and the lads who wait upon us at table, have neither table to feed at nor chair to sit down upon themselves. The boys sleep at night on the hearth by the kitchen fire, and the women upon a rough board bedstead, strewed with a little tree moss. All this shows how very torpid the sense of justice is apt to lie in the breasts of those who have it not awakened by the peremptory demands of others. In the North we could not hope to keep the worst and poorest servant for a single day in the wretched discomfort in which our Negro servants are forced habitually to live.

I received a visit this morning from some of the Darien people. Among them was a most interesting young person, from whose acquaintance, if I have any opportunity of cultivating it, I promise myself much pleasure. The ladies that I have seen since I crossed the Southern line have all seemed to me extremely sickly in their appearance—delicate in the refined term, but unfortunately sickly in the truer one. They are languid in their deportment and speech, and seem to give themselves up, without an effort to counteract it, to the enervating effect of their warm climate. It is undoubtedly a most relaxing and unhealthy one, and therefore requires the more imperatively to be met by energetic and invigorating habits both of body and mind. Of these, however, the Southern ladies appear to have, at present, no very positive idea . . .

Southern ladies

I have, as usual, allowed this letter to lie by, dear E[lizabeth], not in the hope of the occurrence of any event—for that is hopeless—but until my daily avocations allowed me leisure to resume it, and afforded me, at the same time, matter wherewith to do so. I really never was so busy in all my life as I am here. I sit at the receipt of custom (involuntarily enough) from morning till night. No time, no place, affords me a respite from my innumerable petitioners; and whether I be asleep or awake, reading, eating, or walking—in the kitchen, my bedroom, or the parlor—they flock in with urgent entreaties and pitiful stories, and my conscience forbids my ever postponing their business for any other matter; for, with shame and grief of heart I say it, by their unpaid labor

Slave attendants

On the Plantation, 1838–1839

I live—their nakedness clothes me, and their heavy toil maintains me in luxurious idleness. Surely the least I can do is to hear these, my most injured benefactors; and, indeed, so intense in me is the sense of the injury they receive from me and mine, that I should scarce dare refuse them the very clothes from my back, or food from my plate, if they asked me for it.

In taking my daily walk round the banks yesterday, I found that I was walking over violet roots. The season is too little advanced for them to be in bloom, and I could not find out whether they were the fragrant violet or not.

Roswell King

Mr. [Butler] has been much gratified today by the arrival of Mr. K[ing] who, with his father, for nineteen years was the sole manager of these estates, and discharged his laborious task with great ability and fidelity toward his employers. How far he understood his duties to the slaves, or whether, indeed, an overseer can, in the nature of things, acknowledge any duty to them, is another question. He is a remarkable man, and is much respected for his integrity and honorable dealing by everybody here. His activity and energy are wonderful; and the mere fact of his having charge of for nineteen years, and personally governing, without any assistance whatever, seven hundred people scattered over three large tracts of land, at a considerable distance from each other, certainly bespeaks efficiency and energy of a very uncommon order. The character I had heard of him from Mr. [Butler] had excited a great deal of interest in me, and I was very glad of this opportunity of seeing a man who for so many years had been sovereign over the poor people here. I met him walking on the banks with Mr. [Butler] as I returned from my own ramble, during which nothing occurred or appeared to interest me, except, by-the-by, my unexpectedly coming quite close to one of those magnificent scarlet birds which abound here, and which dart across your path like a winged flame. Nothing can surpass the beauty of their plumage, and their voice is excellently melodious—they are lovely.

My companions, when I do not request the attendance of my friend Jack, are a couple of little terriers, who are endowed to perfection with the ugliness and the intelligence of their race; they are of infinite service on the plantation, as, owing to the immense quantity of grain, and chaff, and such matters, rats and mice abound in the mills and storehouses. I crossed the threshing floor today—a very large square, perfectly level, raised by artificial means about half a foot from the ground, and covered equally all over, so as to lie quite smooth, with some preparation of tar. It lies immediately between the house and the steam mill, and on it much of the Negroes' work is done—the first threshing is given to the rice, and other labors are carried on. As I walked across it today, passing through the busy groups, chiefly of women, that covered it, I came opposite to one of the drivers, who held in his hand his whip, the odious insignia of his office. I took it from him; it was a short stick of moderate size, with a thick square leather thong attached to it. As I held it in my hand, I did not utter a word; but I conclude, as is often the case, my face spoke what my tongue did not, for the driver said: "Oh, missis, me use it for measure; me seldom strike nigger with it." For one moment I thought I must carry the hateful implement into the house with me. An instant's reflection, however, served to show me how useless such a proceeding would be. The people are not mine, nor their drivers, nor their whips. I should but have impeded, for a few hours, the man's customary office, and a new scourge would have been easily provided, and I should have done nothing, perhaps worse than nothing.

After dinner I had a most interesting conversation with Mr. K[ing]. Among other subjects, he gave me a lively and curious description of the yeomanry of Georgia, more properly termed pinelanders. Have you visions now of well-to-do farmers with comfortable homesteads, decent habits, industrious, intelligent, cheerful, and thrifty? Such, however, is not the yeomanry of Georgia. Labor being here the especial portion of slaves, it is thenceforth degraded, and considered unworthy of all but slaves. No white man, therefore, of any class puts hand to work of any kind soever. This is an exceedingly dignified way of proving their gentility for the lazy planters who prefer an idle life of semistarvation and barbarism to the degradation of doing anything themselves; but the effect on the poorer whites of the country is terrible. I speak now of the scattered white population, who, too poor to

Yeomen

On the Plantation, 1838–1839

possess land or slaves, and having no means of living in the towns, squat (most appropriately is it so termed) either on other men's land or government districts—always here swamp or pine barren—and claim masterdom over the place they invade till ejected by the rightful proprietors. These wretched creatures will not, for they are whites (and labor belongs to blacks and slaves alone here), labor for their own subsistence. They are hardly protected from the weather by the rude shelters they frame for themselves in the midst of these dreary woods. Their food is chiefly supplied by shooting the wildfowl and venison, and stealing from the cultivated patches of the plantations nearest at hand. Their clothes hang about them in filthy tatters, and the combined squalor and fierceness of their appearance is really frightful. This population is the direct growth of slavery. The planters are loud in their execrations of these miserable vagabonds; yet they do not see that so long as labor is considered the disgraceful portion of slaves, these free men will hold it nobler to starve or steal than till the earth, with none but the despised blacks for fellow laborers. The blacks themselves—such is the infinite power of custom—acquiesce in this notion, and, as I have told you, consider it the lowest degradation in a white to use any exertion. I wonder, considering the burdens they have seen me lift, the digging, the planting, the rowing, and the walking I do, that they do not utterly contemn me, and, indeed, they seem lost in amazement at it.

Talking of these pinelanders—gypsies, without any of the romantic associations that belong to the latter people—led us to the origin of such a population, slavery; and you may be sure I listened with infinite interest to the opinions of a man of uncommon shrewdness and sagacity, who was born in the very bosom of it, and has passed his whole life among slaves. If anyone is competent to judge of its effects, such a man is the one; and this was his verdict: "I hate slavery with all my heart; I consider it an absolute curse wherever it exists. It will keep those states where it does exist fifty years behind the others in improvement and prosperity."

Farther on in the conversation he made this most remarkable observation: "As for its being an irremediable evil—a thing not to be helped or got rid of—that's all nonsense; for, as soon as people become convinced that it is their interest to get rid of it, they will soon find the means to do so, depend upon it."

And undoubtedly this is true. This is not an age, nor yours a country, where a large mass of people will long endure what they perceive to be injurious to their fortunes and advancement. Blind as people often are to their highest and truest interests, your countryfolk have generally shown remarkable acuteness in finding out where their worldly progress suffered let or hindrance, and have removed it with laudable alacrity. Now the fact is not at all as we at the North are sometimes told, that the Southern slaveholders deprecate the evils of slavery quite as much as we do; that they see all its miseries; that, moreover, they are most anxious to get rid of the whole thing, but want the means to do so, and submit most unwillingly to a necessity from which they cannot extricate themselves. All this I thought might be true before I went to the South, and often has the charitable supposition checked the condemnation which was indignantly rising to my lips against these murderers of their brethren's peace. A little reflection, however, even without personal observation, might have convinced me that this could not be the case. If the majority of Southerners were satisfied that slavery was contrary to their worldly fortunes, slavery would be at an end from that very moment; but the fact is—and I have it not only from observation of my own, but from the distinct statement of some of the most intelligent Southern men that I have conversed with—the only obstacle to immediate abolition throughout the South is the immense value of the human property, and, to use the words of a very distinguished Carolinian, who thus ended a long discussion we had on the subject: "I'll tell you why abolition is impossible: because every healthy Negro can fetch a thousand dollars in the Charleston market at this moment." And this opinion, you see, tallies perfectly with the testimony of Mr. K[ing] . . .

Mr. [Butler] was called out this evening to listen to a complaint of overwork from a gang of pregnant women. I did not stay to listen to the details of their petition, for I am unable to command myself on such occasions, and Mr. [Butler] seemed positively degraded in my eyes as he stood enforcing upon these women the necessity of their fulfilling their appointed tasks. How honorable he would have appeared to me begrimed with the sweat and soil of the coarsest manual labor, to what he then seemed, setting forth to these wretched, ignorant women, as a duty, their unpaid exacted labor! I turned away in bitter disgust. I hope this sojourn among Mr. [Butler]'s slaves may not lessen my respect for him, but I fear it; for the details of slaveholding are so unmanly, letting alone every other consideration, that I know not how anyone with the spirit of a man can condescend to them.

I have been out again on the river, rowing. I find nothing new. Swamps crowned with perfect evergreens are the only land (that's Irish!) about here, and, of course, turn which way I will, the natural features of river and shore are the same. I do not weary of these most exquisite watery woods, but you will of my mention of them, I fear. Adieu ... [GP]

[January 1839]

Dearest E[lizabeth],

I received early this morning a visit from a young Negro called Morris, who came to request permission to be baptized. The master's leave is necessary for this ceremony of acceptance into the bosom of the Christian Church; so all that can be said is, that it is to be hoped the rite itself may not be indispensable for salvation, as, if Mr. [Butler] had thought proper to refuse Morris's petition, he must infallibly have been lost, in spite of his own best wishes to the contrary. I could not, in discoursing with him, perceive that he had any very distinct ideas of the advantages he expected to derive from the ceremony; but perhaps they appeared all the greater for being a little vague. I have seldom seen a more pleasing appearance than that of this young man; his figure was tall and straight, and his face, which was of a perfect oval, rejoiced in the grace, very unusual among his people, of a fine high forehead, and the much more frequent one of a remarkably gentle and sweet expression. He was, however, jet-black, and certainly did not owe these personal advantages to any mixture in his blood. There is a certain African tribe from which the West Indian slave market is chiefly recruited, who have these same characteristic features, and do not at all present the ignoble and ugly Negro type, so much more commonly seen here. They are a tall, powerful people, with remarkably fine figures, regular features, and a singularly warlike and fierce disposition, in which respect they also differ from the race of Negroes existing on the American plantations. I do not think Morris, however, could have belonged to this tribe, though perhaps Othello did, which would at once settle the difficulties of those commentators who, abiding by Iago's very disagreeable suggestions as to his purely African appearance, are painfully compelled to forego the mitigation of supposing him a Moor and not a Negro.

Did I ever tell you of my dining in Boston, at the H[odgkinson]'s on my first visit to that city, and sitting by Mr. John Quincy Adams, who, talking to me about Desdemona, assured me, with a most serious expression of sincere disgust, that he considered all her misfortunes as a very just judgment upon her for having married a "nigger?" I think, if some ingenious American actor of the present day, bent upon realizing Shakespeare's finest conceptions, with all the advantages of modern enlightenment, could contrive to slip in that opprobrious title, with a true South Carolinian anti-abolitionist expression, it might really be made quite a point for Iago, as, for instance, in his first soliloquy—"I hate the nigger," given in proper Charleston or Savannah fashion, I am sure would tell far better than "I hate the Moor." Only think, E[lizabeth], what a very new order of interest the whole tragedy might receive, acted throughout from this standpoint, as the Germans call it in this country, and called *Amalgamation, or the Black Bridal* . . . [*GP*]

January 21, 1839

My Dearest E[lizabeth],
A rather longer interval than usual has elapsed since I last wrote to you, but I must beg you to excuse it. I have had more than a usual amount of small daily occupations to fill my time; and, as a mere enu-

meration of these would not be very interesting to you, I will tell you a story which has just formed an admirable illustration for my observation of all the miseries of which this accursed system of slavery is the cause, even under the best and most humane administration of its laws and usages. Pray note it, my dear friend, for you will find, in the absence of all voluntary or even conscious cruelty on the part of the master, the best possible comment on a state of things which, without the slightest desire to injure and oppress, produces such intolerable results of injury and oppression.

We have, as a sort of under nursemaid and assistant of my dear M[argery], whose white complexion, as I wrote you, occasioned such indignation to my Southern fellow travelers, and such extreme perplexity to the poor slaves on our arrival here, a much more orthodox servant for these parts, a young woman named Psyche, but commonly called Sack, not a very graceful abbreviation of the divine heathen appellation. She cannot be much over twenty, has a very pretty figure, a graceful, gentle deportment, and a face which, but for its color (she is a dingy mulatto), would be pretty, and is extremely pleasing, from the perfect sweetness of its expression; she is always serious, not to say sad and silent, and has always an air of melancholy and timidity, that has frequently struck me very much, and would have made me think some special anxiety or sorrow must occasion it, but that God knows the whole condition of these wretched people naturally produces such a deportment, and there is no necessity to seek for special or peculiar causes to account for it. Just in proportion as I have found the slaves on this plantation intelligent and advanced beyond the general brutish level of the majority, I have observed this pathetic expression of countenance in them, a mixture of sadness and fear, the involuntary exhibition of the two feelings, which I suppose must be the predominant experience of their whole lives, regret and apprehension, not the less heavy, either of them, for being, in some degree, vague and indefinite—a sense of incalculable past loss and injury, and a dread of incalculable future loss and injury.

I have never questioned Psyche as to her sadness, because, in the first place, as I tell you, it appears to me most natural, and is observable in all the slaves whose superior natural or acquired intelligence allows of their filling situations of trust or service about the house and family; and, though I cannot and will not refuse to bear any and every tale of suffering which these unfortunates bring to me, I am anxious to spare both myself and them the pain of vain appeals to me for redress and help, which, alas! it is too often utterly out of my power to give them. It is useless, and, indeed, worse than useless, that they should see my impotent indignation and unavailing pity, and hear expressions of compassion for them, and horror at their condition, which might only prove incentives to a hopeless resistance on their part to a system, under the hideous weight of whose oppression any individual or partial revolt must be annihilated and ground into the dust. Therefore, as I tell you, I asked Psyche no questions; but, to my great astonishment, the other day M[argery] asked me if I knew to whom Psyche belonged, as the poor woman had inquired of her with much hesitation and anguish if she could tell her who owned her and her children. She has two nice little children under six years old, whom she keeps as clean and tidy, and who are sad and as silent as herself. My astonishment at this question was, as you will readily believe, not small, and I forthwith sought out Psyche for an explanation. She was thrown into extreme perturbation at finding that her question had been referred to me, and it was some time before I could sufficiently reassure her to be able to comprehend, in the midst of her reiterated entreaties for pardon, and hopes that she had not offended me, that she did not know herself who owned her. She was, at one time, the property of Mr. K[ing], the former overseer, of whom I have already spoken to you, and who has just been paying Mr. [Butler] a visit. He, like several of his predecessors in the management, has contrived to make a fortune upon it (though it yearly decreases in value to the owners, but this is the inevitable course of things in the Southern states), and has purchased a plantation of his own in Alabama, I believe, or one of the Southwestern states. Whether she still belonged to Mr. K[ing] or not she did not know, and entreated me, if she did, to endeavor to persuade Mr. [Butler] to buy her. Now you must know that this poor woman is the wife of one of Mr. [Butler]'s slaves, a fine, intelligent, active, excellent young

On the Plantation, 1838–1839

129

man, whose whole family are among some of the very best specimens of character and capacity on the estate. I was so astonished at the (to me) extraordinary state of things revealed by poor Sack's petition, that I could only tell her that I had supposed all the Negroes on the plantation were Mr. [Butler]'s property, but that I would certainly inquire, and find out for her, if I could, to whom she belonged, and if I could, endeavor to get Mr. [Butler] to purchase her, if she really was not his. Now, E[lizabeth], just conceive for one moment the state of mind of this woman, believing herself to belong to a man who in a few days was going down to one of those abhorred and dreaded Southwestern states, and who would then compel her, with her poor little children, to leave her husband and the only home she had ever known, and all the ties of affection, relationship, and association of her former life, to follow him thither, in all human probability never again to behold any living creature that she had seen before; and this was so completely a matter of course that it was not even thought necessary to apprise her positively of the fact, and the only thing that interposed between her and this most miserable fate was the faint hope that Mr. [Butler] *might have* purchased her and her children. But if he had, if this great deliverance had been vouchsafed to her, the knowledge of it was not thought necessary; and with this deadly dread at her heart she was living day after day, waiting upon me and seeing me, with my husband beside me, and my children in my arms in blessed security, safe from all separation but the one reserved in God's great providence for all His creatures. Do you think I wondered any more at the woebegone expression of her countenance, or do you think it was easy for me to restrain within prudent and proper limits the expression of my feelings at such a state of things? And she had gone on from day to day enduring this agony, till I suppose its own intolerable pressure and M[argery]'s sweet countenance and gentle sympathizing voice and manner had constrained her to lay down this great burden of sorrow at our feet.

I did not see Mr. [Butler] until the evening; but, in the meantime, meeting Mr. O[den], the overseer, with whom, as I believe I have already told you, we are living here, I asked him about Psyche, and who was her proprietor, when, to my infinite surprise, he told me that *he* had bought her and her children from Mr. K[ing], who had offered them to him, saying that they would be rather troublesome to him than otherwise down where he was going. "And so," said Mr. O[den], "as I had no objection to investing a little money that way, I bought them." With a heart much lightened, I flew to tell poor Psyche the news, so that, at any rate, she might be relieved from the dread of any immediate separation from her husband. You can imagine better than I can tell you what her sensations were; but she still renewed her prayer that I would, if possible, induce Mr. [Butler] to purchase her, and I promised to do so.

Early the next morning, while I was still dressing, I was suddenly startled by hearing voices in loud tones in Mr. [Butler]'s dressing room, which adjoins my bedroom, and the noise increasing until there was an absolute cry of despair uttered by some man. I could restrain myself no longer, but opened the door of communication and saw Joe, the young man, poor Psyche's husband, raving almost in a state of frenzy, and in a voice broken with sobs and almost inarticulate with passion, reiterating his determination never to leave this plantation, never to go to Alabama, never to leave his old father and mother, his poor wife and children, and dashing his hat, which he was wringing like a cloth in his hands, upon the ground, he declared he would kill himself if he was compelled to follow Mr. K[ing]. I glanced from the poor wretch to Mr. [Butler], who was standing, leaning against a table with his arms folded, occasionally uttering a few words of counsel to his slave to be quiet and not fret, and not make a fuss about what there was no help for. I retreated immediately from the horrid scene, breathless with surprise and dismay, and stood for some time in my own room, with my heart and temples throbbing to such a degree that I could hardly support myself. As soon as I recovered myself I again sought Mr. O[den], and inquired of him if he knew the cause of poor Joe's distress, he then told me that Mr. [Butler], who is highly pleased with Mr. K[ing]'s past administration of his property, wished, on his departure for his newly acquired slave plantation, to give him some token of his satisfaction, *and had made him a present* of the man Joe, who had just received the intelligence that he was to go down to Alabama with his new owner the next day, leaving father, mother, wife, and children behind. You will not wonder that the man required a little judicious soothing under such circumstances, and you will also, I hope, admire the humanity of the sale of his wife and children by the owner who was going to take him to Alabama, because *they* would be encumbrances rather than otherwise down there. If Mr. K[ing] did not do this after he knew that the man was his, then Mr. [Butler] gave him to be carried down to the South after his wife [and] children were sold to remain in Georgia. I do not know which was the real transaction, for I have not had the heart to ask; but you will easily imagine which of the two cases I prefer believing.

When I saw Mr. [Butler] after this most wretched story became known to me in all its details, I appealed to him, for his soul's sake, not to commit so great a cruelty. Poor Joe's agony while remonstrating with his master was hardly greater than mine while arguing with him upon this bitter piece of inhumanity—how I cried, and how I adjured, and how all my sense of justice, of mercy, and of pity for the poor wretch, and of wretchedness at finding myself implicated in such a state of things, broke in torrents of words from my lips and tears from my eyes! God knows such a sorrow at seeing anyone I belonged to commit such an act was indeed a new and terrible experience to me, and it seemed to me that I was imploring Mr. [Butler] to save himself more than to spare these wretches. He gave me no answer whatever, and I have since thought that the intemperate vehemence of my entreaties and expostulations perhaps deserved that he should leave me as he did without one single word of reply; and miserable enough I remained.

Toward evening, as I was sitting alone, my children having gone to bed, Mr. O[den] came into the room. I had but one subject in mind; I had not been able to eat for it. I could hardly sit still for the nervous distress which every thought of these poor people filled me with. As he sat down looking over some accounts, I said to him: "Have you seen Joe this afternoon, Mr. O[den]?" (I give you our conversation as it took place.)

"Yes, ma'am; he is a great deal happier than he was this morning."

"Why, how is that?" asked I, eagerly.

"Oh, he is not going to Alabama. Mr. K[ing] heard that he had kicked up a fuss about it" (being in despair at being torn from one's wife and children is called *kicking up a fuss;* this is a sample of overseer appreciation of human feelings), "and said that if the fellow wasn't willing to go with him, he did not wish to be bothered with any niggers down there who were to be troublesome, so he might stay behind."

"And does Psyche know this?"

"Yes, ma'am, I suppose so."

I drew a long breath; and whereas my needle had stumbled through the stuff I was sewing for an hour before, as if my fingers could not guide it, the regularity and rapidity of its evolutions were now quite edifying. The man was for the present safe, and I remained silently pondering his deliverance and the whole proceeding, and the conduct of everyone engaged in it, and, above all, Mr. [Butler]'s share in the transaction, and I think, for the first time, almost a sense of horrible personal responsibility and implication took hold of my mind, and I felt the weight of an unimagined guilt upon my conscience; and yet, God knows, this feeling of self-condemnation is very gratuitous on my part, since when I married Mr. [Butler] I knew nothing of these dreadful possessions of his, and even if I had I should have been much puzzled to have formed any idea of the state of things in which I now find myself plunged, together with those whose well-doing is as vital to me almost as my own.

With these agreeable reflections I went to bed. Mr. [Butler] said not a word to me upon the subject of these poor people all the next day, and in the meantime I became very impatient of this reserve on his part, because I was dying to prefer my request that he would purchase Psyche and her children, and so prevent any future separation between her and her husband, as I supposed he would not again attempt to make a present of Joe, at least to anyone who did not wish to be *bothered* with his wife and children. In the evening I was again with Mr. O[den] alone in the strange, bare, wooden-walled sort of shanty which is our sitting room, and revolving in my mind the means of res-

On the Plantation, 1838–1839

cuing Psyche from her miserable suspense, a long chain of all my possessions, in the shape of bracelets, necklaces, brooches, earrings, etc., wound in glittering procession through my brain, with many hypothetical calculations of the value of each separate ornament, and the very doubtful probability of the amount of the whole being equal to the price of this poor creature and her children; and then the great power and privilege I had foregone of earning money by my own labor occurred to me, and I think, for the first time in my life, my past profession assumed an aspect that arrested my thoughts most seriously. For the last four years of my life that preceded my marriage I literally coined money, and never until this moment, I think, did I reflect on the great means of good, to myself and others, that I so gladly agreed to give up forever for a maintenance by the unpaid labor of slaves—people toiling not only unpaid, but under the bitter conditions the bare contemplation of which was then wringing my heart. You will not wonder that when, in the midst of such cogitations, I suddenly accosted Mr. O[den], it was to this effect: "Mr. O[den], I have a particular favor to beg of you. Promise me that you will never sell Psyche and her children without first letting me know of your intention to do so, and giving me the option of buying them."

Mr. O[den] is a remarkably deliberate man, and squints, so that, when he has taken a little time in directing his eyes to you, you are still unpleasantly unaware of any result in which you are concerned; he laid down a book he was reading, and directed his head and one of his eyes toward me and answered: "Dear me, ma'am, I am very sorry—I have sold them."

My work fell down on the ground, and my mouth opened wide, but I could utter no sound, I was so dismayed and surprised; and he deliberately proceeded: "I didn't know, ma'am, you see, at all, that you entertained any idea of making an investment of that nature; for I'm sure, if I had, I would willingly have sold the woman to you; but I sold her and her children this morning to Mr. [Butler]."

My dear E[lizabeth], though [Mr. Butler] had resented my unmeasured upbraidings, you see they had not been without some good effect, and though he had, perhaps justly, punished my violent outbreak of indignation about the miserable scene I witnessed by not telling me of his humane purpose, he had bought these poor creatures, and so, I trust, secured them from any such misery in future. I jumped up and left Mr. O[den] still speaking, and ran to find Mr. [Butler], to thank him for what he had done, and with that will now bid you good-by. Think, E[lizabeth], how it fares with slaves on plantations where there is no crazy English woman to weep, and entreat, and implore, and upbraid for them, and no master willing to listen to such appeals . . .

A very valuable slave called Shadrach was seized with a disease which is frequent, and very apt to be fatal here—peripneumonia; and, in spite of all that could be done to save him, sank rapidly, and died after an acute illness of only three days. The doctor came repeatedly from Darien, and the last night of the poor fellow's life [Mr. Butler] himself watched with him. I suppose the general low diet of the Negroes must produce some want of stamina in them; certainly, either from natural constitution or the effect of their habits of existence, or both, it is astonishing how much less power of resistance to disease they seem to possess than we do. If they are ill, the vital energy seems to sink immediately. This rice cultivation, too, although it does not affect them as it would whites—to whom, indeed, residence on the rice plantation after a certain season is impossible—is still, to a certain degree, deleterious even to the Negroes. The proportion of sick is always greater here than on the cotton plantation, and the invalids of this place are not unfrequently sent down to St. Simons to recover their strength, under the more favorable influences of the sea air and dry sandy soil of Hampton Point.

Yesterday afternoon the tepid warmth of the air and glassy stillness of the river seemed to me highly suggestive of fishing, and I determined, not having yet discovered what I could catch with what in these unknown waters, to try a little innocent paste bait—a mystery his initiation into which caused Jack much wonderment. The only hooks I had with me, however, had been bought in Darien—made, I should think, at the North expressly for this market; and so villainously bad were they, that, after trying them and my patience a reasonable time, I gave up the attempt and took a lesson in paddling instead.

Death of a slave

Among other items Jack told me of his own fishing experience was that he had more than once caught those most excellent creatures, Altamaha shad, by the fish themselves leaping out of the water and landing, as Jack expressed it, to escape from the porpoises, which come in large schools up the river to a considerable distance, occasioning, evidently, much emotion in the bosoms of the legitimate inhabitants of these muddy waters. Coasting the island on our return home, we found a trap, which the last time we examined it was tenanted by a creature called a mink, now occupied by an otter. The poor beast did not seem pleased with his predicament; but the trap had been set by one of the drivers, and, of course, Jack would not have meddled with it except upon my express order, which, in spite of some pangs of pity for the otter, I did not like to give him, as, in the extremely few resources of either profit or pleasure possessed by the slaves, I could not tell at all what might be the value of an otter to his captor.

Slave funeral

Yesterday evening the burial of the poor man Shadrach took place. I had been applied to for a sufficient quantity of cotton cloth to make a winding sheet for him, and just as the twilight was thickening into darkness I went with Mr. [Butler] to the cottage of one of the slaves whom I may have mentioned to you before—a cooper of the name of London, the head of the religious party of the inhabitants of the island, a Methodist preacher of no small intelligence and influence among the people—who was to perform the burial service. The coffin was laid on trestles in front of the cooper's cottage, and a large assemblage of the people had gathered round, many of the men carrying pine-wood torches, the fitful glare of which glanced over the strange assembly, where every pair of large white-rimmed eyes turned upon [Mr. Butler] and myself; we two poor creatures, on this more solemn occasion, as well as on every other when these people encounter us, being the objects of admiration and wonderment, on which their gaze is immovably riveted. Presently the whole congregation uplifted their voices in a hymn, the first high wailing notes of which—sung all in unison, in the midst of these unwonted surroundings—sent a thrill through all my nerves. When the chant ceased, cooper London began a prayer, and all the people knelt down in the sand, as I did also. Mr.

[Butler] alone remained standing in the presence of the dead man and of the living God to whom his slaves were now appealing. I cannot tell you how profoundly the whole ceremony, if such it could be called, affected me; and there was nothing in the simple and pathetic supplication of the poor black artisan to check or interfere with the solemn influences of the whole scene. It was a sort of conventional Methodist prayer, and probably quite as conventional as all the rest was the closing invocation of God's blessing upon their master, their mistress, and our children; but this fairly overcame my composure, and I began to cry very bitterly; for these same individuals, whose implication in the state of things in the midst of which we are living, seemed to me as legitimate a cause for tears as for prayers.

When the prayer was concluded we all rose, and, the coffin being taken up, proceeded to the people's burial ground, when London read aloud portions of the funeral service from the Prayer Book—I presume the American Episcopal version of our Church service, for what be read appeared to be merely a selection from what was perfectly familiar to me; but whether he himself extracted what he uttered I did not inquire. Indeed, I was too much absorbed in the whole scene, and the many mingled emotions it excited of awe and pity, and an indescribable sensation of wonder at finding myself on this slave soil, surrounded by my slaves, among whom again I knelt while the words proclaiming to the living and the dead the everlasting covenant of freedom, "I am the resurrection and the life," sounded over the prostrate throng, and mingled with the heavy flowing of the vast river sweeping, not far from where we stood, through the darkness by which we were now encompassed (beyond the immediate circle of our torch-bearers). There was something painful to me in [Mr. Butler]'s standing while we all knelt on the earth; for, though in any church in Philadelphia he would have stood during the praying of any minister, here I wished he would have knelt, to have given his slaves some token of his belief that—at least in the sight of that Master to whom we were addressing our worship—all men are equal.

The service ended with a short address from London upon the subject of Lazarus, and the confirmation which the story of his resurrection afforded our hopes. The words were simple and rustic, and of course uttered in the peculiar sort of jargon which is the habitual Negro speech; but there was nothing in the slightest degree incongruous or grotesque in the matter or manner, and the exhortations not to steal, or lie, or neglect to work well for massa, with which the glorious hope of immortality was blended in the poor slave preacher's closing address, was a moral adaptation, as wholesome as it was touching, of the great Christian theory to the capacities and consciences of his hearers. When the coffin was lowered the grave was found to be partially filled with water—naturally enough, for the whole island is a mere swamp, off which the Altamaha is only kept from sweeping by the high dikes all round it. This seemed to shock and distress the people, and for the first time during the whole ceremony there were sounds of crying and exclamations of grief heard among them. Their chief expression of sorrow, however, when Mr. [Butler] and myself bade them good night at the conclusion of the service, was on account of my crying, which appeared to affect them very much, many of them mingling with their "Farewell, good night, massa and missis," affectionate exclamations of "God bless you, missis; don't cry!" "Lor, missis, don't you cry so!"

Mr. [Butler] declined the assistance of any of the torchbearers home, and bade them all go quietly to their quarters; and as soon as they had dispersed, and we had got beyond the fitful and unequal glaring of the torches, we found the shining of the stars in the deep blue lovely night sky quite sufficient to light our way along the dikes. I could not speak to [Mr. Butler], but continued to cry as we walked silently home; and, whatever his cogitations were, they did not take the usual form with him of wordy demonstration, and so we returned from one of the most striking religious ceremonies at which I ever assisted . . .

Local gentry

This morning I went over to Darien upon the very female errands of returning visits and shopping. In one respect (assuredly in none other) our life here resembles existence in Venice: we can never leave home for any purpose or in any direction but by boat—not, indeed, by gondola, but the sharp-cut, well-made light craft in which we take our walks on the water is a very agreeable species of conveyance. One of my visits this morning was to a certain Miss [Orallie Troup, who lived with an uncle in Darien], whose rather grandiloquent name and very striking style of beauty exceedingly well became the daughter of an ex-governor of Georgia. As for the residence of this princess, it was like all the planters' residences that I have seen, and such as a well-to-do English farmer would certainly not inhabit. Occasional marks of former elegance or splendor survive sometimes in the size of the rooms, sometimes in a little carved woodwork about the mantel-pieces or wainscotings of these mansions; but all things have a Castle Rackrent air of neglect, and dreary, careless untidiness, with which the dirty, barefooted negro servants are in excellent keeping . . .

It seems to me too—but upon this point I can not, of course, judge as well as the persons accustomed to and acquainted with the physical capacities of their slaves—that the labor is not judiciously distributed *Slaves' physical qualities* in many cases—at least not as far as the women are concerned. It is true that every able-bodied woman is made the most of in being driven afield as long as, under all and any circumstances, she is able to wield a hoe; but, on the other hand, stout, hale, hearty girls and boys, of from eight to twelve and older, are allowed to lounge about, filthy and idle, with no pretense of an occupation but what they call "tend baby," i.e., see to the life and limbs of the little slave infants, to whose mothers, working in distant fields, they carry them during the day to be suckled, and for the rest of the time leave them to crawl and kick in the filthy cabins or on the broiling sand which surrounds them, in which industry, excellent enough for the poor babies, these big lazy youths and lasses emulate them. Again, I find many women who have borne from five to ten children rated as workers, precisely as young women in the prime of their strength who have had none; this seems a cruel carelessness. To be sure, while the women are pregnant their task is diminished, and this is one of the many indirect inducements held out to reckless propagation, which has a sort of premium offered to it in the consideration of less work and more food, counterbalanced by none of the sacred responsibilities which hallow and ennoble the relation of parent and child; in short, as their lives are for the part those of mere animals, their increase is literally mere animal breeding, to which every encouragement is given, for it adds to the master's live-stock and the value of his estate . . .

This morning, instead of my usual visit to the infirmary, I went to look at the work and workers in the threshing mill: all was going on actively and orderly under the superintendence of headman Frank, with whom, and a very sagacious clever fellow who ages the steam power of the mill, and his honorably distinguished Engineer Ned, I had a small chat. There is one among various drawbacks to the comfort and pleasure of our intercourse with these colored "men and brethren," at least in their slave condition which certainly exercises my fortitude not a little. The swarms of fleas that cohabit with these sable dependents of ours are—well—incredible; moreover, they are by no means the only or most objectionable companions one borrows from them; and I never go to the infirmary, where I not infrequently am requested to look [at] very dirty limbs and bodies in very dirty draperies, without coming away with a strong inclination to throw myself into the water, and my clothes into the fire, which last would be expensive. I do not suppose that these hateful consequences of dirt and disorder are worse here than among the poor and neglected human creatures who swarm in the lower parts of European cities; but my call to visit them has never been such as that which constrains me to go daily among these poor people, and although on one or two occasions I have penetrated into fearfully foul and filthy abodes of misery in London, I have never rendered the same personal services to their inhabitants that I do to Mr. [Butler]'s slaves, and so have not incurred the same amount of entomological inconvenience.

After leaving the mill I prolonged my walk, and came, for the first time, upon one of the "gangs," as they are called, in full field work. Upon my appearance and approach there was a momentary suspension of labor, and the usual chorus of screams and ejaculations of welcome, affection, and infinite desires for infinite small indulgences. I was afraid to stop their work, not feeling at all sure that urging a conversation with me would be accepted as any excuse for an uncompleted task, or avert the fatal infliction of the usual award of stripes; so I hurried off and left them to their hoeing.

On my way home I was encountered by London, our Methodist preacher, who accosted me with a request for a Prayer Book and Bible, and expressed his regret at hearing that we were so soon going to St. Simons. I promised him his holy books, and asked him how he had learned to read, but found it impossible to get him to tell me. I wonder if he thought he should be putting his teacher, whoever he was, in danger of the penalty of the law against instructing the slaves, if he told me who he was; it was impossible to make him do so, so that, besides his other good qualities, he appears to have that most unusual one of all in an uneducated person—discretion. He certainly is a most remarkable man.

After parting with him, I was assailed by a small gang of children, clamoring for the indulgence of some meat, which they besought me to give them. Animal food is only allowed to certain of the harder working men, hedgers and ditchers, and to them only occasionally, and in very moderate rations. My small cannibals clamored round me for flesh, as if I had had a butcher's cart in my pocket, till I began to laugh, and then to run, and away they came, like a pack of little black wolves, at my heels, shrieking: "Missis, you gib me piece meat—missis, you gib me meat," till I got home.

At the door I found another petitioner, a young woman named Maria, who brought a fine child in her arms, and demanded a present of a piece of flannel. Upon my asking her who her husband was, she replied, without much hesitation, that she did not possess any such appendage. I gave another look at her bonny baby, and went into the house to get the flannel for her. I afterward heard from Mr. [Butler] that she and two other girls of her age, about seventeen, were the only instances on the island of women with illegitimate children.

After I had been in the house a little while, I was summoned out again to receive the petition of certain poor women in the family way to have their work lightened. I was, of course, obliged to tell them that I could not interfere in the matter; that their master was away, and that, when he came back, they must present their request to him: they said they had already begged "massa," and he had refused, and they thought, perhaps, if "missis" begged "massa" for them, he would lighten their task. Poor "missis," poor "massa," poor woman, that I am to have such prayers addressed to me! I had to tell them that, if they had already spoken to their master, I was afraid my doing so would be of no use, but that when he came back I would try; so, choking with crying, I turned away from them, and re-entered the house, to the chorus of "Oh, thank you, missis! God bless you, missis!" E[lizabeth], I think an improvement might be made upon that caricature published a short time ago, called the "Chivalry of the South." I think an elegant young Carolinian or Georgian gentleman, whip in hand, driving a gang of "lusty women," as they are called here, would be a pretty version of the "Chivalry of the South"—a little coarse, I am afraid you will say. Oh! quite horribly coarse, but then so true—a great matter in works of art, which nowadays appear to be thought excellent only in proportion to their lack of ideal elevation. That would be a subject, and a treatment of it, which could not be accused of imaginative exaggeration, at any rate.

In the evening I mentioned the petitions of these poor women to Mr. O[den], thinking that perhaps he had the power to lessen their tasks. He seemed evidently annoyed at their having appealed to me; said that their work was not a bit too much for them, and that constantly they were shamming themselves in the family way in order to obtain a diminution of their labor. Poor creatures! I suppose some of them do; but, again, it must be a hard matter for those who do not, not to obtain the mitigation of their toil which their condition requires; for their assertion and their evidence are never received: they can't be believed, even if they were upon Death, say their white taskmasters; why? because they have never been taught the obligations of an oath, to whom made, or wherefore binding; and they are punished both directly and indirectly for their moral ignorance, as if it were a natural and incorrigible element of their character, instead of the inevitable result of their miserable position. The oath of any and every scoundrely fellow with a white skin is received, but not that of such a man as Frank, Ned, old Jacob, or cooper London.   [GP]

[February 14, 1839]

Dearest E[lizabeth],

. . . After my survey, as I walked home, I came upon a gang of lusty women, as the phrase is here for women in the family way; they were engaged in burning stubble, and I was nearly choked while receiving the multitudinous complaints and compliments with which they overwhelmed me. After leaving them, I wandered along the river side of the dike homeward, rejoicing in the buds and green things putting forth their tender shoots on every spray, in the early bees and even the less amiable wasps busy in the sunshine with flowers (weeds I suppose they should be called), already opening their sweet temptations to them, and giving the earth a spring aspect, such as it does not wear with you in Massachusetts till late in May . . .

On my return home I was met by a child (as she seemed to me) carrying a baby, in whose behalf she begged me for some clothes. On making some inquiry, I was amazed to find that the child was her own: she said she was married, and fourteen years old; she looked much younger even than that, poor creature. Her mother, who came up while I was talking to her, said she did not herself know the girl's age; how horridly brutish it all did seem, to be sure . . .

I asked Abraham [a Butler slave] what sum his grandfather paid for his freedom: he said he did not know, but he supposed a large one, because of his being a "skilled carpenter," and so a peculiarly valuable chattel. I presume, from what I remember Major M—— [unidentified] and Dr. [James] H[olmes] saying on the subject of the market value of Negroes in Charleston and Savannah, that such a man in the prime of life would have been worth from 1500 to 2000 dollars. However, whatever the man paid for his ransom, by his grandson's account, fourteen years after he became free, when he died, he had again amassed money to the amount of 700 dollars, which he left among his wife and children, the former being a slave on Major [Butler]'s estate, where the latter remained by virtue of that fact slaves also. So this man not only bought his own freedom at a cost of *at least* 1000 dollars, but left a little fortune of 700 more at his death; and then we are told of the

*Industri-
ousness of
a slave*

universal idleness, incorrigible sloth, and brutish incapacity of this inferior race of creatures, whose only fitting and Heaven-appointed condition is that of beasts of burden to the whites. I do not believe the whole low white population of the State of Georgia could furnish such an instance of energy, industry, and thrift as the amassing of this laborious little fortune by this poor slave, who left, nevertheless, his children and grandchildren to the lot from which he had so heroically ransomed himself; and yet the white men with whom I live and talk tell me, day after day, that there is neither cruelty nor injustice in this accursed system . . .

Planter women

[I was] called into the house to receive the return visit of old Mrs. S[palding, mistress of the nearby plantation, Ashantilly]. As usual the appearance, health, vigor, and good management of the children were the theme of wondering admiration; as usual, my possession of a white nurse the theme of envious congratulation; as usual, I had to hear the habitual senseless complaints of the inefficiency of colored nurses. If you are half as tired of the sameness and stupidity of the conversation of my Southern female neighbors as I am, I pity you; but not as much as I pity them for the stupid sameness of their most vapid existence, which would deaden any amount of intelligence, obliterate any amount of instruction—and render torpid and stagnant any amount of natural energy and vivacity. I would rather die—rather a thousand times—than live the lives of these Georgia planters' wives and daughters . . . [*GP*]

[February 17]

St. Simons

My letter has been interrupted, dear E[lizabeth], by the breaking up of our residence on the rice plantation, and our arrival at St. Simons, whence I now address you. We came down yesterday afternoon, and I was thankful enough of the fifteen miles' row to rest in, from the labor of leave-taking, with which the whole morning was taken up, and which, combined with packing and preparing all our own personalities and those of the children, was no sinecure. At every moment one or other of the poor people rushed in upon me to bid me good-by;

many of their farewells were grotesque enough, some were pathetic, and all of them made me very sad. Poor people! how little I have done, how little I can do for them.

I had a long talk with that interesting and excellent man, cooper London, who made an earnest petition that I would send him from the North a lot of Bibles and Prayer Books; certainly the science of reading must be much more common among the Negroes than I supposed, or London must look to a marvelously increased spread of the same hereafter. There is, however, considerable reticence upon this point, or else the poor slaves must consider the mere possession of the holy books as good for salvation and as effectual for spiritual assistance to those who cannot as to those who can comprehend them. Since the news of our departure has spread, I have had repeated eager entreaties for presents of Bibles and Prayer Books, and to my demurrer of "But you can't read, can you?" have generally received for answer a reluctant acknowledgment of ignorance, which, however, did not always convince me of the fact. In my farewell conversation with London I found it impossible to get him to tell me how he had learned to read: the penalties for teaching them are very severe—heavy fines, increasing in amount for the first and second offense, and imprisonment for the third. Such a man as London is certainly aware that to teach the slaves to read is an illegal act, and he may have been unwilling to betray whoever had been his preceptor even to my knowledge; at any rate, I got no answers from him but: "Well, missis, me learn; well, missis, me try"; and finally: "Well, missis, me 'spose Heaven help me"; to which I could only reply that I knew Heaven was helpful, but very hardly to the tune of teaching folks their letters. I got no satisfaction.

Old Jacob, the father of Abraham, cook John, and poor Psyche's husband, took a most solemn and sad leave of me, saying he did not expect ever to see me again. I could not exactly tell why, because, though he is aged and infirm, the fifteen miles between the rice plantation and St. Simons do not appear so insuperable a barrier between the inhabitants of the two places, which I represented to him as a suggestion of consolation.

I have worked my fingers nearly off with making, for the last day or

*Slave
literacy*

two, innumerable rolls of coarse little baby clothes, layettes for the use of small newborn slaves; M[argery] diligently cutting and shaping, and I as diligently stitching. We leave a good supply for the hospitals, and for the individual clients besides who have besieged me ever since my departure became imminent.

Our voyage from the rice to the cotton plantation was performed in the *Lily*, which looked like a soldier's baggage wagon and an emigrant transport combined. Our crew consisted of eight men. Forward in the bow were miscellaneous livestock, pots, pans, household furniture, kitchen utensils, and an indescribable variety of heterogeneous necessaries. Enthroned upon beds, bedding, tables, and other chattels, sat that poor pretty chattel Psyche, with her small chattel children. Midships sat the two tiny free women [Sarah and Fan] and myself, and in the stern Mr. [Butler] steering. And "all in the blue unclouded weather" we rowed down the huge stream, the men keeping time and tune to their oars with extemporaneous chants of adieu to the rice island and its denizens. Among other poetical and musical comments on our departure recurred the assertion, as a sort of burden, that we were "parted in body, but not in mind," from those we left behind. Having relieved one set of sentiments by this reflection, they very wisely betook themselves to the consideration of the blessings that remained to them, and performed a spirited chant in honor of Psyche and our bouncing black housemaid, Mary.

At the end of a fifteen miles' row we entered one among a perfect labyrinth of arms or branches, into which the broad river ravels like a fringe as it reaches the sea, a dismal navigation along a dismal tract, called Five Pound, through a narrow cut or channel of water divided from the main stream. The conch was sounded, as at our arrival at the rice island, and we made our descent on the famous long-staple cotton island of St. Simons, where we presently took up our abode in what had all the appearance of an old, half-decayed, rattling farmhouse.

This morning, Sunday, I peeped round its immediate neighborhood, and saw, to my inexpressible delight, within hail, some noble-looking evergreen oaks, and close to the house itself a tiny would-be garden, a plot of ground with one or two peach trees in full blossom, tufts of silver narcissus and jonquils, a quantity of violets and an exquisite myrtle bush; wherefore I said my prayers with especial gratitude . . .

I observed, among the numerous groups that we passed or met, a *Mulattoes* much larger proportion of mulattoes than at the rice island; upon asking Mr. [Butler] why this was so, he said that there no white person could land without his or the overseer's permission, whereas on St. Simons, which is a large island containing several plantations belonging to different owners, of course the number of whites, both residing on and visiting the place, was much greater, and the opportunity for intercourse between the blacks and whites much more frequent. While we were still on this subject, a horrid-looking filthy woman met us with a little child in her arms, a very light mulatto, whose extraordinary resemblance to Driver Bran (one of the officials who had been duly presented to me on my arrival, and who was himself a mulatto) struck me directly. I pointed it out to Mr. [Butler], who merely answered, "Very likely his child." "And," said I, "did you never remark that Driver Bran is the exact image of Mr. K[ing]?"

"Very likely his brother," was the reply: all which rather unpleasant state of relationships seemed accepted as such a complete matter of course, that I felt rather uncomfortable, and said no more about who was like who, but came to certain conclusions in my own mind as to a young lad who had been among our morning visitors, and whose extremely light color and straight, handsome features and striking resemblance to Mr. K[ing] had suggested suspicions of a rather unpleasant nature to me, and whose sole-acknowledged parent was a very black negress of the name of Minda. I have no doubt at all, now, that he is another son of Mr. K[ing], Mr. [Butler]'s paragon overseer . . .

I find here an immense proportion of old people; the work and the *Cotton* climate of the rice plantation require the strongest of the able-bodied *planting* men and women of the estate. The cotton crop is no longer by any means as paramount in value as it used to be, and the climate, soil, and labor of St. Simons are better adapted to old, young, and feeble cultivators than the swamp fields of the rice island. I wonder if I ever told you of the enormous decrease in value of this same famous sea-island long staple cotton. When Major [Butler], Mr. [Butler]'s grandfather, first sent the produce of this plantation where we now are to England, it was of so fine a quality that it used to be quoted by itself in the Liverpool cotton market, and was then worth half a guinea a pound; it is now not worth a shilling a pound. This was told me by the gentlemen in Liverpool who has been factor for this estate for thirty years. Such a decrease as this in the value of one's crop, and the steady increase at the same time of a slave population, now numbering between 700 and 800 bodies to clothe and house, mouths to feed, while the land is being exhausted by the careless and wasteful nature of the agriculture itself, suggests a pretty serious prospect of declining prosperity; and, indeed, unless these Georgia cotton-planters can command more land, or lay abundant capital (which they have not, being almost all of them are head and ears in debt) upon that which has already spent its virgin vigor, it is a very obvious thing that they must all very soon be eaten up by their own property. The rice plantations are a great thing to fall back upon under these circumstances, and the rice crop is now quite as valuable, if not more so, than the cotton one on Mr. [Butler]'s estates, once so famous and prosperous through the latter.

I find any number of all but superannuated men and women here, whose tales of the former grandeur of the estate and family are like things one reads in novels. One old woman, who crawled to see me, and could hardly lift her poor bowed head high enough to look in my face, had been in Major [Butler]'s establishment in Philadelphia, and told with infinite pride of having waited upon his daughters and granddaughters, Mr. [Butler]'s sisters. Yet here she is, flung by like an old rag, crippled with age and disease, living, or rather dying by slow degrees in a miserable hovel, such as no decent household servant would at the North, I suppose, ever set their foot in. The poor old creature complained bitterly to me of all her ailments and all her wants. I can do little, alas! for either . . .

I had a curious visit this morning from half a dozen of the women, among whom were Driver Morris's wife and Venus (a hideous old goddess she was, to be sure), Driver Bran's mother. They came especially to see the children, who are always eagerly asked for, and hugely admired by their sooty dependents.

These poor women went into ecstasies over the little white pickaninnies, and were loud and profuse in their expressions of gratitude to Massa [Butler] for getting married and having children, a matter of thankfulness which, though it always makes me laugh very much, is a most serious one to them; for the continuance of the family keeps the estate and slaves from the hammer [of an auctioneer], and the poor wretches, besides seeing in every new child born to their owners a security against their own banishment from the only home they know, and separation from all ties of kindred and habit, and dispersion to distant plantations, not unnaturally look for a milder rule from masters who are the children of their fathers' masters. The relation of owner and slave may be expected to lose some of its harsher features, and, no doubt, in some instances, does so, when it is on each side the inheritance of successive generations. And so [Mr. Butler]'s slaves laud, and applaud, and thank, and bless him for having married, and endowed their children with two little future mistresses . . .

My dearest E[lizabeth], I write to you today [February 26] in great depression and distress. I have had a most painful conversation with Mr. [Butler], who has declined receiving any of the people's petitions through me. Whether he is wearied with the number of these prayers and supplications, which he would escape but for me, as they probably would not venture to come so incessantly to him, and I, of course, feel bound to bring every one confided to me to him, or whether he has been annoyed at the number of pitiful and horrible stories of misery and oppression under the former rule of Mr. K[ing], which have come to my knowledge since I have been here, and the grief and indignation caused, but which cannot, by any means, always be done away with, though their expression may be silenced by his angry exclamations of: "Why do you listen to such stuff?" "Why do you believe such trash? don't you know the niggers are all d—d liars?" etc. I do not know; but he desired me this morning to bring him no more complaints or requests of any sort, as the people had hitherto had no such advocate, and had done very well without, and I was only kept in an incessant state of excitement with all the falsehoods they "found they could make me believe." How well they have done without my advocacy, the conditions which I see with my own eyes, even more than their pitiful petitions, demonstrate; it is indeed true that the sufferings of those who come to me for redress, and, still more, the injustice done to the great majority who cannot, have filled my heart with bitterness and indignation that have overflowed my lips, till, I suppose, [Mr. Butler] is weary of hearing what he has never heard before, the voice of passionate expostulation and importunate pleading against wrongs that he will not even acknowledge, and for creatures whose common humanity with his own I half think he does not believe; but I must return to the North, for my condition would be almost worse than theirs—condemned to hear and see so much wretchedness, not only without the means of alleviating it, but without permission even to represent it for alleviation: this is no place for me, since I was not born among slaves, and cannot bear to live among them.

Freedom   Perhaps, after all, what he says is true: when I am gone they will fall back into the desperate uncomplaining habit of suffering, from which my coming among them, willing to hear and ready to help, has tempted them. He says that bringing their complaints to me, and the sight of my credulous commiseration, only tend to make them discontented and idle, and brings renewed chastisement upon them; and that so, instead of really befriending them, I am only preparing more suffering for them whenever I leave the place, and they can no more cry to me for help. And so I see nothing for it but to go and leave them to their fate; perhaps, too, he is afraid of the mere contagion of freedom which breathes from the very existence of those who are free; my way of speaking to the people, of treating them, or living with them, the appeals I make to their sense of truth, of duty, of self-respect, the infinite compassion and the human consideration I feel for them—all this, of course, makes my intercourse with them dangerously suggestive of relations far different from anything they have ever known; and, as Mr. O[den] once almost hinted to me, my existence among slaves was an element of danger to the "institution." If I should go away, the human sympathy that I have felt for them will certainly never come near them again.

I was too unhappy to write any more, my dear friend, and you have been spared the rest of my paroxysm, which hereabouts culminated in the blessed refuge of abundant tears. God will provide. He has not forgotten, nor will He forsake these His poor children; and if I may no longer minister to them, they yet are in His hand, who cares for them more and better than I can . . .

This morning [February 28] I had a visit from two of the women, Charlotte and Judy, who came to me for help and advice for a complaint, which it really seems to me every other woman on the estate is cursed with, and which is a direct result of the conditions of their existence; the practice of sending women to labor in the fields in the third week after their confinement is a specific for causing this infirmity, and I know no specific for curing it under these circumstances. As soon as these poor things had departed with such comfort as I could give them, and the bandages they especially begged for, three other sable graces introduced themselves, Edie, Louisa, and Diana; the former told me she had had a family of seven children, but had lost them all through "ill luck," as she denominated the ignorance and ill treatment which were answerable for the loss of these, as of so many other poor little creatures their fellows. Having dismissed her and Diana with the sugar and rice they came to beg, I detained Louisa, whom I had never seen but in the presence of her old grandmother, whose version of the poor child's escape to, and hiding in the woods, I had a desire to compare with the heroine's own story.

She told it very simply, and it was most pathetic. She had not finished her task one day, when she said she felt ill, and unable to do so, and had been severely flogged by Driver Bran, in whose "gang" she then was. The next day, in spite of this encouragement to labor, she had again been unable to complete her appointed work; and Bran having told her that he'd tie her up and flog her if she did not get it done, she had left the field and run into the swamp.

"Tie you up, Louisa!" said I; "what is that?"

She then described to me that they were fastened up by their wrists to a beam or a branch of a tree, their feet barely touching the ground, so as to allow them no purchase for resistance or evasion of the lash, their clothes turned over their heads, and their backs scored with a leather thong, either by the driver himself, or, if he pleases to inflict their punishment by deputy, any of the men he may choose to summon to the office; it might be father, brother, husband, or lover, if the overseer so ordered it. I turned sick, and my blood curdled listening to these details from the slender young slip of a lassie, with her poor piteous face and murmuring, pleading voice.

"Oh," said I, "Louisa; but the rattlesnakes—the dreadful rattlesnakes in the swamps; were you not afraid of those horrible creatures?"

"Oh, missis," said the poor child, "me no tink of dem; me forget, all 'bout dem for de fretting."

"Why did you come home at last?"

"Oh, missis, me starve with hunger, me most dead with hunger before me came back."

"And were you flogged, Louisa?" said I, with a shudder at what the answer might be.

"No, missis, me go to hospital; me almost dead and sick so long, 'spec Driver Bran him forgot 'bout de flogging."

I am getting perfectly savage over all these doings, E[lizabeth], and really think I should consider my own throat and those of my children well cut if some night these people were to take it into their heads to clear off scores in that fashion.

Slaves
watch
Kemble
write

The Calibanish wonderment of all my visitors at the exceedingly coarse and simple furniture and rustic means of comfort of my abode is very droll. I have never inhabited any apartment so perfectly devoid of what we should consider the common decencies of life; but to them, my rude chintz-covered sofa and common pine-wood table, with its green baize cloth, seem the adornings of a palace; and often in the evening, when my bairns are asleep, and M[argery] up stairs keeping watch over them, and I sit writing this daily history for your edification, the door of the great barn-like room is opened stealthily, and one after another, men and women came trooping silently in, their naked feet falling all but inaudibly on the bare boards as they betake themselves to the hearth, where they squat down on their hams in a circle, the bright blaze from the huge pine logs, which is the only light of this half of the room, shining on their sooty limbs and faces, and making them look like a ring of ebony idols surrounding my domestic hearth. I have had as many as fourteen at a time squatting silently there for nearly half an hour, watching me writing at the other end of the room. The candles on my table give only light enough for my own occupation, the fire-light illuminates the rest of the apartment; and you can not imagine any thing stranger than the effect of all these glassy whites of eyes and grinning white teeth turned toward me, and shining in the flickering light. I very often take no notice of them at all, and they seem perfectly absorbed in contemplating me. My evening dress probably excites their wonder and admiration no less than my rapid and continuous writing, for which they have sometimes expressed compassion, as if they thought it must be more laborious than hoeing; sometimes at the end of my day's journal I look up and say suddenly, "Well, what do you want?" when each black figure springs up at once, as if moved by machinery; they all answer me, "Me come say ha do (how d'ye do), missis" and then they troop out as noiselessly as they entered, like a procession of sable dreams, and I go off in search, if possible, of whiter ones . . .

The women who visited me yesterday evening were all in the family-way, and came to entreat of me to have the sentence (what else can I call it?) modified which condemns them to resume their labor of hoeing in the fields three weeks after their confinement. They knew, of course, that I can not interfere with their appointed labor, and therefore their sole entreaty was that I would use my influence with Mr. [Butler] to obtain for them a month's respite from labor in the field after childbearing. Their principal spokeswoman, a woman with a bright sweet face, called Mary, and a very sweet voice, which is by no means an uncommon excellence among them, appealed to my own experience; and while she spoke of my babies and my carefully tended, delicately nursed, and tenderly watched confinement and convales-

Pregnant women

cence, and implored me to have a kind of labor given to them less exhausting during the month after their confinement, I held the table before me so hard in order not to cry that I think my fingers ought to have left a mark on it. At length I told them that Mr. [Butler] had forbidden me to bring him any more complaints from them, for that he thought the ease with which I received and believed their stories only tended to make them discontented, and that, therefore, I feared I could not promise to take their petitions to him; but that he would be coming down to "the Point" [Hampton Point, where the cotton was grown] soon, and that they had better come then some time when I was with him, and say what they had just been saying to me; and with this, and various small bounties, I was forced, with a heavy heart, to dismiss them; and when they were gone, with many exclamations of, "Oh yes, missis, you will, you will speak to massa for we; God bless you, missis, we sure you will!" I had my cry out for them, for myself, for us. All these women had had large families, and all of them had lost half their children, and several of them had lost more . . .

Before closing this letter, I have a mind to transcribe to you the entries for to-day recorded in a sort of day-book, where I put down very succinctly the number of people who visit me, their petitions and ailments, and also such special particulars concerning them as seem to me worth recording. You will see how miserable the physical condition of many of these poor creatures is; and their physical condition, it is insisted by those who uphold this evil system, is the only part of it which is prosperous, happy, and compares well with that of Northern laborers. Judge from the details I now send you; and never forget, while reading them, that the people on this plantation are well off, and consider themselves well off, in comparison with the slaves on some of the neighboring estates.

Miscarriages and pregnancies

Fanny has had six children; all dead but one. She came to beg to have her work in the field lightened.

Nanny has had three children; two of them are dead. She came to implore that the rule of sending them into the field three weeks after confinement might be altered.

Leah, Caesar's wife, has had six children; three are dead.

Sophy, Lewis's wife, came to beg for some old linen. She is suffering fearfully; has had ten children; five of them are dead. The principal favor she asked was a piece of meat, which I gave her.

Sally, Scipio's wife, has had two miscarriages and three children born, one of whom is dead. She came complaining of incessant pain and weakness in her back. This woman was a mulatto daughter of a slave called Sophy, by a white man of the name of Walker, who visited the plantation.

Charlotte, Renty's wife, had had two miscarriages, and was with child again. She was almost crippled with rheumatism, and showed me a pair of poor swollen knees that made my heart ache. I have promised her a pair of flannel trousers, which I must forthwith set about making.

Sarah, Stephen's wife—this woman's case and history were alike deplorable. She had had four miscarriages, had brought seven children into the world, five of whom were dead, and was again with child. She complained of dreadful pains in the back, and an internal tumor which swells with the exertion of working in the fields; probably, I think, she is ruptured. She told me she had once been mad and had ran into the woods, where she contrived to elude discovery for some time, but was at last tracked and brought back when she was tied up by the arms, and heavy logs fastened to her feet, and was severely flogged. After this she contrived to escape again, and lived for some time skulking in the woods, and she supposes mad, for when she was taken again she was entirely naked. She subsequently recovered from this derangement, and seems now just like all the other poor creatures who come to me for help and pity. I suppose her constant childbearing and hard labor in the fields at the same time may have produced the temporary insanity.

Sukey, Bush's wife, only came to pay her respects. She had had four miscarriages; had brought eleven children into the world, five of whom are dead.

Molly, Quambo's wife, also only came to see me. Hers was the best account I have yet received; she had had nine children, and six of them were still alive.

This is only the entry for to-day, in my diary, of the people's complaints and visits. Can you conceive a more wretched picture than that which it exhibits of the conditions under which these women live? . . .

Curse of slavery

As I looked at those trees [drowned orange trees] a wild wish rose in my heart that the river and the sea would swallow up and melt in their salt waves the whole of this accursed property of ours. I am afraid the horror of slavery with which I came down to the South, the general theoretic abhorrence of an Englishwoman for it, has gained, through the intensity it has acquired, a morbid character of mere desire to be delivered from my own share in it. I think so much of these wretches that I see, that I can hardly remember any others; and my zeal for the general emancipation of the slave has almost narrowed itself to this most painful desire that I and mine were freed from the responsibility of our share in this huge misery; and so I thought, "Beat, beat, the crumbling banks and sliding shores, wild waves of the Atlantic and the Altamaha! Sweep down and carry hence this evil earth and these homes of tyranny, and roll above the soil of slavery, and wash my soul and the souls of those I love clean from the blood of our kind!" But I have no idea that Mr. [Butler] and his brother would cry amen to any such prayer. Sometimes, as I stand and listen to the roll of the great ocean as it surges on the farther side of Little St. Simons Island, a small green screen of tangled wilderness that interposes between this point and the Atlantic, I think how near our West Indian Islands and freedom are to these unfortunate people, many of whom are expert and hardy boatmen, as far as the mechanical management of a boat goes; but, unless Providence were compass and steersman too, it avails nothing that they should know how near their freedom might be found, nor have I any right to tell them if they could find it, for the slaves are not mine, they are Mr. [Butler]'s . . .

Sexual exploitation

I have been interrupted by several visits, my dear E[lizabeth], among other, one from a poor creature called Judy, whose sad story and condition affected me terrible . . . She told me a miserable story of her former experience on the plantation under Mr. K[ing]'s overseership. It seems that Jem Valiant (an extremely difficult subject, a mulatto lad, whose valor is sufficiently accounted for now by the influence of the mutinous white blood) was her first-born, the son of Mr. K[ing], who forced her, flogged her severely for having resisted him, and then sent her off as a farther punishment, to Five Pound—a horrible swamp in a remote corner of the estate, to which the slaves are sometimes banished for such offenses as are not sufficiently atoned for by the lash. The dismal loneliness of the place to these poor people, who are as dependent as children upon companionship and sympathy, makes this solitary exile a much-dreaded infliction; and this poor creature said that, bad as the flogging was, she would sooner have taken that again than the dreadful lonely days and nights she spent on the penal swamp of Five Pound.

I make no comment on these terrible stories, my dear friend, and tell them to you as nearly as possible in the perfectly plain, unvarnished manner in which they are told to me. I do not wish to add to, or perhaps I ought to say take away from, the effect of such narrations by amplifying the simple horror and misery of their bare details . . . [GP]

[March 4, 1839]

Another of my visitors had a still more *dismal* story to tell; her name was Die; she had had sixteen children, fourteen of whom were dead; she had had four miscarriages: one had been caused with falling down with a very heavy burden on her head, and one from having her arms strained up to be lashed. I asked her what she meant by having her arms tied up. She said their hands were first tied together, sometimes by the wrists, and sometimes, which was worse, by the thumbs, and they were then drawn up to a tree or post, so as almost to swing them off the ground, and then their clothes rolled round their waist, and a man with a cowhide stands and stripes them. I give you the woman's words. She did not speak of this as of any thing strange, unusual, or especially horrid and abominable; and when I said, "Did they do that to you when you were with child?" she simply replied, "Yes, missis." And to all this I listen—I, an English woman, the wife of the man who owns these wretches, and I can not say, "That thing shall not be done again;

*Whipping
and
miscarriage*

that cruel shame villainy shall never be known here again." I gave the woman meat and flannel, which were what she came to ask for, and remained choking with indignation and grief long after they had all left me to my most bitter thoughts . . .

After my return home I had my usual evening reception, and, among other pleasant incidents of plantation life, heard the following agreeable anecdote from a woman named Sophy, who came to beg for some rice. In asking her about her husband and children, she said she had never had any husband; that she had had two children by a white man of the name of Walker, who was employed at the mill on the rice island; she was in the hospital after the birth of the second child she bore this man, and at the same time two women, Judy and Sylla, of whose children Mr. K[ing] was the father, were recovering from their confinements. It was not a month since any of them had been delivered, when Mrs. K[ing] came to the hospital, had them all severely flogged, a process which she personally superintended, and then sent them to Five Pound—the swamp Botany Bay [Australian penal colony] of the plantation, of which I have told you—with further orders to the drivers to flog them every day for a week. Now, E[lizabeth], if I make you sick with these disgusting stories, I can not help it; they are the life itself here; hitherto I have thought these details intolerable enough, but this apparition of a female fiend in the middle of this hell I confess adds an element of cruelty which seems to me to surpass all the rest. Jealousy is not an uncommon quality in the feminine temperament; and just conceive the fate of these unfortunate women between the passions of their masters and mistresses, each alike armed with power to oppress and torture them. Sophy went on to say that Isaac was her son by Driver Morris, who had forced her while she was in her miserable exile at Five Pound. Almost beyond my patience with this string of detestable details, I exclaimed—foolishly enough, heaven knows—"Ah, but don't you know—did nobody ever tell or teach any of you that it is a sin to live with men who are not your husbands?"

Alas! E[lizabeth], what could the creature answer but what she did, seizing me at the same time vehemently by the wrist: "Oh yes, missis, we know—we know all about dat well enough but we do any thing to get our poor flesh some rest from de whip; when he made me follow him into de bush, what use me tell him no? He have strength to make me."

I have written down the woman's words; I wish I could write down the voice and look of abject misery with which they were spoken. Now you will observe that the story was not told to me as a complaint; it was a thing long past, and over, of which she only spoke in the natural course of accounting for her children to me. I make no comment; what need, or can I add, to such stories?—But how is such a state of things to endure? And again, how is it to end?

While I was pondering, as it seemed to me, at the very bottom of the Slough of Despond, on this miserable creature's story, another woman came in (Tema), carrying in her arms a child the image of the mulatto Bran; she came to beg for flannel. I asked her who was her husband. She said she was not married. Her child is the child of Brick-layer Temple, who has a wife at rice island. By this time, what do you think of the moralities, as well as the amenities of slave life? These are the conditions which can only be known to one who lives among them; flagrant acts of cruelty may be rare, but this ineffable state of ut-ter degradation, this really *beastly* existence, is the normal condition of these men and women, and of that no one seems to take heed . . .

Slave immorality

I must tell you that I have been delighted, surprised, and the very least perplexed, by the sudden petition on the part of our young waiter, Aleck, that I will teach him to read. He is a very intelligent lad of about sixteen, and preferred his request with an urgent humility that was very touching. I told him I would think about it. I mean to do it. I will do it; and yet, it is simply breaking the laws of the government under which *I* am living. Unrighteous laws are made to be broken—*perhaps*—but then, you see, I am a woman, and Mr. [Butler] stands between me and the penalty. If I were a man, I would do that and many a thing besides, and doubtless should be shot some fine day from behind a tree by some good neighbor, who would do the com-munity a service by quietly getting rid of a mischievous incendiary; and I promise you, in such a case, no questions would be asked, and my lessons would come to a speedy and silent end; but teaching slaves

Teaching slaves to read

to read is a finable offense, and I am *feme couverte* [legal status of married women], and my fines must be paid by my legal owner, and the first offense of the sort is heavily fined, and the second more heavily fined, and for the third, one is sent to prison. What a pity it is I can't begin with Aleck's third lesson, because going to prison can't be done by proxy, and that penalty would light upon the right shoulders! I certainly intend to teach Aleck to read. I certainly won't tell Mr. [Butler] any thing about it. I'll leave him to find it out, as slaves, and servants, and children, and all oppressed, and ignorant, and uneducated and unprincipled people do; then, if he forbids me, I can stop—perhaps before then the lad may have learned his letters. I begin to perceive one most admirable circumstance in this slavery: you are absolute on your own plantation. No slaves' testimony avails against you, and no white testimony exists but such as you choose to admit. Some owners have a fancy for maiming their slaves, some brand them, some pull out their teeth, some shoot them a little here and there (all details gathered from advertisements of runaway slaves in Southern papers); now they do all this on their plantations, where nobody comes to see, and I'll teach Aleck to read, for nobody is here to see, at least nobody whose seeing I mind; and I'll teach every other creature that wants to learn. I haven't much more than a week to remain in this blessed purgatory; in that last week perhaps I may teach the boy enough to go on alone when I am gone . . .

Mixed-race children

Before reaching the house I was stopped by one of our multitudinous Jennies with a request for some meat, and that I would help her with some clothes for Ben and Daphne, of whom she had the sole charge; these are two extremely pretty and interesting-looking mulatto children, whose resemblance to Mr. K[ing] had induced me to ask Mr. [Butler], when first I saw them, if he did not think they must be his children. He said they were certainly like him, but Mr. K[ing] did not acknowledge the relationship. I asked Jenny who their mother was. "Minda." "Who their father?" "Mr. K[ing]." "What! old Mr. K[ing]?" "No, Mr. R[oswell] K[ing]." "Who told you so?" "Minda, who ought to know." "Mr. K[ing] denies it." "That's because he never has looked upon them nor done a thing for them." "Well, but he acknowledged

Renty as his son, why should he deny these?" "Because old master was here then when Renty was born, and he made Betty tell all about it, and Mr. K[ing] had to own it; but nobody knows any thing about this, and so he denies it"—with which information I rode home . . .   [GP]

Sunday, April 14th.

My Dear E[lizabeth],

. . . I know that the Southern men are apt to deny the fact that they do live under an habitual sense of danger; but a slave population, coerced into obedience, though unarmed and half fed, is a threatening source of constant insecurity, and every Southern woman to whom I have spoken on the subject has admitted to me that they live in terror of their slaves. Happy are such of them as have protectors like J[ohn] C[ouper, the owner of Cannon's Point next to Butler's home, a great favorite of Kemble's]. Such men will best avoid and best encounter the perils that may assail them from the abject, human element, in the control of which their noble faculties are sadly and unworthily employed.   [GP]

Wednesday, 17th April.

I once heard a conversation between Mr. O[den] and Mr. K[ing], the two overseers of the plantation on which I was living, upon the question of taking slaves, servants, necessary attendants, into the Northern states; Mr. O[den] urged the danger of their being "got hold of," i.e. set free by the abolitionists, to which Mr. K[ing] very pertinently replied: "Oh, stuff and nonsense; I take care, when my wife goes North with the children, to send Lucy with her; *her children are down here, and I defy all the abolitionists in creation to get her to stay North.*" Mr. K[ing] was an extremely wise man.   [GP]

This was Kemble's last entry in her plantation journal. She and her husband returned to Philadelphia very much estranged.

On the Plantation, 1838–1839

Troubled Times
1840–1867

Philadelphia
January 15, 1840

[My Dearest Harriet]

Loneliness I have nothing to tell you; my life externally is *nothing;* and who can tell the inward history of their bosom—that internal life, which is often so strangely unlike the other? Suppose I inform you that I have just come from a ride of an hour and a half; that I went out of the city by Broad Street, and returned by Islington Lane and the Ridge Road— how much the wiser will you be? that the roads were frozen hard as iron, and here and there so sheeted with ice that I had great difficulty in preventing my horse from slipping and falling down with me, and, being quite alone, without even a servant, I wondered what I should do if *he* did. I have a capital horse, whom I have christened Forester, after the hero of my play, and who grins with delight, like a dog, when I talk to him and pat him. He is a bright bay, with black legs and mane, tall and large, and built like a hunter, with high courage and good temper. I have had him four years, and do not like to think what would become of me if anything were to happen to him. It would be necessary that I should commit suicide, for his fellow is not to be found in "these United States." Dearest Harriet, we hope to come over to England next September; and if your sister will invite me, I will come and see you some before I re-cross the Atlantic. I am very anxious about my father, and still more anxious about my sister, and feel heart-weary for the sight of some of my own people, places, and things; and so, Fate prospering, to speak heathen, I shall go *home* once more in the autumn of this present 1840: till when, dearest Harriet, God bless you!   [*LL*]

Philadelphia
February 9, 1840

[Dear Mrs. Jameson]
J[ohn] B[utler] and his brother [Pierce] have just started for Georgia, leaving his wife and myself in forlorn widowhood, which (the providence of railroads and steamboats allowing) is not to last more than three months. I have been staying nearly three months in their house in town, expecting every day to depart for the plantation; but we have procrastinated to such good effect that the Chesapeake Bay is now unnavigable, being choked up with ice, and the other route involving seventy miles of night traveling *on the worst road in the United States* (think what that means!), it has been judged expedient that the children and myself should remain behind—I am about, therefore, to return with them to the Farm, where I shall pass the reminder of the winter,—how, think you? Why, reading Gibbon's *Decline and Fall*, which I have never read yet, and which I now intend to study with classical atlas, Bayle's dictionary, the Encyclopedia, and all sorts of "aids to beginners." How quiet I shall be! I think perhaps I may die some day, without so much as being aware of it; and if so, beg to record myself in good season, before that imperceptible event.   [*LL*]

Butler Place
October 26, 1840

[Dearest Harriet],

On publishing Georgia journal

You ask me if I ever write any journal, or anything else now. The time that I passed in the South was so crowded with daily and hourly occupations that, though I kept a regular journal, it was hastily written, and received constant additional notes of things that occurred, and that I wished to remember inserted in a very irregular fashion in it?~~I think I should like to carry this journal down to Georgia with me this winter; to revise, correct, and add whatever my second experience might furnish to the chronicle. It has been suggested to me that such an account of a Southern plantation might be worth publishing; but I think such a publication would be a breach of confidence, an advantage taken on my part of the situation of trust, which I held on the estate. As my condemnation of the whole system is unequivocal, and all my illustrations of its evils must be drawn from our own plantation, I do not think I have a right to exhibit the interior management and economy of that property to the world at large, as a sample of Southern slavery, especially as I did not go thither with any such purpose. This winter I think I shall mention my desire upon the subject before going to the South, and of course any such publication must then depend on the acquiescence of the owners of the estate. I am sure that no book of mine on the subject could be of as much use to the poor people on Butler's Island as my residence among them; and I should therefore, be very unwilling to do anything that was likely to interfere with that: although I have sometimes been haunted with the idea that it was an imperative duty, knowing what I know, and having seen what I have seen, to do all that lies in my power to show the dangers and evils of this frightful institution. And the testimony of a planter's wife, whose experience has all been gathered from estates where the slaves are universally admitted to be well treated, should carry with it some authority. So I am occupying myself, from time to time, as my leisure allows, in making a fair copy of my Georgia Journal . . .

Here are two of your questions answered: the third is—whether I *Antislavery sentiment* let the slave question rest more than I did? Oh yes; for I have come to the conclusion that no words of mine could be powerful enough to dispel clouds of prejudice which early habits of thought, and the general opinion of society upon this subject have gathered round the minds of the people I live among. I do not know whether they ever think or read about it, and my arguments, though founded in this case on pretty sound reason, are apt to degenerate into passionate appeals, the violence of which is not calculated to do much good in the way of producing convictions in the minds of others~~~

Even if the property were mine, I could exercise no power over it; nor could our children, after our death, do anything for those wretched slaves, under the present laws of Georgia. All that any one could do, would be to refrain from using the income derived from the estates, and return it to the rightful owners—that is the earners of it. Had I such property, I think I would put my slaves at once quietly upon the footing of free laborers, paying them wages, and making them pay me rent and take care of themselves. Of course I should be shot by my next neighbor (against whom no verdict would be found except "Serve her right!") in the first week of my experiment; but *if I wasn't*, I think, reckoning only the meanest profit to be derived from the measure, I should double the income of the estate in less than three years~~~I am more than ever satisfied that God and Mammon would be equally propitiated by emancipation.

You ask me whether I take any interest in the Presidential election. *Election of Harrison* Though I have not room left for my reasons—and I have some, besides that woman's reason, sympathy with the politics of the man I belong to. The party coming into power are, I believe, at heart less democratic than the other; and while the natural advantages of this wonderful country remain unexhausted (and they are apparently inexhaustible), I am sure the Republican Government is by far the best for the people themselves, besides think it is the best in the abstract, as you know I do. God bless you, my dearest Harriet[.]   [*LL*]

In late 1840 Kemble was informed that her father was ill, and in December 1840 she and her husband and children sailed to England. They spent over two years abroad.

Harley Street, London
May 14, 1842

Women earning income

My Dearest Hal [Kemble's nickname for Harriet St. Leger],
You ask whether it is a blessing or a curse not to provide one's own means of subsistence. I think it is a great blessing to be able and allowed to do so. But I dare say I am not a fair judge of the question, for the feeling of independence and power consequent upon earning large sums of money has very much destroyed my admiration for any other mode of support; and yet certainly my *pecuniary* position now would seem to most people very preferable to my former one; but having *earned* money, and therefore most legitimately *owned* it, I never can conceive that I have any right to the money of another person~~~I cannot help sometimes regretting that I did not reserve out of my former earnings at least such a yearly sum as would have covered my personal expenses; and having these notions, which impair the comfort of *being maintained*, I am sometimes sorry that I no longer possess my former convenient power of coining. I do not think I should feel so uncomfortable about inheriting money, though I had not worked for it; for, like any other free gift, I think I should consider that legitimately my own, just like any other present that was made me . . . [*LL*]

Harley Street
May 30, 1842

My Dearest Harriet,
I have just finished a letter to you, in which I tell you that I have sketched out the skeleton of another tragedy . . . You ask me what has moved me to this mental effort. My milliner's bill, my dear; which, being £97 sterling, I feel extremely inclined to pay out of my own brains; for, though they received a very severe shock, and one of rather para-

lyzing effect, upon my being reminded that whatever I write is not my own legal property, but that of another, which, of course, upon consideration, I know; I cannot, nevertheless, persuade myself that that which I invent—create, in fact—can really belong to any one but myself; therefore, if anything I wrote could earn for me £97, I am afraid I should consider that I, and no one else, had paid my bill.

In thinking over the position of women with regard to their right to own earnings, I confess to something very like wrathful indignation; impotent wrath and vain indignation, to be sure—not the less intense for that, however, for the injustice is undoubtedly great. That a man whose wit could not keep him half a week from starving should claim as his the result of a mental process such as that of composing a noble work of imagination—say *Corinne*, for example—seems too beneficent a provision of the law for the protection of male *superiority*. It is true, that by our marriage bargain, they feed, clothe, and house us, and are answerable for our debts (not my milliner's bill, though, if I can prevent it), and so, I suppose, have a right to pay themselves as best they can out of all we are or all we can do. It is a pretty severe puzzle, and a deal of love must be thrown into one or other or both scales to make the balance hang tolerably even.

Madame de Stael, I suppose, might have said to Rocca, "If my brains are indeed yours, why don't you write a book like *Corinne* with them?" You know though he was perfectly amiable, and she married him for love, he was an intellectual zero; but perhaps the man who, acknowledging her brilliant intellectual superiority, could say, "Je l'aimerai tant, qu'elle finira par, m'aimer" [I will love her so much that, in the end, she will love me], deserved to be master even of his wife's brains~~~I wish women could be dealt with, not mercifully, nor compassionately, nor affectionately, but *justly;* it would be so much better—for men . . . [*LL*]

Kemble and Butler returned to America in 1843, but their relationship deteriorated. Gossip about Butler's infidelities resulted in scandal.

Philadelphia
May 20, 1844

No, my dearest Hal [Harriet], the day is never long, but always short, even when I rise before six~~~I have a vivid consciousness of an increased perception of the minor goods of existence, in the midst of its greatest evils, and things that till now have been mere enjoyments to me now appear to me in the light of positive blessings.

My delight in everything beautiful increases daily, and I now count and appreciate the inumerable alleviations that life has in every twenty-four hours, even in its seasons of severest trial.

A spirit of greater thankfulness is often engendered by suffering itself; it is one of the "sweet uses of adversity," and mitigates it immensely.

A beautiful flower was brought me to-day; and while I remained absorbed in contemplating it, it seemed to me a very angel of consolatory admonition. God bless you, dearest friend. How full of sources of comfort He has made this lovely woe-world!   [LL]

Philadelphia
July 14, 1844

Daily routine

. . . You ask me if I apportion my time among my various occupations with the same systematic regularity as formerly. I endeavour to do so but find it almost impossible~~~I read but very little. My leisure is principally given to my German, in which I am making some progress. I walk with the children morning and evening; I still play and sing a little at some time or other of the day, and write interminable letters to people afar off, who I wish were nearer. I walk before breakfast with the children, i.e., from seven till eight. Three times a week I take them to the market to buy fruits and flowers, an errand I like as well as they do. The other mornings we walk in the square opposite this house. After breakfast they leave me for the morning, which they now pass with their governess or nurse. For the last two months I have ridden every day, but have unhappily disabled my horse for the present, poor fellow! by galloping him during a sudden heavy rain-shower over a slippery road, in which process he injured one of his hip-joints, not incurably, I trust, but so as to deprive me of him for at least three months.

I shall now walk after breakfast, as, my rides being suppressed, my walks with the chicks are not exercise enough for me. After that, I prepare for my German lesson (which I take three times a week) and write letters—I take the children out again at half-past six, and at half-past seven come in to my dinner; after dinner I go to my piano, and generally sit at it or read until I go to bed, which I do early—*et voila!*

Almost all the people I know are out of town now, and I do not see a human creature; the heat is intense and the air foul and stifling, and we are gasping for breath and withering away in this city atmo-sphere~~~ [*LL*]

For the rest of 1844 and well into 1845, Butler and Kemble became even more estranged. Finally, in September 1845, Kemble left her husband and departed for England, leaving her children behind.

Mortimer Street, London
October 3, 1845

[My Dear Harriet]
Heaven be praised, my American letters are finished!—eleven long ones, eleven shillings' worth. I am sure somebody (but at this moment I don't rightly know who) ought to pay me eleven shillings for such a batch of work. So now I have nothing to do but answer your daily calls, my dearest Hal, which "nothing," as I write it, looks like a bad joke. If you expect me, however, to write you a long letter on the heels of that heavy American budget, you deceive yourself, my dear friend, and the truth is not in you.

In the first place, I have nothing to say except that I am well and intensely interested by everything about me. I am very sorry to have neglected sending you *Arnold* [his Life, just published at that time], but it shall be done this day.

London, with its distracting quantity of *things to do*, is already lay-ing hold of me; and the species of vertigo which I experience after my lonely American existence, at finding myself once more overwhelmed with visits, messages, engagements, and endless notes to read and answer, is pitiable. I feel as if I had been growing idiotic out there [in Philadelphia], my life here is such an amazing contrast.   [*LL*]

Mortimer Street, London
November 20, 1845

. . . Thus far, my dearest Harriet, when your letter of the 19th—yesterday (you see I did look at the date)—was brought to me. It is certainly most miserable to consider what horrible things men contrive to make of the mutual relations which might be so blest. I do not know if I am misled by the position from which I take my observations, but it seems to me that one of the sins most ripe in the world is the *mis*use, or *dis*use, of the potent and tender ties of relationship and kindred . . . [*LL*]

London
November 21, 1845

[My Dearest Harriet]

Marital separation

I receive infinite advice on all hands about my perplexed affairs, all of it most kindly meant, but little of it, alas! available to me. Some of it, indeed, appears to me so worldly, so false, and so full of compromise between right and wrong for the mere sake of expediency; sometimes for cowardice, sometimes for peace, sometimes for pleasure, sometimes for profit, sometimes for mere social consideration,—the whole system (for such it is) accepted and acknowledged as a rule of life— that, as I sit listening to these friendly suggestions, I am half the time shocked at those who utter them, and the other half shocked at myself for being shocked at people so much my betters~~~My abiding feeling is that I had better go back to my beloved Lenox, to the side of the "Bowl" (the Indian name of a beautiful small lake between Lenox and Stockbridge), among the Berkshire hills, where selfishness and moral cowardice and worldly expediency exist in each man's practice no doubt quite sufficiently; but where they are not yet universally recognized as a social system, by the laws of which civilized existence should be governed. You know, "a bad action is a thousand times preferable to a bad principle" . . . [LL]

The Hoo, Welwyn, Herts
December, 1845

My Dearest Hal,

God knows I am admonished to patience, both by my own helplessness and the inefficiency of those who, it seems to me, ought to be able to help me~~~Doubtless, my father reasonably regrets the independence which I might by this time have earned for myself in my profession, and feels anxious about my unprovided future. I have written to Chorley [Henry Chorley, literary critic for the *Athenaeum*], the only person I know to whom *I* can apply on the subject, to get me some means of publishing the few manuscript verses I have left in some magazine or other~~~If I cannot succeed in this, I shall try if I can publish my "English Tragedy," and make a few pounds by it. It is a wretchedly uncomfortable position, but compared with all that has gone before, it is *only* uncomfortable . . . [LL]

Publishing efforts

In late 1845 Kemble joined her sister's family in Rome for a year.

Rome
Saturday, January 10 [1846]

I had seen my sister's children asleep in their cribs last night; cooing and chirping woke me in the morning. While I was still in my dressing-gown [Edward Sartoris, Kemble's brother-in-law] called me out to see the view. We are on the very top of the Pincio; Rome lay like a map at our feet, bathed far and with glorious sunlight, against which on the opposite horizon the stone pines of the Doria Pamfili spread out their dark roofs. Our apartment reminds me extremely of all the houses I ever was in the southern states of America—large lofty rooms, with not a window or door that can shut, and those that do, giving one one's death by the imperfect manner in which they close,—a great deal more than if they stood for ever wide open; coarse common carpets laid over a layer of straw; in short, the whole untidy discomfort which characterizes the dwellings of all southern people, as far as my observation goes.

Now for the chapter of compensations: my bed-room door and window open upon a terraced garden at least forty-feet above the street, full of orange and lemon trees, magnolias, myrtles, oleanders and camellias, roses and violets, in blossom; a fountain of the aqua felice trickles under the superintendence of a statue into a marble shell, and thence escapes under the garden. The view from thence of the Eternal City and its beauteous girdle of hills surpasses all description, and the twin towers of the Trinita rise close to it up into the blue sky, which looks through the belfry arches as through windows down into my sleeping-room. The colored tiles of all our ante-rooms and passages enchant me; so do the gay painted ceilings. The little room where I bathe is a perfect delight to me, with its latin inscription on the lintel, its marble bath, its walls covered with fresco Cupids and dolphins, and altars with flames, and baskets with flowers, all strung together by waving patterns of wreaths and garlands. This afternoon we drove through the streets of Rome, out to a place that was once *one of* the innumerable Cenci possessions, but which is the light over radiant and tender; the warmth and balmy softness of the atmosphere— everything was perfect enchantment. Everything was graceful, harmonious, and delightful to the eye, and soothing beyond expression to the mind. Presently came two of the beautiful mouse-colored oxen of the campagna, slowly, through the arched gateway of the farm-yard, and, leaning their serious-looking heads upon the stone basin, drank soberly, with their great eyes fixed on us, who sat upon the hem of the fountain; I for the first time in my life, almost comprehending the delight of listless inactivity. As the water ran lullingly by my side, and between the grey shafts of the tall pine-trees, and beneath the dark arches of their boughs, the distant landscape, formed into separate and distinct pictures of incomparable beauty, arrested by my delighted eyes. Yes, I think I actually could be content to sit on that fountain's edge, and do nothing but listen and look for a whole summer's afternoon. But no more—"up, and be doing," is the impulse for ever with me; when I ask myself, both sadly and scornfully, what? both my nature and my convictions repeat the call, "up, and be doing;" for surely there is something to be done from morning till night, and to find out what, is the appointed work of the onward-tending soul.

Returning home, the arches of the aqueducts were all gilt within the sunset. How beautiful they are, those great chains, binding the mountains to the plain, with their veins of living water! The links are broken, and the graceful line intercepted, and the flowing element within withdrawn to its heart in the mountains, and now they are only the most beautiful ruins in the whole world. Sometimes, when seen from a height which commanded a long stretch of their course, they reminded me of the vertebrae of some great serpent, whose marrow was the living water, of which Rome drank for centuries. We returned to the city by the beautiful Porta Maggiore . . . [*YC*]

Sunday, 11th January [1846]

We drove up the Monte Mario to a beautiful villa, formerly the Villa Mellini, now called the Villa Falconieri; from this place the view of Rome, the Tiber, the hills, the campagna, and the *sea,* most glorious. The house stands like a fortress, on the very top of a precipitous hill, which is crowned with ramparts of ilex and cypress. Here (as everywhere) we were pursued by the shameless, wretched pauperism that disgusts and palm one the whole time, and makes the ruined aspect of the great outward things about one cheerful, compared with the abject degradation of that which God has made in his own image. Oh! I would not live among these people for anything in the world; and when I think of England and of America, I thank God that I was born in the one, and shall live in the other. [*YC*]

Italian villas

April 20 [1846]

My friend has given me a charming little Sicilian song, of which the
following is a free translation. The pathetic and graceful idea is, however, a thousand tunes more appropriately clothed in the soft dialect
from which I have transferred it:

> I planted in my heart one seed of love,
>   Water'd with tears, and watched with sleepless care;
> It grew—and when I look'd that it should prove
>   A gracious tree, and blessed harvests bear,
> Blossom nor fruit was there to crown my pain,
>   Tears, cares, and labor all had been in vain;
> And yet I dare not pluck it from my heart,
>   Lest with the deep-struck root my life depart.   [YC]

Frascati
Summer 1846

*Workers'
wages*

I could not discover such a thing as a fly-loom in all Frascati; but
women working at exceedingly clumsy and wretched old hand-looms
told me, that one paul a day, that is about five pence, was the most that
they could earn with their utmost diligence. So antiquated a machine
as a hand-loom, I suppose, could hardly be found now in Philadelphia;
but a worker there at the fly-loom earns, without the slightest
difficulty, a dollar and a half or between six and seven shillings a day;
the wages of handicraftsmen and artisans, such as carpenters, bricklay-
ers, and masons, in these small villages in the vicinity of Rome, are
very fair, amounting to about a scudo a day; not, indeed, equal to the
nine dollars a week of an industrious American journeyman, but still,
compared with the agricultural wages, excellent.

*American
cost of
living*

In speaking, as I perpetually do, of the extraordinary advantage
workmen in America enjoy over the same class in England, and other
countries in Europe, I do not wish at all to be understood to state, that
they can live more cheaply on the other side of the Atlantic; for directly the reverse is the case, as I have been repeatedly assured by num-

bers of the working classes who had emigrated from England to America, and who found living there much dearer than in the old country. The only item of expenditure that is really cheap in Philadelphia and its neighborhood, is food. Provisions are infinitely cheaper than in England; and if men could live by bread alone, the difference between the costliness of existence in the New and old world would indeed be immense. But almost everything else necessary for physical existence is either as dear or dearer than in England;—all materials for and articles of clothing infinitely dearer and by no means so good; all implements of industry, whether mechanical or agricultural, infinitely dearer and not so good; fuel as dear, or dearer; and house-rent for the poorer classes much upon the same scale in both countries. With regard to the advantage that his fortune; a chance which of course involved its opposite chance of sudden ruin,—it will easily be conceived how absolutely destructive such a state of things must be of everything like habits of economy or the regular management and careful administration of certain means.

I have heard American women repeatedly say, that their husbands *American financial speculation* never informed them of anything relating to their affairs; that they had not remotest idea of the amount of their income; and that it was the most unusual thing among them for a woman to be at all aware of the extent of her husband's means. To English lawyers', physicians', clergymen's, or professional men's wives, whose task it is invariably to hold the proportion between their husband's income and the necessary outlay of their families, this state of things appears incredible; but it ceases to be so singular, when one reflects that a man engaged in wild speculations, which may at any moment double or treble his fortune or sweep from him the bare means of existence, cannot very well consider himself possessed of any fixed income, or reckon his certain means at any specific sum. Nor is it very likely that any man would care to burden the heart and mind of his wife, in the midst of her domestic duties and anxieties, with the intense nervous expectation—the incessant tension of acute apprehension—of a condition hovering perpetually between such reverses of fortune . . . [YC]

Troubled Times, 1840–1867

Frascati, Italy
September 2, 1846

[My Dearest Harriet]

I think that the women who have contemplated any equality between the sexes have almost all been unmarried, for while the father disposes of the children whom he maintains, and which thus endows him with the power of supreme torture, what mother's heart is proof against the tightening of that screw? At any rate, what number of women is ever likely to be found so organized or so principled as to resist the pressure of this tremendous power? My sister, in speaking to me the other day of what she would or would not give up to her husband of conscientious conviction of right, wound up by saying, "But sooner than lose my children, there is *nothing* that I would not do;" and in so speaking she undoubtedly uttered the feeling of the great majority of women~~~

My dearest Hal, I have kept no journal since I have been abroad but such as could be published verbatim. I have kept no record of my own life; I have long felt that to chronicle it would not assist me in enduring it~~~Indeed, since I came to Italy, I should have kept no diary at all, but that my doing so was suggested to me as a possible means of earning something towards my present support, and with that view I have noted what I have seen, much to my own disgust and dissatisfaction; for I feel very strongly my own inability to give any fresh interest to a mere superficial description of things and places seen and known by everybody, and written about by all the world and his wife, for the last hundred years. Nevertheless, I have done it; because I could not possibly neglect any means whatever that were pointed out to me of helping myself, and relieving others from helping me~~~ [*LL*]

In December 1846 Kemble returned to London and to the stage, to earn a living.

Park Place, St. James's London
February 1st, 1847

[My Dearest Harriet]
I feel almost certain, my dear Hal, that it will be better for me to be alone when I come out at Manchester than to have you with me, even if in all other respects it were expedient you should be there. My strength is much impaired, my nerves terribly shattered, and to see reflected in eyes that I love that pity for me which I shall feel only too keenly for myself, on the first night of my return to the stage, might, I fear, completely break down my courage. I am glad for this reason that I am to come out at Manchester, where I know nobody, and not in London, where, although I might not distinguish them, I should know that not a few who cared for me, and were sorry for me, were among my spectators. I am now so little able to resist the slightest appeal to my feelings that, at the play (to which I have been twice lately), the mere sound of human voices simulating distress has shaken and affected me to a strange degree, and this in pieces of a common and uninteresting description. A mere exclamation of pain or sorrow makes me shudder from head to foot. Judge how ill prepared I am to fulfill the task I am about to undertake~~~

Return to the stage

This, however, is one of the most painful aspects of my work. It has a more encouraging one. It is an immense thing for me to be still able to work at all, and keep myself from helpless dependence upon any one~~~The occupation, the mere business of the business, will, I am persuaded, be good rather than bad for me; for though one may be strong against sorrow, sorrow and inactivity combined are too much for any strength. Such a burden might not kill one, but destroy one's vitality to a degree just short of, and therefore worse than death— crush, instead of killing and releasing one~~~. [*LL*]

Albion Hotel, Manchester
February 5, 1847

[My Dearest Harriet]
I have a desire for mental culture, only equalled by my sense of my profound ignorance, and the feeling of how little knowledge is attained even by scholars leading the most active and assiduously studious existences.

My delight in my own superficial miscellaneous reading is not so much for the information I retain (for I forget, or at least seem to do so, much of what I read), as for the sense of mental activity produced at the time, by reading; and though I forget much, something doubtless remains, upon the whole.

Knowledge, upon any subject, is an enchanting curiosity to me; fine writing on elevated subjects is a source of the liveliest pleasure to me; in all kinds of good poetry I find exquisite enjoyment; and not having a particle of satisfaction in letter-writing for its own sake, I cannot admit any parallel between reading and writing (whatever I might think of arithmetic). I have sometimes fancied, too, that but for the amount of letter-writing I perform, I might (perhaps) write carefully and satisfactorily something that might (perhaps) be worth reading, something that might (perhaps) in some degree approach my standard of a tolerably good literary production—some novel or play, some work of imagination—and that my much letter-writing is against this; but I dare say this is a mistaken notion, and that I should never, under any circumstances, write anything worth anything . . . [*LL*]

Albion Hotel, Manchester
February 17, 1847

My Dear Lady Dacre,
I acted Julia in *The Hunchback* last night (the first time for thirteen years) . . . I am so far satisfied with my last night's experiment, that I

think it has proved that my strength will serve to go through this sort of labor for a couple of years; and I hope during that time, by moving from one place to another, that my attraction may hold out sufficiently to enable me to secure the small capital upon which I can contrive to live independently . . . [*LL*]

Manchester
February 18, 1847

[My Dearest Hal]
Oh, my dear Hal, I strive to judge of my position as reasonably as I can! I do hope that in spite of the loss of youth, of person, and feeling (which latter communicates itself even to acting), I may be able to fill some parts better than I did formerly . . . My physical power of voice and delivery is not diminished, which is good for tragedy; my self-possession is increased, which ought to be good for comedy; and I do trust I may succeed, at least sufficiently to be able, by going from one place to another, and returning to America when I have worn out my public favor here—say, in two years,—to make what will enable me to live independently, though probably upon very small means.

I write this after my first night's performance, and I trust my views are not unreasonable. How I wondered at myself, as I stood at the side scene the other night, without any quickening of the pulse or beating of the heart—thanks to the other experiences I have gone through, which have left me small sensibility for stage apprehensions; and yet I could hardly have believed it possible that I should have been as little nervous as I was. When I went on, however, I had to encounter the only thing I had dreaded; and the loud burst of public welcome (suggestive of how many associations, and what a contrast!) shocked me from head to foot, and tried my nerves to a degree that affected my performance unfavorably through several scenes. [*LL*]

Railway Station, Hull
December 4, 1847

[My Dearest Harriet]

I have been spending the afternoon crying over the tender mercies of English Christmas to their pauper population, till my eyes smart, and itch, and ache, and I shall have neither sight nor voice to read *Coriolanus,* which I must do this evening. To this Hull Railway Hotel is attached a magnificent Railway Station (or rather *vice versa*), shaped like a horseshoe, with a spacious broad pavement, roofed with a sky-light all round, making a noble ambulatory, of which I have availed myself every day since I have been here for my walking exercise~~~

I was just starting for my walk to-day, when in came old Mr. Frost, my Hull employer, President of the Literary and Scientific Institution, before which I am giving my present readings, the principal lawyer, and, I believe, Mayor of Hull,—a most charming, accomplished, courteous old gentleman of seventy years and upwards, who, finding that I was about to walk, proposed to accompany me, and we descended to that Station.

As we paced up and down, I remarked, lying in a corner, what I took at first for a bundle of rags. On looking again, however, I perceived there was a live creature in the rags—a boy, whose attitude of suffering and weariness, as he crouched upon the pavement, was the most wretched thing you can imagine. I knelt down by him, and asked him what ailed him: he hardly lifted his face from his hands, and said, "Headache;" and then, coughing horribly, buried his miserable face again. Mr. Frost, seeing I still knelt by, began to ask him questions; and then followed one of those piteous stories which make one smart all over while one listens to them; parental desertion, mother marrying a second time, cruelty from the step-father, beating, starving, and final abandonment. He did not know what had become of them; they had gone away to avoid paying their rent, and left this boy to shift for himself. "How long ago is that?" said Mr. Frost. "Before snow," said the lad,—the snow has been gone a fortnight and more from this neighborhood, and for all that time the child, by his own account, has wandered up and down, living by begging, and sleeping in barns and stables and passages. The interrogatory was a prolonged one: my friend Mr. Frost is slow by age, and cautious by profession, and a man by nature, and so not irresistibly prompted to seize up such an unfortunate at once in his arms and adopt it for his own. In the course of his answers the boy, among other things, said, "I wouldn't mind only for little brother." "How old is he?" "Going on two years." "Where is he?" "Mother got him." "Oh, well, then, you needn't fret about him; she'll take care of him." "No, she won't; he won't be having nothing to eat, I know he won't." And the boy covered his face again in a sullen despair that was pitiful to see. Now, you know, Hal, this boy was not begging; he did not come to us with a pathetic appeal about his starving little brother: he was lying, starving himself, and stupefied, with his head covered over, buried in his rags when I spoke to him; and this touching reminiscence of his poor little step-brother came out in the course of Mr. Frost's interrogatory accidentally, and made my very heart ache. The boy had been in the workhouse for two years, with his mother, before she married this second husband; and, saying that he had been sent to school, and kindly treated, and well fed in the workhouse, I asked him if he would go back thither, and he said yes. So, rather to Mr. Frost's amazement I think, I got a cab, and put the child in, and with my kind old gentleman—who, in spite of evident repugnance to such closed quarters with the poor tatterdemalion, would by no means leave me alone in the adventure—we carried the small forsaken soul to the workhouse, where we got him, with much difficulty, temporarily received. The wife of the master of the poor-house knew the boy again, and corroborated much of what he had told us, adding that he was a good boy enough while he was there with his mother; but—would you believe it, Hal? also told us that this poor little creature had come to their gate the night before, begging admittance; but that, because he had not a *certain written order* from a certain officer, the rules of the establishment prevented their receiving him, and he had been turned away *of course*. I was in a succession of convulsions of rage and crying all this time, and so adjured and besought poor old Mr. Frost to take instant measures for helping the little outcast, that when we left him by the workhouse fire, the woman having gone to get him some food, and I returned blaspheming and blubbering to my inn, he, Mr. Frost, went off in search of a principal police-officer of Hull from whom he hoped to obtain some further information about the child, which he presently brought back to me. "Oh, yes, the magistrate knew the child; he had *sent him to prison* already several times, for being found lying at night on the wharves and about the street." So this poor little wretch was *sent to prison* because literally he had no where to lay his head!~~~I wouldn't be a man for anything! They are so cruel, without even knowing that they are so: the habit of seeing sin and suffering is such a *heart-hardener*. Well, the boy is safe in the workhouse now, and is, according to his own wish and inclination, either to be sent to sea or put out apprentice to some trade. I have pledged one of my readings for purposes of outfit or entrance-fee, and Mr. Frost has promised me not to lose sight of the child, so I hope he is rescued from sin and suffering for the present, and perhaps for the future . . . [*LL*]

Begun at Norwich/
Finished at Yarmouth
December 21, 1847

I do but poorly at Norwich, my dearest Hal, in body and estate, having a wretched influenza, sore throat, sore chest, and cold in my head, through which I am obliged to stand bare-necked and bare-armed, bare-headed and almost bare-footed (for the thin silk stockings and satin shoes are a poor protection), on the stage, to houses, I am sorry to say, as thin as my stockings; so that the money return for all this fatigue, discomfort, and expense is but inconsiderable, i.e., by comparison, for undoubtedly it is a fair harvest for such grain as I sow.

My mind rather thrives upon this not too prosperous condition of my body and estate, inasmuch as I naturally make some effort to be courageous and cheerful, and therefore do better in that respect than when I was cheerful and needed no courage, while you were spoiling me at St. Leonard's with all your love for me, and Dorothy with all her love for you.

In half an hour I leave this place for Yarmouth, where I act to-night, and to-morrow. The manager has made an arrangement with me to act at his theatres at Lynn and Cambridge next week, so that instead of returning to London the day after to-morrow, I shall not do so until Friday, 28th.

I should, I believe, find it very difficult indeed to be economical, and yet I suppose that if I felt the duty and necessity of it I should be more so than I am. The saving of money without any special motive for it does not appear to me desirable, any more than self-denial without a sufficient motive—and I do not call mere mortification such—appears to me reasonable. I do not feel called upon to curtail the comforts of my daily life, for in some respects it is always miserable, and in many respects inevitably very uncomfortable; and while I am laboring to spare sacrifice and disgrace to others, I do not see any very strong motive for not applying a sufficient portion of the money I work so hard for, to make my wandering and homeless life as endurable as I can . . .

An actor's life

I have a sort of lost-child feeling whenever I go to a strange place, that very few people who know me would give me credit for; but that's because they don't know me.

King Street, London
Saturday and Sunday March 11th and 12th, 1848

Dearest Hal,
My father tells me he has definitely renounced all idea of reading [offering Shakespearean readings] again, so I took heart of grace to ask him to lend me the plays he read from . . . My father's marks are most elaborate, but the plays are cruelly sacrificed to the exigencies of the performance—as much maimed, I think as they are for stage representation. My father has executed this inevitable mangling process with extreme good judgment and taste; but it gives me the heart-ache for all that. But he was *timed*, and that impatiently, by audiences who would barely sit two hours in their places, and required that the plays should

Shake-spearean readings

be compressed into the measure of their intellectual *short*-suffering capacity . . . [*LL*]

Kemble returned to America in 1848. She and Pierce Butler were divorced in 1849, and she continued a successful career as a Shakespearean reader in the United States and England.

Rochester, New York
February 4, 1850

My Dearest Arthur [Arthur Malkin, a friend and fellow mountain climber in the Alps],

I think I shall certainly be in England in the autumn. I have not yet quite finished making my fortune, in spite of the magnificent accounts of my wealth with which the newspapers abound, and I think I shall come and put the finishing stroke to it among my own people.

American divorce law

With regard to the American law of divorce, about which you inquire, it is different in different parts of the country; the several States have each their own independent government, jurisdiction, and institutions, and deal with matters matrimonial as with various others, according to their own peculiar laws. Pennsylvania, you know, is greatly peopled by Germans, and the divorce law there follows that of Germany, which itself is founded on the French Code Napoleon; it admits divorce on the plea of desertion (non-cohabitation) on the part of husband or wife for a space of two consecutive years. I believe a joint appeal may procure a separation from the legislature upon the ground of absolute incompatibility of temper and character, and also that a legal separation of person and property is sometimes allowed for other reasons. None of these processes of relief from the bonds of matrimony are available to Roman Catholics in America any more than elsewhere. Marriage is one of the sacraments of their church, to be annulled only by the authority of the Pope. The greater facility of obtaining divorce in the State of Pennsylvania occasionally induces citizens of other States to appeal to the Philadelphia tribunals. In Massachusetts, where the English law prevails, divorce is granted only for cause of adultery.   [FR]

In 1856, when her daughter Sarah turned twenty-one, Kemble was reunited with her.

New York, New York
November 29, 1857

[My Dear Arthur]
The best part of my year is over, the summer with S[arah], who returns to Philadelphia for the winter months on the 1st of December; after that, I shall resume my readings, and work hard, probably the whole time, till the summer months come round again, bringing for me the one blossom of my year.

I find living in America very, very irksome to me in many respects, and I am often sadder than I ought to be, when I think that my home for the rest of my life must certainly be here, even if I should revisit my own country, of which at present I see not the remotest chance. My child does not appear to wish to visit Europe, and all idea of her doing so is strongly opposed . . .

It is not likely, my dear Arthur, let me live as I will, that I shall ever be a rich woman, if I am to live in America; the cost of one's existence here is something fabulous, and the amount of discomfort one obtains for money, that purchases a liberal allowance of luxury as well as comfort in Europe, is by no means a small item of annoyance in one's daily life. For instance, I have just arrived in New York, where I shall probably spend the greater part of the winter at a hotel, and have been making inquiry as to prices of rooms, etc. I have had a very lofty, airy, cheerful, good-sized drawing-room, with three large looking-glasses set in superb frames, green-and-gold satin curtains and furniture, and carpet and rug of all the splendidest colours in the rainbow. The bedroom, which goes with this magnificent trumpery, is a small closet without curtains to the window or bed, no fireplace (and the range of

Cost of living in America

the winter thermometer in New York is from zero to twenty-one degrees below it), a bed pushed against the door, so that the latter cannot open, a washing-stand, which is a fixture, i.e. a corner cupboard, containing a waste-pipe and plug in a sunk marble basin, with a turncock above it, because that saves the housemaid the trouble of emptying slops, there is not even room or any substitute for a towel-horse. Does not the juxtaposition of such a drawing-room and such a bedroom speak volumes for the love of finery and ignorance of all decent comfort, which are alike semi-barbarous. For this accommodation and a bedroom for Marie [her maid] I am expected to pay sixteen guineas a week, so that you see, let me work as I will, it is not possible for me to save much where my mere board and lodging are at such rates, and everything else, carriage-hire, clothes, etc., are on the same extravagant scale. I cannot help thinking sometimes of the amount of comfort, enjoyment, and pleasure of all sorts I could command almost anywhere on the continent of Europe for the expense that here cannot procure me what we call the decencies of life, simply because they are not to be procured; and then I think that my children are dear to me in the most literal sense of the word . . .   [FR]

Lenox, Massachusetts
May 8, 1860

[Dear Arthur]

America divided

The United States schism, my dear Arthur, has become a wide yawning cleft, like your favourite Swiss abysms, with a mad tumult of folly and wickedness, and none but Vie Male on either side of it. The whole spirit of the people is gone, it seems to me Slavery has made the Southerners insane egotists, and the pursuit of gain has made the Northerners incapable egotists. Manliness, patriotism, honour, loyalty, appear to have been stifled out of these people by material success and their utter abdication to mere material prosperity. A grievous civil war, shattering their financial and commercial idols, and compelling them to find the connection between public safety and private virtue, may be the salvation of the country; a blessed, bitter blast of adversity, checking the insolent forwardness of their national spring, may yet perhaps preserve them from that which really seemed impending over the land—unripe rottenness, decay without duration, or exertion to excuse and account for it, the most amazing and deplorable unworthiness of the most glorious advantages that have ever yet belonged to any nation in the world . . . [FR]

Lenox, Massachusetts
November 24, 1860

[Dear Arthur]
We are in all the distraction and uproar of the presidential election. The southern states are loud in vehement threats of secession, if the republican candidate is elected; but their bluster is really lamentably ludicrous, for they are without money, without credit, without power, without character—in short, *sans* everything, but so many millions of slaves, *sans* good numbers of whom they would also be the very moment they cut themselves adrift from the protection of the North . . . [FR]

Lincoln's election

Lenox, Massachusetts
September 15, 1861

[Dear Arthur]
Our daily talk is of fights and flights, weapons and wounds. The stars and stripes flaunt their gay colours from every farm roof among these peaceful hills, and give a sort of gala effect to the quiet New England villages, embowered in maple and elm trees, that would be pretty and pleasing but the grievous suggestions they awake of bitter civil war, of the cruel interruption of an unparalleled national prosperity, of impending danger and insecurity, of heavy immediate taxation, of probable loss of property, and all the evils, public and personal, which spring from the general disorganization of the government, and disrupture of the national ties.

Pierce Butler's arrest

How nearly I am affected by all these disturbances you can imagine, when I tell you that Mr. B[utler] is a state prisoner, that he was arrested a month ago on a charge of high treason, and that my children left me the beginning of last week to visit him in a fortress, at the entrance of the Bay of New York, to which they obtained access only by a special order from the President, and where they were only permitted to see Mr. B[utler] in the presence of one of the officers of the fort. All this sounds strange enough, does it not? The charge against him is that he acted as an agent for the Southerners in a visit he paid to Georgia this spring, having received large sums of money for purchase and transmission of arms. Knowing Mr. B[utler]'s Southern sympathies, I think the charge very likely to be true; whether it can be proved or not is quite another question, and I think it probable, that, if it is not proved, Mr. B[utler] will still be detained till the conclusion of the war, as he is not likely to accept any oath of allegiance tendered to him by this government, being a determined democrat and inimical, both on public and private grounds, to Mr. Lincoln and his ministers.

The state of the country is very sad, and I fear will long continue to grieve and mortify its well wishers; but of the ultimate success of the North, I have not a shadow of a doubt. I hope to God that neither England nor any other power from the other side of water will meddle in the matter—but, above all, not England; and thus, after some bad and good fighting, and an unlimited amount of brag and bluster on both sides, the South, in spite of a much better state of preparation, of better soldiers, better officers, and above all, a much more unanimous and venomous spirit of hostility, will be obliged to knock under to the infinitely greater resources and less violent but much more enduring determination of the North. With the clearing away of this storm, slavery will be swept from among the acknowledged institutions of America, and I trust that republican and not democratic principles may prevail to the extent of modifying in some degree the exercise of the franchise, and *weighting* the right of suffrage with some qualifications which may prevent an Irish Roman Catholic celt, not two removes from a brute, from exercising the same influence in a public election that a New England Puritan farmer does, who is probably the most intelligent man of his class that can be found anywhere in the world.

I have nothing to tell you of myself. The summer is passing rapidly away, and as pleasantly as the many and inevitable discomforts of American house-keeping may allow. My children are both with me, but not, I am sorry to say, my grandchild. S[arah] having come up to Lenox to recruit health and strength, and judging it best therefore to leave her baby with its father, who, being a doctor, is competent to the charge. She will probably return to her home, husband, and child in about a fortnight; but Mr. B[utler]'s incarceration will be likely to throw F[an] entirely upon my charge. Perhaps, if she does not (mis)bestow herself in marriage in the mean time, she will return to Europe with me next year . . .   [FR]

Kemble spent time with Fan abroad, and in 1863, while in England, she published A Journal of a Residence on a Georgian Plantation. *She was in London when the war ended and returned to the States only after Pierce Butler's death in 1867.*

Later Life
1868–1893

Butler Place
August 30, 1868

[My Dear Arthur]

Return to Butler Place

Your letter reached me at this place, the home of my very sad married life, and I am writing to you now in the room where my children were born—my room, as it is once more called. It is full twenty-six years since I last inhabited it. When my children ceased to be among the richest girls in America (which they once were), and had to leave this place, to which they were extremely attached, to go and live in a Philadelphia boarding-house, this place was let for a term of years, to people who took no care of it, let it get completely out of order, and neglected even to keep the pleasure-grounds tidy or house in repair; and so it remained, getting more and more dilapidated and desolate, and passing through a succession of equally careless and dishonest hands until last April, when the lease of the last tenant who had taken it expired. This gentleman's wife died here about two years ago, whereupon he left the place, shut up the house, leaving it and his furniture to rot together, and when, early in May, I came hither to look at its condition, it seemed to me too damp and too dreadfully out of repair, for F[an] to find it possible to inhabit it during the summer, which I knew to be her purpose . . .

I have spent a very peaceful and happy week here in this my former purgatory, and leave it with infinite reluctance to-morrow, to start on a three month's tour in the West, reading as I run, as far as Niagara, the great lakes, and the Mississippi. I hope to be home again, that is, with my children, the last week in November, and to spend the winter and spring quietly in Philadelphia, and I do hope most fervently to see the Alps next summer . . .   [FR]

Philadelphia
January 26, 1869

[Dear Arthur]
I suppose from what I know of my own rate of earning, or as you say "manufacturing" *greenbacks* that the amount of Mr. Dickens's earnings has been probably as violently exaggerated as that of mine was. Of mine I will now give you the history. In six months I have earned seven thousand pounds in greenbacks (that is, about four thousand three hundred pounds in gold). During those six months my expenses of living amounted to twelve hundred pounds in greenbacks (about nine hundred in real money), which leaves me in round numbers six thousand pounds in greenbacks, or four thousand in real money to invest. I do not know whether that comes up to or exceeds what you supposed my earnings to have amounted to, but it falls ludicrously short of the sum which popular report has rewarded my exertions with . . .

Theatrical earnings

I had a letter from F[an] to-day from the plantation, written in rather a depressed state of spirits. The old leaven of personal attachment which survived for a short while among the negroes after their emancipation, or perhaps the natural timidity of absolute ignorance which possessed and paralyzed them at first, is rapidly passing away, and they are asserting their natural and divine right to cultivate happiness (that is, idleness) instead of cotton and rice at any price; and F[an], who over-estimated the strength of their old superstitions, is beginning to despond very much. For my own part, the result seems to

Curse of slavery

me the only one to have been rationally expected, and I have no hope whatever that as long as one man, once a planter, and one man, once a slave, survives, any successful cultivation of the southern estates be achieved. Indeed, it seems to me most probable that, like other regions long cursed by the evil deeds of their inhabitants, the plantations be gradually restored to the wild treasury of natural and the land "enjoy its sabbaths" as a wilderness, peopled with snakes, for perhaps a good half century yet. I do not know why the roots of slavery should be grubbed out of the soil a day sooner. It is unlucky, no doubt, for the present holders of southern property, but then the world has laws, and I do not know that the planters of the southern states were sufficiently meritorious folks to have earned a miracle, especially a very immoral one for their heirs.   [FR]

Rittenhouse Square, Philadelphia
February 14, 1874

[My Beloved Harriet]

Editing letters

I have only come as far as 1832 in my Memoirs, and my letters to you, from the provincial towns, where my father and I were acting during the summer of that year.

I have no intention whatever of undertaking any literary work of any sort, but this of my Reminiscences. I have no mental vigour, and not physical energy left. Looking over my letters, and copying portions of them, affords me a certain amount of quiet amusement and occupation daily. Letters which could have revived any distressing associations were all destroyed when first I received the box containing my whole correspondence with you; and though occasionally, in going back over all my life in those I have preserved, I still find details that sadden me, I have hitherto derived more interest and entertainment than anything else from the whole retrospect; and my depression has nothing whatever to do with that, though I think it is the physical result of the nervous strain of my whole life. All the early excitement, and all the subsequent trouble and sorrow, and all the prolonged exercise of that capacity for superficial emotion—these causes have

shaken, I might almost say, shattered, my nervous system to such a degree, that the frequent depression I suffer from seems to me simply the
inevitable result of such an existence as mine has been, on such a temperament... [FR]

Rittenhouse Square, Philadelphia
March 9, 1874

[My Dearest Harriet]
I have never been able to believe in any return of prosperity for any *Postwar*
part of the southern country till the whole generation of former plant- *South*
ers and slaves had died out. There must be almost a new heaven and a
new earth throughout the whole of that land before it can recover
from the leprosy in which it has been steeped for nearly a hundred
years. Its moral, social, and political condition is now one of such corruption that decay and dissolution must, I believe, do their utmost
work of destruction before the first vital breath of resurrection or renewed life can stir there. Of course, I hoped, but never quite believed,
in the success of the first experiment of freedom, though all my in-
stinctive and rational faith in God's laws and government was against
such expectation. Can you reflect upon the condition of that plantation, as it was within my experience, and think it reasonable to imagine that the sudden abolition of slavery, by the means of the war and
the President's proclamation, could cancel the action of all the previous influences that had reigned for a hundred years upon the place
and people?
    While I have been writing the last sentence I have seen something
that I think worth telling you. A wretched looking girl, evidently a beg-
gar, has just emptied out upon the pavement, by the square railings
opposite my window, about a dozen large pieces of bread from a bas-
ket, and run off, leaving them there. She is a member no doubt of a
whole army of beggars who now infest this city, going from house to
house carrying baskets, with piteous stories of starvation, and receiving money and food, bread and meat, from charitable persons. How
little of real starvation exists in their case, or indeed at even in the

poorest class of the community, is proved by the fact that they constantly throw away the food they have thus received, and nothing is commoner than to see in the gutters and on the pavements great slices of bread and butter and quarter and half loaves of bread. A small street vagabond has just stopped to examine these fragments of food, and amused himself with kicking them hither and thither, finally stamping upon and grinding several of them to powder. The birds of the square are already making their profit by them.

My poor coloured man-servant is behaving very steadily and keeping his pledge hitherto unbroken. Of course I lock up every drop of wine and beer with the greatest care, and cannot help hoping that his coming into my service may be the means of rescuing him and his family from the ruin into which his drunkenness would probably have plunged them all; it would be a great delight if it should prove so . . . [FR]

Rittenhouse Square, Philadelphia
March 21, 1874

[My Dearest Harriet]

Southern party politics

Before the war, the Southern slave-holders were undoubtedly the most influential politicians in the United States. Whether as great landowners their position was more favourable for the formation of political capacity than that of the hard-working Northern men of business I do not know; but the Democratic party, which the war all but annihilated, was formed in the South, and was led and supported by Southern statesmen, who controlled the whole government of the country, with the view of upholding their own peculiar institution of slavery, until the West and North threw off their despotism it was that in effect), and the war destroyed, for the time being, all Southern influence in the councils and government of the country. Since its termination, the South has been politically annihilated; the slave-holders are gone, and no class of men has come forward to represent in any way their influence. A territorial aristocracy, of course, always has some good elements out of which to make leaders and governors, and the power

and capacity of the planters (though not their way of applying them), as efficient political men and statesmen of ability, are a great loss in the working of the government. The freeing the blacks was a mere *consequence* of the war, and cannot in any way account for the present low average of the men who constitute congress, except as the sweeping away of the Southern slaveholders abolished a class of men who, for various reasons, were especially adapted to political life. The great difficulty here at the north is, that men of character and ability cannot afford to sacrifice their personal interests to becoming working politicians; and those who do the business of the State are, as a rule, inferior in honesty and capacity to the great majority of the people whom they represent (or, I should say, *mis*represent) and rule. It is a most extraordinary state of things, of which it is difficult to see the remedy or foresee the result. The scandalous dishonesty and incapacity of the present men in power, however, is making the whole country restive under a sense of disgrace; but, unfortunately (I cannot say, fortunately), the prosperity of the country is such that the misgovernment and abuses do not press sufficiently hard upon any large body of men to make ardent reformers of them. A pure patriot may lead a charge against a corrupt government for righteousness' sake; but his followers must be people who have a grievance and a gain to spur them on. Here the pure patriot, who could spare the time to lead a crusade against the government, would be difficult, and his followers impossible, to find; for the grievances and the gains do not come home sufficiently to the business and bosoms of any sufficiently large mass of people to give rise to any effectual action of reform. The bulk of the people are too well off to care how bad their government is. Heavy as the taxation is, they are able to bear it, and corrupt and degraded as the present result of the system is, in many respects, it is always in the immediate power of the people to make a change when their "machinery" doesn't work to their satisfaction. Of course the higher-minded and better-educated people are neither pleased with nor proud of their government just now; but the "majority" is not a *nice* creature, and it, apparently, is contented with time, things will mend, and the country, by dint of its material circumstances and its institutions (mal-administered as they are), is wonderfully prosperous and fortunate in its conditions. It is not patriotism, but the grossest ignorance and selfishness, that opposes free trade in America; but by degrees the advantages of it are beginning to dawn upon men's minds, though convincing people of a future gain, in the face of an immediate loss, is a difficult process. After all, England was protectionist, within my recollection; and nothing seems stranger then the delusions of other people, when they have ceased to be our own.

I never thought the Southerners *gentlemen* in contradistinction to the Northerners; they were aristocrats, men of comparative leisure, by position, landowners and slaveholders, but certainly not for any of those reasons necessarily *gentlemen.* I know nothing whatever of either their condition or that of their former dependents now. Both, I imagine, are miserably abiding, and must long continue to abide, the deplorable results of their former mutually baneful relation . . . [FR]

Rittenhouse Square, Philadelphia
April 20, 1874

[My Dearest Harriet]

Women's rights

I believe women, at present, have no political rights in the United States, any more than in England. My impression is, that in very early times of the republic, the state laws of New Jersey (you know the several states have all their own peculiar laws) allowed women to be voters. Whether the privilege has since been taken from them or not I do not know; but I never heard of their claiming the exercise of it. Now, however, I imagine several of the states may take measures for allowing the suffrage to women; and I dare say they will obtain it, if they choose to do so, all over the country, where certainly the most curious anomalies exist, with regard to large bodies of (so-called) citizens of the United States.

Racial segregation

The negroes are now all exalted to that dignity, and vote accordingly; moreover, the negroes are at this moment sitting as members of the state legislature of South Carolina: in spite of which, my man-servant, a very decent-looking, respectably dressed individual, was not allowed here to purchase a ticket for any part of the theatre to which I went the other night, and was turned from the door with the announcement that *people of colour* were not admitted even to the gallery there. This man votes, and is to all intents and purposes politically, though not socially, a citizen of the United States.

The present attitude of the government, and aspect of public affairs in this country, is afflicting enough in all conscience to every one interested in it. I am grieved, indignant, and ashamed at the conduct and character of the present administration, but have not lost my faith in the fundamental principles of right, truth, and justice. The future of this country is an enormous problem for any one to guess at; its condition in many respects, at present, is lamentable and disgraceful . . . [*FR*]

York Farm, Branchtown
August 2, 1874

My Dearest H[arriet],
I quite agree with you that a woman's nursing her own infant is the right thing both for mother and child, whatever modern theorists may say to the contrary; indeed, I am by no means charmed with modern theories in these matters, and moreover, for my own part, am of [the] opinion that the year in which a mother holds her baby at her breast and sees it looking up into her eyes is a sufficient compensation even for the most miserable marriage?~~I am now told, with regard to the scrupulous care with which a woman's diet was formerly regulated, with a view to its effect upon her child, that that is a mere nonsensical superstition, an exploded old woman's fanatical fallacy; that whatever agrees with the mother is sure to agree with the child, and that is to become inured by experience from the very first to the effect of every variety in its nurse's diet,—to which I can only reply, "it may be so," it was different in my time. Mais nous avons change tout cela . . . [*FR*]

Joys of motherhood

York Farm, Branchtown
February 10, 1875

My Dearest H[arriet],

Plantation crops
The last letters from the plantation were [in] every way cheerful and pleasant. They had no overseer, and Mr. [James] L[eigh, her daughter Fan's husband] was looking after the work of the estate himself, and so industriously and efficiently, that they were in a state of greater forwardness with all their spring processes of planting than they had been for years before so early in the season; and are in this respect better off than any of the neighbouring planters. F[an] herself had been planting a hundred orange trees, a most admirable outlay of labour, for besides the lovely flowers and fruit for their own enjoyment, the oranges are worth three guineas a barrel, here at the north, and are becoming quite a valuable crop.

Financial panic
My dearest H[arriet], many years must pass before the United States becomes over-populated. There is just now considerable distress in the Atlantic cities, proceeding from the money difficulties and bad financial administration of the government, and the impediments and restrictions put upon trade and commerce by the foolish tariff duties—a system of recruiting the revenue really almost ludicrous in the inefficiency of the result, compared with the enormous abuses it has given rise to.

A number of temporary influences combining together are just now depressing trade and manufacturers in the northern and eastern states, and many people are out of work in the cities; but as for this vast country being already over-peopled, the bare idea makes one smile, when one thinks of its immense extent and incalculable resources . . .

I went to pay S[arah] a visit this morning . . . and we discussed the arrangement of the furniture in my old drawing-room, in my old home; and as I find myself thus once again all but inhabiting this my former "house of woe," I am occasionally seized with a bewildering sense of surprise, and, overwhelmed, with a sudden flood of reminiscence and association, feel almost inclined to doubt my own identity.   [FR]

York Farm, Branchtown
October 1, 1875

[My Beloved Harriet]
I am still occupying my time with preparing my Memoirs for the *Editing* press. This has nothing whatever to do, however, with what I am pub- *letters* lishing, as I do not intend extending that record beyond the period of my leaving the stage, if even I continue it so far. That would only take me to the year 1832, and you may judge what a task the whole selection and copying of matter is, when *I* tell you that at present I am still extracting from letters of only 1843.

I wonder if I told you that, at Mr. L[eigh, Kemble's son-in-law]'s instigation, I had bought myself a printing machine [a typewriter], by means of which I print, instead of write my daily task of copying, and as it is a very ingeniously contrived machine, which is worked merely by striking keys as one plays on a piano, it is a great relief from the fatigue of constant writing. It is an admirable invention, and affords me a great deal of satisfaction in the process of working it. I got it principally in hopes that S[arah], who writes a great deal too much, would use it, but she says it would fidget her to such a degree that the nervous irritation it would cause her would quite militate against any relief from fatigue in employing it. This has been a great disappointment to me, as I should never have gone to the expense of such an apparatus for myself . . .   [FR]

York Farm, Branchtown
April 25, 1876

My Dearest Harriet,
I am sorry to say that in F[an]'s last letter she mentioned a circumstance which is likely to operate very unfavourably against either the

sale or lease of their rice plantation. F[an] says that the New Orleans and Louisiana planters are now to a great extent giving up the cultivation of cotton and sugar, which have been hitherto the staple products of that state, and are taking to cultivate rice upon a scale which will be seriously injurious to the Georgia rice-planters, and greatly diminish the value of the rice growing estates there. I believe I am superstitious about that Georgia property. I have a feeling that it is never to be prosperous or profitable to those who own or inherit it. I shall rejoice when Mr. L[eigh] has turned his back upon it, and resumed his own proper position and vocation in his own country, though I am afraid as long as it is theirs F[an] will never be contented anywhere else, and unless the plantation is absolutely parted with, I fear she will always be desiring and endeavouring to return there.

The American International Exhibition, in honour of the Centennial Celebration, which takes place in Philadelphia, and is to open early next month, is occupying everybody here entirely.

I take very little interest in it. I have seen our own two great London exhibitions, and the great Paris one, and thought them all oppressive, overwhelming, distracting, and fatiguing, and, with all their wonder and beauty, unsatisfactory to the last degree. And the disgraceful character and condition of the present American government [referring to Grant's scandal-ridden administration] is so distressing to all who really love and respect the country, as I do, that I cannot help regretting this challenge, sent abroad to foreign nations, to come here and admire this country, when it seems to me essentially less admirable than it has ever been, and to be really in a humiliating and degraded position, morally, whatever its material prosperity may be . . . [FR]

In 1877 Kemble returned to London to live, accompanying her daughter's family, the Leighs, who were settling in England.

Grosvenor Street, London
February 3, 1883

My Dear Arthur,

You asked me some questions with regard to the sale of the slaves on our southern property, which I could not immediately answer, for with a very vivid recollection of much tribulation in my middle life, the details of a great deal of sorrow are, thank God, dim in the distance, and from the blessed effect of many happier years.

The former slaves, for they were all free when my children inherited the estate, may have been some that were not carried to Savannah for sale, or they may have been former slaves of their aunt, Mrs. John Butler, their uncle's widow, who owned part of the property. At the time of the sale of those who had been *my* slaves, the [London] *Times* newspaper devoted two long columns to the account of the circumstance and their proprietor, supposed to be interesting to English readers, on account of their connection with me, and during the war, on its being mentioned that their owner was in trouble in the North for his southern *proclivities,* there was rather a sarcastic article on his having, by that sale, sagaciously taken abolition by the forelock, which was not true. The slaves were sold to pay their owner's debts, his own estimate of which amounted to one hundred thousand pounds, the result of gambling on the Stock Exchange. The sale of his slaves, to which he was compelled, caused him extreme pain and mortification. I do not know how much or how little of this his children know, but the condition of things, liable to such results, can neither be held happy for slaves or slaveholders.

Believe me, always affectionately yours,
Fanny Kemble

Kemble lived the rest of her life in London and died there in 1893. She is buried at Kensal Green Cemetery.

Fanny Kemble's Published Works

Frances the First: An Historical Drama. London: John Murray, 1832.

Frances the First: A Tragedy in Five Acts. New York: Peabody & Co., 1832.

Journal of Frances Anne Kemble. 2 vols. Philadelphia: Carey, Lea & Blanchard, 1835.

Journal of Residence in America. 2 vols. London: John Murray, 1835.

The Star of Seville. London: Saunders & Otley, 1835.
New York: Saunders & Otley, 1837.

Poems. Philadelphia: John Pennington, 1844.
London: H. Washbourne, 1844.

A Year of Consolation. 2 vols. London: Edward Moxon, 1847.
New York: Wiley & Putnam, 1847.

The Christmas Tree and Other Tales. London: John W. Parker & Son, 1856.

Poems. Boston: Ticknor & Fields, 1859.

Plays. London: Longman, Green, Longman, Roberts & Green, 1863.

Journal of a Residence on a Georgian Plantation. London: Longman, Green, Longman, Roberts & Green, 1863.
New York: Harper & Bros., 1863.

Records of a Girlhood. 3 vols. London: Richard Bentley & Son, 1878.
New York: Henry Holt & Co., 1879.

Records of Later Life. London: Richard Bentley & Son, 1881.
New York: Henry Holt & Co., 1882.

Notes upon Some of Shakespeare's Plays. London: Richard Bentley & Son, 1882.

Poems. London: Richard Bentley & Son, 1883.

Far Away and Long Ago. London: Richard Bentley & Son, 1889.
New York: Henry Holt & Co., 1889.

The Adventures of Mr. John Timothy Homespun in Switzerland. London: Richard Bentley & Son, 1889.

Further Records. 2 vols. London: Richard Bentley, 1890.
New York: Henry Holt & Co., 1891.

Acknowledgments

Many people supplied me with crucial information for the preparation of this edition. Thanks to Lisa Cardyn, Robert Forbes, Heather Hathaway, Jessica Betts, Virginia Gould, Mr. and Mrs. John W. Stokes II, James Butler, and Cynthia Larson.

In the final stages of this project both the Charles Warren Center at Harvard University, under the direction of Laurel Ulrich, and the Gilder Lehrman Center at Yale University, under the direction of David Brion Davis, generously offered me affiliation and library access that proved critical to my completion of the volume.

Harvard University Press remains a splendid team, with which any author is lucky to work. I wish to thank Elizabeth Suttell and Donna Bouvier for their invaluable assistance. Aida Donald deserves more gratitude than I can ever hope to repay. She has been a good friend for the past two decades, and her patience and support on this project were saintly. She is an editor's editor, and I remain in her debt.

Without my son Drew's technical assistance, and my son Ned's constant cheer, this volume never would have been completed. They are exceptional boys, who luckily bear striking resemblance to their father, Daniel Colbert.

Index

Rome, 171–173; wages in, 174
Rose (slave), 101, 105, 108, 116, 118

Sally (slave), 155
Salmonia, 41
"Sambo," 16
Sanitary Commission, 5
Sartoris, Adelaide (Kemble), 35, 171
Sartoris, Edward, 171
Savannah (Ga.), 97, 127, 143
Scipio (slave), 155
Scott, John Anthony, 16
sea-island cotton, 147–148
secession, 187
Sedgwick, Catharine, 8, 81
Sedgwick, Elizabeth Dwight, 12, 98
Semiramis, 32
sexual exploitation, 15, 157, 158–159
Shadrach (slave), 135
Shakers, 89
Shakespeare, William, 2, 4, 19, 28, 56, 59, 64,
    87, 127, 183
shipboard travel, 38–40
Siddons, Sarah, 1, 33, 51, 59, 64
slaveholders, 16, 62, 83, 100, 125, 126, 194–
    195, 200; acknowledgment of slave off-
    spring, 160–161; cruelty to slaves, 160; fear
    of insurrections, 57, 161; slave offspring,
    15
slavery, 2, 83, 93, 124–125, 165, 186–187,
    192; task system, 100
slaves, 110, 150, 201; babies, 118; clothing,
    115, 146; diet, 119–120; drivers, 112; es-
    cape, 155; families separated by sale, 127–
    135; funerals, 136–138; gangs, 140; infant
    mortality, 154–155, 157; infirmaries for,
    102, 104, 107, 108, 110, 117; miscarriages,
    14, 104, 155–156, 157; motherhood, 101,
    109; parents, 116; petitions of, 141, 149–
    150; pregnancies, 125, 139, 143, 153; prices
    of, 125, 143; religion, 126; taught to read,
    56, 145, 159–160. *See also* sexual exploita-
    tion; slaveholders; slavery
snakes, 96, 152
Sophy (slave), 155, 158
South, 83, 90, 92, 95, 125, 156, 164, 172, 186,
    188; postbellum society in, 191–196
South Carolina, 56, 64, 100, 196

Spalding, Mrs., 144
St. Leger, Harriet, 8, 10, 12, 18, 22, 37, 92
St. Leonard's, 182
St. Simons Island (Ga.), 20, 106, 135, 141,
    144, 145, 146, 147
steamboat travel, 50, 54–55, 61–62
Stephen (slave), 155
suffrage, 196–197
Sukey (slave), 155
Swiss Family Robinson, 19

Taylor, Jeremy, 84
Tema (slave), 159
Temple (slave), 159
Ten Years on a Georgian Plantation (1883), 18
terriers, 122
Titian, 59
Trelawny, Edward, 72, 73, 74–75
Trollope, Frances, 55
Troup, Orallie, 139
typewriter, 199

Union cause, 5, 14, 188

Van Buren, Martin, 51
Venice, 138
Venus (slave), 148
Virginia, 118

Walker, 158
Washington, D.C., 7, 62
waterfalls, 73, 76
Webster, Daniel, 62
whipping, 108, 111–112, 123, 151, 152, 157
Wilson, Dorothy, 90, 182
Wister, Owen, Jr., 5, 189
Wister, Sarah (Butler). *See* Butler, Sarah
    (Wister)
women's intellect, 31, 69–70
women's status, 90, 166–167, 176, 184–185;
    in England, 83. *See also* legal status of
    women
workers, 174–175
Wuthering Heights, 11, 19

Yarmouth (U.K.), 183
Year of Consolation, A (1847), 10
yeomanry, 120, 123–124

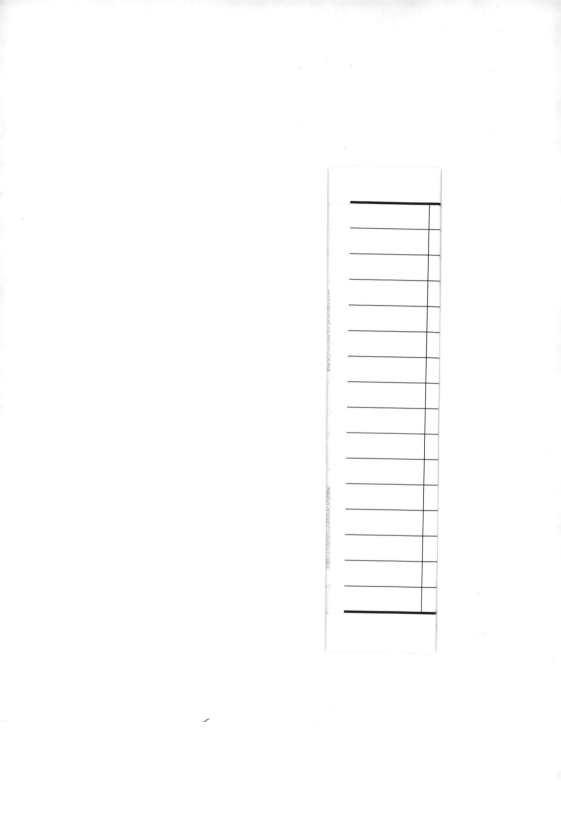